Chopin Studies

This book contains detailed documentary and analytical studies of the music of Chopin, representing the most recent research of leading scholars in the field.

The first three essays, by Jeffrey Kallberg, Wojciech Nowik and Jim Samson, are concerned with the composer's intentions as revealed in autograph sources. The next group of four essays, by William Kinderman, Eugene Narmour, William Rothstein and Zofia Chechlińska, deal analytically with different aspects of Chopin's musical language, ranging from large-scale tonal planning and the interpretation of harmonic dissonance to phrase rhythm and texture. The final three essays are case studies, by Jean-Jacques Eigeldinger, John Rink and Carl Schachter, of individual works: the Preludes op. 28, the *Barcarolle*, and the Fantasy op. 49.

Chopin Studies

EDITED BY
JIM SAMSON

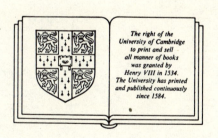

The right of the
University of Cambridge
to print and sell
all manner of books
was granted by
Henry VIII in 1534.
The University has printed
and published continuously
since 1584.

Cambridge University Press

CAMBRIDGE

NEW YORK   PORT CHESTER

MELBOURNE   SYDNEY

Published by the Press Syndicate of the University of Cambridge
The Pitt Building, Trumpington Street, Cambridge CB2 1RP
40 West 20th Street, New York, NY 10011–4211, USA
10 Stamford Road, Oakleigh, Melbourne 3166, Australia

First published 1988
Reprinted 1991

Printed in Great Britain at
the University Press, Cambridge

British Library cataloguing in publication data
Chopin studies.
1. Chopin, Frédéric – Criticism and
interpretation
I. Samson, Jim
786.1'092'4   ML410.C54

Library of Congress cataloguing in publication data
Chopin studies.
Includes index.
1. Chopin, Frédéric, 1810–1849 – Criticism and interpre-
tation. I. Samson, Jim.
ML410.C54C48   1988   86.1'092'4   87–25614

ISBN 0 521 30365 6

ME

Contents

Contents

Preface

The conception of this book owes much to the numerous specialised studies of major nineteenth-century composers which have appeared in recent years, each of them drawing together in a single volume the documentary and analytical researches of leading scholars in the field. In particular there have been major studies of Beethoven, Schubert and Brahms, and it is to be hoped that the present volume will not be the last to challenge this Austro-German bias.

Like its predecessors it is thematic only in a rather loose sense. The first three chapters form a unit in that they are all in different ways concerned with the composer's intentions as revealed in autograph sources. Jeffrey Kallberg's study tells us much about Chopin's own understanding of the genre which occupied him most consistently throughout his composing life. In the process it affords some insight into the problems facing nineteenth-century composers generally as they sought to reconcile generic stability and stylistic change. Wojciech Nowik addresses just a single work. By examining all surviving sources for the *Berceuse*, he demonstrates that changes of substance occurred at a surprisingly late stage of the source chain and that these changes had some bearing on Chopin's view of the 'ideal' reception of his music. My own chapter examines the tonal structure of the Polonaise-fantasy both in its final form and as Chopin first conceived it.

The next four chapters also form a group in that they deal analytically with particular aspects of Chopin's musical language. The chapters by William Kinderman and Eugene Narmour are concerned with pitch structures. Kinderman examines large-scale tonal planning in three major works, while Narmour attempts a radical reassessment of the roles played by vertical and horizontal elements in Chopin's music, a reassessment which necessitates some novel methodology. The contributions by William Rothstein and Zofia Chechlińska examine areas of musical language which are less directly dependent on precise pitch content, phrase rhythm and texture respectively.

The final three chapters are case-studies of individual works. Jean-Jacques Eigeldinger draws upon a wide range of historical, theoretical and analytical data to support his interpretation of the preludes as a unified cycle. John Rink and Carl Schachter are less eclectic, relying predominantly on the theories of Heinrich Schenker in their close-to-the-text analyses of the *Barcarolle* and the Fantasy op. 49.

One interesting, and largely unplanned, feature of the book is the recurrence of specific genres in changing analytical contexts, such that radically different perspectives are taken on the same pieces. Thus we have three studies of the mazurkas, three of the nocturnes and two of the Fantasy op. 49. Such cross-referencing has in certain instances proved illuminating.

Anglo-American prejudices reveal themselves clearly in the concentration on genesis, style and structure in the present volume. Extensive areas of Chopin research have been excluded, notably questions of performance practice, social history, musical 'poetics' and reception. It is hoped that at some future date we may produce a second volume of *Chopin studies*. If so, a central aim will be to widen the scope of our investigation to embrace at least some of these topics.

Exeter 1987

JIM SAMSON

The problem of repetition
and return in Chopin's mazurkas

JEFFREY KALLBERG

The sources reveal one omnipresent fact: Chopin revised habitually. He altered works extensively already when he commenced composing at the keyboard, and he continued to revise abundantly when he first notated with pen and paper the ideas conceived at the piano. He revamped continuously through successive stages of manuscripts, though addressing different varieties of problems and correcting less frequently in the second or third autograph of the same work. Publication in no way hindered him. He made changes to proofs, as well as to students' copies of his published editions, and he requested publishers to alter printed texts. Chopin's habits have left a complex welter of changes, yet there is more to complicate matters. Though he revised constantly, he did not always do so consistently: sometimes he altered one engraver's manuscript or printed edition, and not another.

Revision, basic to his compositional method, thus creates a special burden for careful students of Chopin. Whether musicologist, theorist, editor or pianist, all will eventually confront Chopin's authorial changes. His tendency continually to emend compositions, coupled with his practice of making different changes in contemporaneous sources of the same works, in essence make the revisions to a work part of its esthetic property. The elucidation of Chopin's music often requires an understanding of his revisions.

Discussions of Chopin's extensive alterations and variants date at least as far back as George Sand's exaggerated account of his compositional process in her *Histoire de ma vie*.[1] Yet much of this commentary has been cast in purely descriptive terms; textual differences have merely been tallied rather than

---

[1] See George Sand, *Oeuvres autobiographiques*, ed. Georges Lubin, 2 vols. (Paris, 1978), ii, 446. The chapter on Chopin was written in late 1854.

1

plumbed for their compositional meaning. Recently, however, scholars have begun to pay greater attention to the wide-ranging musical issues Chopin's revisions encompass.[2]

These recent studies have largely concentrated on compositional difficulties and issues in specific compositions. Because of the nature both of the surviving sources and the changes made in them – individual sources tend to contain revisions unique to the work they transmit – such a focus is for the most part necessary. But not always: in certain situations throughout his career, Chopin pondered the same or related issues in a number of different works. Some of these troubles surfaced in a variety of genres – for example, the very frequent corrections of detail in chord construction – others arose mainly in a particular genre. Studies of such recurring revisions scarcely exist for Chopin. Partly to redress this, I want here to survey one of his perennial generic stumbling blocks: the problem of repetition and return in the mazurkas.

In most music, repetition and return are fundamental elements of structure. Although both concepts depend upon relationships of similarity, repetition – the immediate reiteration of an event – and return – its more distant recurrence – tend to function differently. Leonard B. Meyer has drawn our attention to the essential distinctions between the two.[3] Repetition gives rise to both formal and processive relationships, to feelings of impending change (though these can vary depending upon the context of the repetition), to an awareness of the differences between like events. Return serves to articulate structural units, to emphasise points of arrival and departure, and to draw attention to the similarities between like events.

Given the pervasiveness of repetition and return as constructive principles, why did Chopin struggle with them in one specific genre? For even though corrections pertaining to repetition and return occur now and then in sources for other genres, they appear with such frequency in the mazurkas as to suggest that the relationship of these concepts to this genre is special.[4] After describing the passages and sources where the alterations took place, I want then to investigate some of the reasons why the mazurkas in particular should have invited this kind of compositional revision, to examine the changes undergone

---

[2] Of the several studies that might be mentioned, let me cite only three: Wojciech Nowik, 'Proces twórczy Fryderyka Chopina w świetle jego autografów muzycznych' (Diss., U. of Warsaw, 1978); Nancy S. Morgan, 'Formal Redefinition and the Genesis of the Finale to the Sonata for Violoncello and Piano, opus 65, by Frédéric Chopin' (M.A. thesis, U. of Pennsylvania, 1983); and my 'Chopin's Last Style', *Journal of the American Musicological Society* xxxviii (1985), 264–315.

[3] *Explaining Music: Essays and Explorations* (Berkeley and Los Angeles, 1973), 49–52; 90–7.

[4] One example of such a revision in another genre is found in an early manuscript of the F minor Nocturne op. 55 no. 1 (Paris, Bibliothèque Nationale, MS 109), which lacks the repetitive bars 95–6 of the printed version. Chopin added the missing bars in a scribal copy of the manuscript (Cracow, Biblioteka Jagiellońska)

in Chopin's attitudes toward repetition and return, and to explore the general critical ramifications of these revisions for our understanding of the genre.

The emendations may be parcelled into three broad categories. The first, and least common, contains repetition at the level of the individual bar or phrase. The second encompasses sectional repetition. The third includes sectional return. These divisions are not always neat; the latter two in particular often overlap. Nevertheless, they correspond to the different kinds of issues that Chopin faced in making the revisions, and as such, allow us to gauge the extent of the problem he faced.

1. Low-level repetition

Revisions of one-bar motives occur twice, both times in the codas to mazurkas from Chopin's late period, and both times in the same type of source, a rejected public manuscript.[5] In the G minor autograph of op. 59 no. 3 (a piece eventually published in F♯ minor), conserved in the Pierpont Morgan Library, New York, Chopin inserted a five-bar phrase in place of bar 134 (Example 1). The impulse to insert the phrase was only temporary, for when Chopin later decided to transpose the piece down a semitone, he returned, after some

Example 1. Versions of bars 134ff. in op. 59 no. 3

ORIGINAL

REVISION

---

[5] Chopin's autograph manuscripts may be divided into two main categories: those that he initially intended only for his private use (e.g., sketches), and those that he initially intended to serve some public use (e.g., engraver's manuscripts, gifts). Occasionally, however, his intentions could not be fulfilled; at times, because of the number or type of revisions that he made in an autograph, he was unable to present the document for public viewing. Such autographs I have dubbed 'rejected public manuscripts'; for discussions, see 'The Chopin Sources: Variants and Versions in Later Manuscripts and Printed Editions' (Diss., U. of Chicago, 1982), 172–80; and 'O klasyfikacji rękopisów Chopina', *Rocznik Chopinowski* xvii (1985), 63–96.

hesitation, to his initial version. (That he first began to copy out the repetitive phrase in the F♯ minor version may be seen in the *Stichvorlage* prepared for the Berlin publisher Stern, currently on deposit by the heirs of Stefan Zweig in the British Library.)[6]

An early version of op. 63 no. 1 (Paris, Bibliothèque Nationale, MS 112) lacks bars 88–91 of the piece as it was printed in its first editions (Example 2).

Example 2. Op. 63 no. 1, bars 86ff.: original and revision

These repetitive bars were added in a no longer surviving later source, either an engraver's autograph or a corrected proof.

2. Sectional repetition

Revisions of sectional repetition themselves fall into two groupings: those where the intent of the correction is clear, and those where it is not, due to demonstrable ambiguities in the surviving sources, in the composer's mind, or both.

[6] Gastone Belotti discussed the G minor version in 'Una nuova mazurca di Chopin', *Studi Musicali* vi (1977), 160–206. I countered some of his arguments in 'Compatibility in Chopin's Multipartite Publications', *The Journal of Musicology* ii (1983), 402–4. A facsimile of the Stern manuscript is printed in Krystyna Kobylańska, *Rękopisy Utworów Chopina. Katalog*, 2 vols. (Cracow, 1977), ii, 102–4.

A. Clear revisions

The Breitkopf and Härtel *Stichvorlage* for op. 24 no. 4 (Warsaw, Biblioteka Narodowa, Mus. 216) was initially conceived with first and second endings in place of the present bar 20; the first ending, comprised of two bars, led to a double barline and repeat signs at the beginning of bar 6 (Example 3). Chopin

Example 3. Op. 24 no. 4: original first ending, bar 20

cancelled this literal repeat by covering the first ending of bar 20 with cross-hatches, and scraping away the double bar and repeat signs in bar 6. The locus of the changes (manuscripts destined for German publishers were usually the second or third *Stichvorlagen* prepared), and presence in the deleted bars of a dynamic indication, pedal marks, and slurs (all among the final notations Chopin would normally make on a manuscript) demonstrate that the decision to avoid a literal repetition of the opening section came just before the work was submitted for publication.[7]

Chopin cancelled a sectional repeat in op. 33 no. 4 at an even later stage, well after the piece was published. Three different copies of the French first edition and one of the German that Chopin used in lessons with piano students or gave to family or acquaintances, none apparently dating before 1843 (the work was published in 1838), delete a full scale repeat of the principal thematic section (bars 87–110).[8] Even though two of these exemplars may reflect efforts to bring annotated readings into agreement after Chopin's death, the others remain independent; there can be little doubt that the trimming of the literal repetition of the first large section reflects Chopin's later thoughts on the

---

[7] I have documented Chopin's notational habits when preparing public manuscripts in 'The Chopin Sources', 168–72; and I have discussed the ordinary sequence of manuscripts for publishers when more than one was required in 'Chopin in the Marketplace: Aspects of the International Music Publishing Industry in the First Half of the Nineteenth Century', *Notes* xxxix (1983), 535–69; 795–824.

[8] The editions are identified according to their original owners: Jane Stirling (Paris, Bibliothèque Nationale, Rés. Vma 241 [IV]), Camille Dubois-O'Meara (Paris, Bibliothèque Nationale, Rés. R. 980 [III]), Ludwika Jędrzejewicz (Warsaw, Towarzystwo imienia Fryderyka Chopina, M/175), and Zofia Zaleska-Rosengardt (Paris, Bibliothèque Polonaise, F.N. 15811–44). The Zaleska-Rosengardt exemplar is of the German first edition. Camille Dubois-O'Meara in 1843 was the first of the group to commence her studies with Chopin; hence the earliest date for the correction. (I have derived this date from Bertrand Jaeger, 'Quelques nouveaux noms d'élèves de

proper form for the piece.[9] In schematic terms, he preferred a formal pattern of AAB AB CD A over the original AAB AAB CD A.

The following three corrections may simply represent notational oversights on the part of Chopin; nevertheless, they still shed light on when the composer deemed literal repetition appropriate. Moreover, they are worth considering for text-critical reasons, since a recent edition of the mazurkas has in two of the three instances allowed the changes to stand uncorrected.

The revision in op. 41 no. 3 (in A♭ major) may be the most likely of the three to reflect a real shift in Chopin's conception, rather than a mere lapse (though this is by no means certain). At issue is whether bars 53–60 should be repeated literally, that is, whether the form of the piece should be AAB C AB′ or AAB C ‖:A:‖ B′. The surviving German sources (a copyist's manuscript sent to Breitkopf and Härtel – Warsaw, Biblioteka Narodowa, Mus. 226 – and the edition set from it), and one variant state of the Troupenas first edition (Paris, Bibliothèque Nationale, Ac.p. 2688) lack the repeat. Another variant state of the Troupenas first edition (Paris, Bibliothèque Nationale, Ac.p. 2717) as well as the Wessel first edition enclose the bars within repeat signs. The two states of the Troupenas edition were deposited for purposes of copyright one month apart; that without the repeat dates from December 1840, and that with the repeat from January 1841. This was not the only double deposit of a work by Chopin; in all other instances the second deposit was at least partially necessitated by changes made by the composer in the musical text.[10] Thus the version containing the repeat probably reflects an authorial change, one evidently arrived at when the source used to set the English first edition was prepared (the Wessel edition probably does not derive from the later state of the Troupenas; the English publication was deposited in Stationers' Hall on 1 December 1840, at least one month before the later Troupenas edition).[11]

In op. 50 no. 2, the omission of necessary repeat signs hinges more obviously

Chopin', *Revue de musicologie* lxiv (1978), 76–108.) It is conceivable, though not very likely, that Jędrzejewicz (Chopin's sister) might have received her copy of the mazurka directly from her brother before 1843; were this the case, it would contradict the very plausible hypothesis of Jean-Jacques Eigeldinger that the Jędrzejewicz exemplars were found by her in her brother's apartment when she examined his effects the day of his death. See Jean-Jacques Eigeldinger, *Chopin: Pianist and Teacher*, 3rd, English edn. (Cambridge, 1986), 226. In the same book, p. 150, Eigeldinger first drew my attention to the presence of the cut in all four exemplars.

[9] Jean-Jacques Eigeldinger has demonstrated that the Stirling and Jędrzejewicz exemplars show clear evidence of collusion after Chopin's death. See *Chopin: Pianist and Teacher*, 222–7, and Frédéric Chopin, *Oeuvres pour piano: fac-similé de l'exemplaire de Jane W. Stirling*, ed. Jean-Jacques Eigeldinger and Jean-Michel Nectoux (Paris, 1982), xlii–xliii.

[10] I have elsewhere discussed other double deposits; of the Sonata op. 35, the Impromptu op. 36, and the Nocturnes op. 37, in 'Chopin in the Marketplace', 545–7; and of the Mazurkas op. 63, in 'The Chopin Sources', 322–34.

[11] The Henle edition of op. 41 no. 3 prints the earlier version; it may be easily corrected by adding double bars and repeat dots around bars 53–60.

on Chopin's notational carelessness. The autograph *Stichvorlage* for the French edition (New York, Pierpont Morgan Library) and the English first edition (obviously based on a source deriving from the French autograph) show only double bars without dots at the beginnings of bars 60, 68 and 84. The French and German first editions print double bars and dots. As the edition printed from the French *Stichvorlage* demonstrates, Chopin clearly intended dots to be printed. The oversight probably owed to his occasional habit, when sketching, of signifying repeats only with a double bar.[12]

The inadvertent failure to add dots before a double bar probably accounts as well for the missing repeat in the German autograph *Stichvorlage* and German first edition of op. 59 no. 1. Both the autograph (Mainz, B. Schott und Söhne) and Stern first edition display only a double bar at the end of bar 12, whereas both the Brandus and Wessel first editions show a double bar and repetition dots. Since Chopin probably proofread the French first edition, the repetitive opening probably represents his true intention. The composer rarely, if ever, saw proofs for his German editions, and thus would have had no opportunity to correct his error of omission in the autograph.[13]

B. Ambiguous revisions

All the ambiguous revisions occur in works that date from the early 1830s, and may reflect the young Chopin's uncertainty about appropriate formal plans for the mazurka.

An undated autograph of op. 6 no. 2 (Stockholm, Stiftelsen Musikkulturens Främjande), perhaps presented by Chopin as a gift, transmits a slightly different formal scheme than that found in the published editions of the piece (the autograph also contains other interesting variants from the published versions). The following graph illustrates the differences ('i' signifies 'introduction'):

Autograph: i ‖: A :‖: BA :‖ C i A
Published editions: i ‖: A :‖: BA :‖ C i AA'

The 'fine' in the autograph falls clearly after the first ending of the A section; a second playing of the section cannot follow. The editions do present a second statement of the A section, but a melodically varied one. This variation might suggest that the published version came later than the autograph, if one argued

---

[12] Wojciech Nowik comments on this practice in 'Autografy muzyczny jako podstawa badań źródłowych w Chopinologii', *Muzyka* xvi (1971), 65–84. Occasionally Chopin employed the double bar as a marker of formal division, as, for example, at the beginning of bar 13 in the sketch for op. 56 no. 2 (London, British Library, Add. 47861.A), and at the beginning of bar 17 in the rejected public manuscript of op. 63 no. 1 (Paris, Bibliothèque Nationale, MS 112).

[13] On Chopin's method of publishing in Germany, see Kallberg, 'Chopin in the Marketplace', 795–824. Once again the Henle edition lacks the repeat; again, it may be emended easily with double bars and dots at the end of bar 12.

that the addition constituted a compositional improvement. Unfortunately, no other evidence helps document this hypothesis. The piece is written on paper unique to Chopin; hence it is of no use in dating.[14] The extant sketch of the piece (Paris, Bibliothèque Polonaise, 1109) offers no directions for repetition. Despite my suspicion that the published editions print Chopin's improved version of the piece, the uncertain provenance of the autograph justifies classifying this revision as ambiguous.

Three of the equivocal variants occur in mazurkas from the op. 7 set. Two manuscript versions of op. 7 no. 1 display schemes of repetition that vary from the published editions of the piece. One is an undated autograph given by Chopin to an unknown recipient (currently in the private collection of R. Floersheim). This source gives clear directions on how to execute the repetitions. The other manuscript, undated and in the hand of an unknown scribe, appears in an album that may have been owned by Zofia Walewska (Warsaw, Biblioteka Narodowa, Mus. 970 [BN 6236], fol. 185v–186r). The album contains piano works by composers popular in the 1820s (including Field, Steibelt, Hummel and Weber); this, together with the dates from around 1823 appended to some of the pieces, suggests that this manuscript version may have been copied before the work was published in 1832. In any event, this manuscript gives vague directions for repetition and return. For convenience, I list all the formal schemes, the clear ones in the autograph and printed versions, the possible ones in the scribal manuscript, found in the surviving sources for op. 7 no. 1:

Autograph:		‖:A:‖ B‖:A:‖ C‖:A:‖		
Scribal copy:	1)	‖:A:‖ BA CA	(BA?)	*or*
		‖:A:‖ B‖:A:‖ C‖:A:‖	(B‖:A:‖?)	
	2)	‖:A:‖: BA :‖ CA	(‖:BA:‖?)	*or*
		‖:A:‖: BAA:‖ C‖:A:‖	(‖:BAA:‖?)	
Printed versions:		AA ‖:BA:‖ ‖:CA:‖		

The unknown scribe copied the three sections A, B and C only once; he or she signalled first and second endings for the initial statements of the A section, but afterwards marked only a 'Da Capo' at the conclusion of the B section, and 'Mazur Da Capo' at the end of the C segment. A double bar at the beginning of the B section seems to have repeat dots to its right (i.e., in the equivalent of bar 25), but no such dots appear at the double bar that concludes the

---

[14] The mazurka is transmitted on a single, cream-coloured bifolio; this paper has ten staves with a total span of 143 millimetres, and a staff length of 194 millimetres; it bears a watermark of 'C & I HONIG' plus a shield. Only one other Chopin manuscript known to me has a Honig watermark, an unknown copyist's version of the D major Variations on a theme of Moore for four hands (Cracow, Biblioteka Jagiellońska, Rkp. 1964:1), but the number of staves (12) and their dimensions (total span of 194 millimetres, length of 278 millimetres) differ greatly from the autograph of op. 6 no. 2.

section. The scribe gave no 'Fine' direction, but the double bar after the second ending of A could imply that the piece should end there (in the autograph, Chopin clearly marked 'Fine' after the second ending).

Thus the scribal manuscript leaves unanswered the following questions: (1) Does the double bar with repeat dots before the B section suggest a repetition of B together with A? (2) Does the marking 'Da Capo' after the B section indicate that both the first and second statements of A (with their separate endings) are to be played, or, invoking an unwritten convention, that only the second, harmonically closed, statement of A is to be sounded? (3) Does the marking 'Mazur Da Capo' tell the performer to repeat only the A section, or some permutation of A and B together (in which case question 2 again comes to the fore)?

The questions may ultimately prove to be moot; the manuscript is not in Chopin's hand, and might not reflect in any way his own conception of the form of the piece. Yet since the piece may have been copied in the album before it was published by the composer (further evidence for which may come from the interesting and awkward melodic variants contained in the manuscript), one cannot simply dismiss it either. The version in the album could easily reflect the equivocal state of an early and now-lost Chopin autograph, for the other problematic works from op. 7 show just this type of ambiguity in demonstrably authentic sources.

Op. 7 no. 2 transmits variants in an autograph manuscript, the printed editions, and, possibly, a student's copy of the printed edition. The autograph manuscript, dating from 1830, was a gift to Emilia Elsner; the current whereabouts of this manuscript are not known, but its contents were published in the Supplement to the Breitkopf and Härtel *Gesamtausgabe* in 1902. The version in this manuscript differs sharply from that published by Chopin; for one, it contains an eight-bar introduction (marked 'Duda', or 'Bagpipe') that he did not include in the printed edition.[15] And as concerns repetition, it not only lacks repeat signs in the trio, but also fails to indicate 'Da Capo' after the trio. The printed editions give both of these directions for repetition and return; even so, some ambiguity remains in Chopin's phrase 'D.C. al Fine'. 'Fine' appears at the end of bar 16; as in op. 7 no. 1, it is not entirely clear whether the repeat marked here is to be taken in the Da Capo. Finally, in the Dubois-O'Meara exemplar of op. 7 no. 2, the 'Fine' direction is crossed out in bar 16, and written in ink after the first ending of bar 32. Eigeldinger reports that the hand does not appear to be Chopin's, which might make the change irrelevant.[16] The following graph summarises the variants in formal repetition

[15] Józef Kański, 'W sprawie mazurka A-dur', *Ruch muzyczny* xxvi/5 (8 sierpnia 1982), 7, discusses the textual history and legitimacy of the manuscript version of op. 7 no. 2.
[16] See *Chopin: Pianist and Teacher*, 149.

schemes in op. 7 no. 2 (the subscript '1' refers to a harmonically open ending; the subscript '2' to a harmonically closed ending):

Autograph: i ‖:A_1A_2 :‖: BA_2 :‖   CDC
Published editions: ‖:A_1A_2 :‖: BA_2 :‖   C‖:DC:‖ A_1A_2 *or*
                       ‖:A_1A_2 :‖: BA_2 :‖   C‖:DC :‖: A_1A_2:‖
Dubois-O'Meara: ‖:A_1A_2 :‖: BA_2:‖   C‖:DC:‖ A_1A_2 BA_2 *or*
                       ‖:A_1A_2 :‖: BA_2 :‖   C‖:DC :‖: A_1A_2:‖ BA_2

Does the autograph version (as transmitted to us in the Breitkopf *Gesamtausgabe*) accurately portray Chopin's intentions? While the lack of a formal return to the opening material would be unusual (though not unique – the Mazurka op. 30 no. 2 never returns to its opening theme), the putative conclusion after the A major trio establishes a certain modal symmetry with the A major introduction. Again, though, the possibility remains that, as in op. 7 no. 1, unwritten tradition would have dictated to Emilia Elsner a repeat of at least some of the opening material. The sources remain equivocal.

The divergent readings for op. 7 no. 4 occur between an autograph apparently given as a gift to Wilhelm Kolberg (Warsaw, Warszawskie Towarzystwo Muzyczne, 14/Ch) and the published editions. The following graph portrays the differences:

Autograph: ‖:A:‖ BA   CD A *or*
                 ‖:A :‖ B‖:A:‖ CD ‖:A:‖
Printed editions: AA‖:BAA:‖ CD AA

Once again the autograph is not entirely clear in its use of 'Fine', the issue being whether the double bar and repeat dots that appear directly above it at the end of bar 4 apply to the statements of A that follow B and D. On the other hand, the autograph does clearly lack a repetition of the entire BA or BAA structural unit.[17]

The final ambiguous passage does not really count as a revision, but since the problem is similar to that seen in the op. 7 sources, I include it here. The autograph of the Mazurka in A♭ major (1834), inscribed in the album of Maria Szymanowska (Paris, Muzeum Mickiewicza, 973) and published only in 1930, displays after the second beat of bar 20 what seems to be a double bar with repeat dots on both sides. But, as the editors of both the Paderewski (which also prints a facsimile of the autograph) and Henle editions have pointed out, this sign cannot be taken at face value. One cannot link the second beat of bar 20 with the first beat of bar 5 (where the preceding double bar – without dots – falls) without altering the text in some way. Nor can one connect the

---

[17] The Henle edition, which prints the autograph version of the piece as 'Anhang 1', misplaces the 'Fine' indication, and thus entirely misrepresents the form of the return after the trio as ‖:A :‖ BA. To correct what Henle has printed, one should cross out bars 13–16, add a double bar and 'Dal segno' at the end of bar 12, and add 'Fine' to the end of bar 4.

end of bar 28 (where the following double bar falls, again without repeat dots) with the third beat of bar 20 without substantial alterations in the text. Both the Paderewski and Henle editions solve the problem by shifting the double bar to the end of bar 20, and cancelling the repeat dots after the bar; hence they call only for a repeat of bars 5–20.[18]

Another solution emerges from a later direction in the manuscript. After bar 28, Chopin wrote 'Dal segno al fine, e poi'. The 'segno' falls at the beginning of bar 5; the 'e poi' refers to the concluding bars (bars 44/45–57) that Chopin penned on the following systems. But to what 'fine' does Chopin direct the performer? None is to be found anywhere; the only possible candidate is the apparent double bar with repeat dots in bar 20. The upbeat to bar 45 that begins the 'e poi' section follows beautifully from this point. If we understand the double bar to be an idiosyncratic 'fine' sign, then it would not need to function as a repeat sign at all: bars 5–20 would not be immediately repeated. This solution creates a more formally compact and well-balanced mazurka; no longer does the opening section dwarf the material that follows. Hence I would suggest that the issue of repetition is less ambiguous in this mazurka than in the three previously discussed; nevertheless, since the double bars and repeat dots would have to be understood idiosyncratically if my interpretation of them is correct, some doubt must remain about the proper form of the piece. For comparison, I give the two formal schemes that result from the different solutions (the B section is an eight-bar phrase):

Solution 1: i ‖:A:‖ B A Closing i
Solution 2: i   A   B A Closing i

3. Sectional return

Corrections that uniquely add or subtract sectional returns occur rarely, and only in works from Chopin's maturity. All three examples known to me involve returns of the opening section.

A rejected public manuscript of op. 50 no. 3 (Cracow, Biblioteka Jagiellońska) lacks thirty-two bars present in the published editions. Missing are the equivalent of bars 100–32; in this guise, the reprise is limited to a brief statement of the first theme of the opening section (Example 4), as opposed to the massive ternary complex that comprises the reprise in the *Stichvorlage* (New York, Pierpont Morgan Library) and published editions:

Rejected public manuscript: ‖:A:‖BA CDC A   Coda
Stichvorlage and published editions: ‖:A:‖BA CDC ABA Coda

---

[18] The critical notes to the Paderewski edition register some discomfort with this solution. .

Example 4. Op. 50 no. 3: reprise and opening of coda in rejected public
manuscript

The sketch of the F minor Mazurka (Warsaw, Towarzystwo imienia Fryderyka Chopina, M/235), reconstructed posthumously by Auguste Franchomme and Julian Fontana, and published by the latter as op. 68 no. 4, suggests that Chopin may have changed his concept of the scope of the form in
the course of writing out the manuscript. Although no sketch has been more
extensively discussed in the Chopin literature, the commentary has mostly
focused on the complex final shape of the mazurka; few have noted the traces
of an earlier, more simple, formal design still visible in the manuscript.[19]

[19] The discussions on the F minor Mazurka appear in both articles and editions. They include
Ludwik Bronarski, 'La Dernière Mazurka de Chopin', *Schweizerische Musikzeitung/Revue musicale
suisse* xcv (1955), 380–7; Fryderyk Chopin, *Mazurek f-moll ostatni*, ed. Jan Ekier (Cracow, 1965);
Wojciech Nowik, 'Próba rekonstrukcja *Mazurka f-moll* op. 68 nr. 4 Fryderyka Chopina', *Rocznik
Chopinowski* viii (1969), 44–85; Nowik, 'Chopins Mazurka F moll, op. 68 nr. 4 "Die letzte Inspi-
ration des Meisters"' *Archiv für Musikwissenschaft* xxx (1973), 109–27; Fryderyk Chopin,

To see this design, one must consider the order in which Chopin entered the music on the sketch page. Chopin first penned the A section of the piece on staves 1–4. He then made two abortive attempts at a contrasting section, the first a four-bar melodic sketch on staff 5 (with a brace in the left margin that envelops staff 6), the second a six-bar draft with the heading 'F dur' on staves 8–9. Only on the third try did he arrive at a version worth keeping (for the moment, at least); this he wrote on staves 11–12, again with the heading 'F dur'. The music written on staves 6–7 (continuing to staves 5–6 in the middle of the page) and 13–14, music that significantly expands the contrasting section begun on staves 11–12, could not have formed part of Chopin's original concept of this contrasting section; the shift up to staves 5–6 from staves 6–7 suggests that Chopin had already written out the eventual B section before he notated these staves. In other words, the expanded version of what came to be the C section was written only after Chopin conceived the B section.

This chronology, together with the connecting signs between the end of the A section and the beginning of the C section, and the 'Da Capo' notation at the conclusion of the C section on staves 11–12, all suggest that Chopin first posited a simple ternary form for this mazurka. In this version, a principal F minor section framed a short contrasting section in F major (I reconstruct this original middle section in Example 5). When Chopin then expanded the

Example 5. Op. 68 no. 4: original middle section

The Final Composition: Mazurka in F Minor Op. Posthumous (Fontana Op. 68, no. 4) A Completely New Realization, ed. Ronald Smith (New York, 1975); and Fryderyk Chopin, Mazurka en fa mineur: La Dernière Oeuvre de Chopin, ed. Milosz Magin (Paris, 1983). In my 'Chopin's Last Style', 296–313, I examine all of the above arguments, suggest a new solution to the final form of the mazurka, and propose that the mazurka was not Chopin's 'last thought', but rather a work composed around 1845–6, perhaps originally for inclusion in the eventual op. 63.

mazurka, he did so on all fronts. The principal section assumed a ternary shape of its own, with its contrasting section beginning in Ab major. The original middle section, only eight bars framed by repeat signs, grew to twice that length, with substantial melodic changes being made along the way. In short, the form expanded from a simple A C A scheme to a complex ternary ABA C ABA plan.

In the third correction, Chopin cancelled a far more subtle variety of return. In the Troupenas *Stichvorlage* of op. 41 no. 1 (Paris, Bibliothèque Nationale, MS 113), Chopin originally thought to begin the C section so that it rhymed melodically with the A section (Example 6). This idea occurred to him re-

Example 6. Op. 41 no. 1: original and revised versions of C section in Troupenas *Stichvorlage*

latively late in the genesis of the work; in the sketch for the piece (owned by the heirs of Gregor Piatigorsky), the melody is exactly that of the version ultimately published. Had Chopin kept the motivic parallel, the central section, which is now heard clearly as the middle of a formal arch (AB C BA), might instead initially have been understood as the middle of a rondo-like structure (AB A' BA), though the rest of the section differs sharply from the A material.

The problem of repetition and return in the mazurkas dogged Chopin throughout his creative career. A few general tendencies manifest themselves in the revisions; they help us begin to understand what was musically at stake. Nearly all of the corrections concerned literal or nearly literal reiteration; only the section added at the end of op. 6 no. 2 and the motivic parallel effaced from the middle section of op. 41 no. 1 dealt with substantially varied repetition or return. Moreover, nearly all pertained to repeats of principal sections, either the main theme alone, or the main theme along with any secondary theme that might be attached to it. Only the repeat added to the second half of the middle section in the printed editions of op. 7 no. 2 contradicts this observation; the missing repeat dots in some sources of the middle section of op. 50 no. 2 were probably no more than an oversight.

Thus the heart of the issue for Chopin seems to have been when to restate the principal theme and/or section of a mazurka. His solutions to the problem to some extent differed according to where in a piece it occurred; for this reason, we should consider the revisions by their location.

Twice Chopin altered repeats at the start of a mazurka. In op. 24 no. 4, he removed one; in op. 59 no. 1, he added one. How do we reconcile these apparently contrary decisions? A clue comes from the structure of the theme in the earlier mazurka, for it displays one of the more remarkably constructed opening paragraphs of its genre. The theme of op. 24 no. 4 evolves gradually out of its chromatically contracting introduction, emerging tentatively in the middle voice in bars 5–10 (remaining subordinate to the top line through most of these bars), and attaining the top voice only in bar 11. Once unfolded, it is then stated whole in normal treble-dominated piano texture in bars 13–20. In short, the opening of op. 24 no. 4 has thematic repetition built into it, a very special sort of repetition that incorporates a process of growth. My choice of descriptive metaphors suggests the wisdom of Chopin's decision to cancel the putative repeat. Thematic 'growth' or 'evolution' works effectively only once: the literal repetition of the process would seem redundant.

The thematic structure of op. 24 no. 4 betokens a common purpose to its revision and that in op. 59 no. 1: both leave mazurkas whose opening themes are restated (literally or otherwise) once and only once. And these revisions alert us to an important generic strategy, for repetition is pervasive in the first themes or first sections of mazurkas. Often this repetition is literal or nearly literal, but sometimes it is disguised. Modified repetition becomes more common as Chopin's style matures; op. 24 no. 4 is one of the earlier examples of disguised repetition (and conversely, op. 59 no. 1 is one of the later examples of literal repetition). The techniques for deflecting the repetition grow more subtle. Frequently, for example, repetitions will begin literally, only to veer off in a substantially different melodic direction (in op. 30 no. 4, compare bars 5–12 with bars 13–20; or in op. 50 no. 1, compare bars 1–8 with bars 9–16). Chopin may have originally been drawn to the strategy of literal repetition because the close replication of initial events strongly implies change. Literal repetition at the opening serves as a propulsive device, one that suffuses the mazurka with a unique kind of restless energy.[20] As an opening gambit, it differs sharply from that found in, say, the nocturnes, where thematic restate-

---

[20] In some of his waltzes, Chopin tried similar strategies of initial sectional repetition. But in these works, he tended to vary melodically the initial theme within the section, and so to lessen the propulsive force of the repeat.

ment normally invites lavish ornamentation.[21] His later preference for disguised repetition at the opening of a mazurka probably grew out of a change in his approach to internal and terminal repetition and return; to understand this change, we should turn to the revisions in these areas.

The four revisions of internal repetition suggest a complex web of motivations. Taken together, they might indicate an effort to frustrate a generic sense of patterned repetition after the opening. The changes in op. 33 no. 4 and op. 41 no. 3, for example, work in opposite directions. In the former, the deleted repeat alters a thematic unit otherwise identical to that heard at the beginning of the piece. In the latter, the added repeat precisely duplicates the thematic unit that opened the piece. In both cases, the alterations owe in part to the nature of the following B material.

Until the last two bars, the B section in bars 113–28 of op. 33 no. 4 duplicates that in bars 49–64. Without the revision, in other words, not only would the A section be repeated exactly from the opening, the B material would be as well (that is, bars 1–64 (AAB) = bars 65–128 (AAB)). This vast repeat would exceed any in other mazurkas, and when combined with the motivically repetitive A and B themes in op. 33 no. 4, would lead to a remarkably static mazurka. In other words, it would stall the desired sense of forward motion at the start of a mazurka.

Bars 61–74 of op. 41 no. 3 also imply a full return of the earlier B section (bars 17–32), but the apparent return suddenly stops two bars earlier than expected to end the piece. Chopin's revision in the preceding A section was a masterpiece of psychological planning. His goal was to make the ending of the piece seem as abrupt as possible, and he achieved this goal by making the return of the AAB unit almost identical (until the last two bars) to its initial statement. The original version, by differing from the initial segment, tipped his hand; the revised version avoids any clue (except perhaps for the 'diminuendo' beginning in bar 70) that the piece will conclude where it does.

The internal revisions in op. 7 no. 1 and op. 7 no. 4 occur in sources that, though ambiguous, cannot be dismissed as ephemeral. Now earlier, I stated that the ambiguity in these sources may reflect Chopin's own uncertainty about formal plans in a mazurka. For when one views together all of the sources for op. 7, something of an *ad libitum* approach to form emerges in the set (and the same holds even when one considers only the definitely authentic sources).[22] In addition to the divergent schemes for repeating the internal

[21] In this light, the initial ornamented repeats in op. 17 no. 4 take on additional meaning, for they are not the only strategies in this mazurka to resemble ones found ordinarily in nocturnes. The coda to the piece atypically tends to diffuse tension, in the manner of a nocturne, rather than to increase it, like most mazurkas. The imitation 'harmonics' of bars 117–21 even anticipate the same kind of timbral technique in the Nocturne in Db major op. 27 no. 2.

[22] This character was carried over into the printed set as well; the final number of the set includes the direction 'Dal segno senza Fine': one may finish where one chooses.

statements of the A material in numbers 1 and 4 (no repeat at all; repeat after the contrasting B phrase; repeat BA unit; repeat BAA unit), one must also consider the equally rich array of plans for concluding statements of the A theme.

From these revisions of concluding repetitions in the op. 7 Mazurkas, we begin to understand why the complex of formal variants remained ambiguous. What is striking about these different options for ending the pieces is that none sounds superior to any other. The reason has to do with the treatment of the principal themes when they repeat or return. They tend at best to be only minimally differentiated functionally on successive statements (usually the themes return unchanged); no return to the principal theme is prospectively identifiable as the final one. Thus, it makes little difference if the mazurkas end with the main theme played once alone or twice in succession. In op. 7 no. 1, for example, the endings sound equally abrupt whether the concluding formal segment stands as CA, C‖:A:‖, or ‖:CA:‖.[23] Much the same point may be made about the changes of interior repetition. In other words, the multiple formal schemes that emerge from the op. 7 sources appear to be the logical concomitant of the nature of the themes themselves. Any selection from among these options will ultimately seem rather arbitrary; to some degree, the structures of these pieces are paratactic. The conceptual difficulty of the revisions of concluding and internal repetitions resists easy solution, and properly so: the ambiguity in the sources for these early mazurkas would seem to reflect something essential in the construction of the themes themselves. Indeed, that sectional repetition and return should have been a recurring compositional issue in a genre that features uniquely pervasive reiteration of short melodic and/or rhythmic motives cannot be coincidental.[24]

This is not to imply, however, that attempts to make melodic and formal processes reflect one another were limited to Chopin's earlier mazurkas. The expansion of op. 68 no. 4 from a simple ternary design to a more complex ternary plan can be viewed in this light. The internal structures of the original A theme, the added B section, and especially the expanded C section all return constantly to two-bar motives (different in each section, of course). In the A and B paragraphs, this reiteration is usually altered somehow, most often by

---

[23] The addition of a melodically varied statement of the principal theme to the end of op. 6 no. 2 might seem more justifiable compositionally than any of the versions of the op. 7 mazurkas, for the variation does lead to some functional differentiation among the statements of the A material. Moreover, it creates a mazurka in which the principal material is repeated at each appearance (in its second statement, the A theme is linked to a contrasting B phrase). Yet, as I argued above, the uncertain provenance of the autograph prevents one from identifying as discarded material the formally aperiodic version of the piece it contains.

[24] The repetitive motivic structure of Chopin's mazurka melodies, and the relation of these melodies to models in Polish folk music, have been discussed by H. Windakiewiczowa, 'Wzory ludowej muzyki polskiej w Mazurkach Fryd. Chopina', *Polska Akademja Umiejętności Wydział Filologiczny. Rozprawy* lxi/7 (Cracow, 1926), 1–49; and by Wiaczesław Paschalow, *Chopin a polska muzyka ludowa* (Cracow, 1951).

sequence, sometimes by melodic variation. In the middle section, too, the repetitions are varied, but the chromatic inflections of melody and harmony that Chopin employed here are so striking as to draw further attention to the similarities among them. Only by enlarging the number of statements of the A section to four could Chopin hope to reflect at the level of form the pervasive repetition in the themes of the mazurka. But one problematic result of this expansion, left unsolved perhaps because Chopin abandoned work on the sketch, is a late mazurka whose thematic statements are as undifferentiated as an early one.[25] The close of this mazurka sounds just as arbitrary as one from op. 7.

Again we encounter this arbitrariness, which I mentioned above as one result of the lack of functional differentiation in the themes of the op. 7 set. More pervasive in earlier mazurkas than in later ones, this type of conclusion tends to sound precipitous or premature. What creates this feeling? It may initially have been a by-product of the folk origins of the genre. The folk *mazur, oberek,* and *kujawiak* often lacked a sense of definitive closure, in part because sectional repeats were taken *ad libitum*.[26] In any case, the unexpectedness of some endings probably derives from a property of persistent literal return. In a piece with several literal returns and repetitions of a theme, each statement at once recalls previous occurrences and prefigures ones that presumably will occur in the future. The events become perceptually linked together in an apparently unending chain; the sensation that the references forward and backward in time will continue indefinitely is tempered only by the understanding of conventional duration for the piece at hand.[27] When a piece ends after one of these literal returns, the termination is understood as artificial. There is no real closure – only stopping.

Here then arose a problem for Chopin. Exact, or nearly exact, repetition and return were properties inherent to the genre, yet Chopin occasionally desired in mature works a more decisive feeling of closure. How could he thwart the sensation of suddenness? One strategy was to play on the qualifier 'nearly', and to effect minor changes in the themes that would promote a somewhat stronger sense of terminal closure. The ending to the printed version of op. 7 no. 4 (Example 7), a reprise of the principal theme, differs from the previous statements only in its dynamic level of *forte* (as opposed to *piano*), and in the fermata added to the rest in the penultimate bar. Since both of these changes

[25] I extensively defend the assertion that Chopin abandoned work on the sketch in 'Chopin's Last Style', 296–315. There I surmise that he stopped work on the sketch because of its irreparable musical defects; the problem with terminal closure is by no means the only one in op. 68 no. 4.

[26] See 'Mazurka' in *The New Grove Dictionary of Music and Musicians* (London, 1980), xi, 865.

[27] My attention was drawn to this effect of return by J. Hillis Miller's discussion of Conrad's *Lord Jim* in *Fiction and Repetition: Seven English Novels* (Cambridge, Mass. 1982), 34–5. Miller does not limit the effect to literal return or repetition.

Example 7. Conclusion in printed versions of op. 7 no. 4

fall in the last two bars of the piece, they only barely alleviate the openness of structure. Chopin found far more effective a second course of action, which generated closure through the imposition of an additional phrase or section. Here a sense of firm conclusion is imposed on the process generated by the body of the piece; the chain of references to the repetitive themes is severed, and closural motion substituted in its place.[28] Chopin's first efforts tended to appropriate conventional closing gestures in a single phrase, as in the twice-stated cadential progression and reduced dynamics of the codetta to op. 6 no. 3 (Example 8a), or the echoing effect in the codetta to op. 7 no. 3 (Example 8b).

Example 8.

(a) Codetta to op. 6 no. 3

(b) Codetta to op. 7 no. 3

[28] On closure in repetitive works of poetry and music, see Barbara Herrnstein Smith, *Poetic Closure: A Study of How Poems End* (Chicago, 1968), 98–109; and Lawrence Kramer, *Music and Poetry: The Nineteenth Century and After*, California Studies in 19th Century Music, (Berkeley and Los Angeles, 1984), iii, 25–56.

Soon Chopin came to prefer full-fledged codas when he wanted to impart a firm sense of closure to mazurkas. As he matured, these codas grew longer, more complex, and even would at times introduce very special types of 'new themes'. I have written elsewhere about these codas, and the powerful effect of these new 'epigrammatic' themes.[29] Suffice it to say here that these themes display a bare-boned profile highly atypical with respect to Chopin's normal thematic style; in their utterly unambiguous nature, they maximally promote closure. Chopin deployed them carefully, placing them only at the ends of codas to the final numbers in multipartite sets. What is further notable is that he for the most part used these 'epigrammatic' themes only in mazurkas;[30] surely this owes in large measure to the particular nature of repetition and return in this genre.

One of these long and complex codas (without an 'epigrammatic' theme) probably accounted for the revision in op. 50 no. 3. Chopin's initial reading and his revision differ as to which version of the canonic opening theme will be used to lead into the coda. The two versions were introduced as part of the complex opening section of the mazurka. The first, with its canonic imitation at the octave, is solidly grounded in the tonic. The second, with its canonic imitation at the fifth, hovers on the dominant. Even though both canons arrive at a G♯ major chord after eight bars, the first chord functions as a dominant, and the second as a tonic (Chopin made this clear by adding a seventh to the first chord). In the rejected public manuscript, the first version of the canon led to the coda; its tonic orientation made for a weak link to the processive opening of the coda. The second version of the canon clearly would function better at this join, and to bring about this change, Chopin found it necessary to add the entire section corresponding to the missing parts of the A and B themes. (Conceivably he could have simply altered the canonic structure as it stood in the rejected public manuscript, changing it from the first version to the second, but this would have severely undercut the feeling of reprise after the central section.) In other words, the literal return was added to op. 50 no. 3 in order to prepare the entry of the coda, a coda that, paradoxically, is present in part to counter the formal process generated by the literal return.

While one of the chief functions of the codas in mazurkas was to cap open forms by interrupting the processes generated by principal themes, this is not to say that codas and principal themes were entirely different in their internal structures. Chopin's revisions of low-level repetition draw our attention to

---

[29] See 'Compatibility in Chopin's Multipartite Publications', 404–17.

[30] In other genres, Chopin occasionally wrote conclusions to codas that achieved a similar restriction of means, but without presenting the fully formed type of 'new theme' known in the mazurkas; one such example is the close of the Prelude in D♭ major op. 28 no. 15 (bars 84–9).

similarities of melodic structuring in codas and principal themes. Both repetitive passages fall in codas, and both lead into contrasting repetitive material. Differences in proportion probably account for why Chopin chose in one instance to add the motivic reiteration, and in the other to delete it. The coda to op. 63 no. 1 is short, and the four bars of dotted rhythm are followed by only four bars of a contrasting repetitive motive. The coda to op. 59 no. 3 is much longer; the cancelled repetitive bars would have been followed by twelve bars of two groups of repetitive motives. In op. 59 no. 3, Chopin ran the risk of overwhelming the coda with motivic repetition, while in op. 63 no. 1 the balance seemed more appropriate. These revisions, along with the repetitive melodic structures in other codas to mazurkas, suggest that not just any means of arresting the formal process was acceptable to Chopin, but rather that codas needed to establish a structural link with the body of the mazurka – here the similarities in their melodic formations – in order to function most effectively.

Codas were not the only way Chopin sought to lessen the sense of openness in structure. He also tried different ways of modifying the returns of principal material. Perhaps the most well-known of these strategies is the foreshortened return, where the abbreviation of the principal theme usually leads into an extended coda of the type described above.[31] These condensed returns begin to assume importance in the op. 17 set (both numbers 2 and 4 feature them), and thereafter appear frequently. Chopin's idea in shortening these returns was to provide some functional differentiation among the statements of the principal theme; he tried other ways as well. One was to alter the tonality of the otherwise literal return, as in the restatements of the second half of the principal theme in op. 41 no. 2, or the reprise in op. 59 no. 1. Another was to shift to an imitative texture, as in op. 59 no. 3. Sometimes the return to the principal melody might be nearly literal, but its accompaniment changed to incorporate a dominant pedal, as in op. 63 no. 1. Some mazurkas combine these techniques; one example is op. 41 no. 4. Like other changes in Chopin's approach to literal repetition, these modifications in return occurred with greater frequency as he matured.

Finally, one last type of evidence demonstrates the shift in the mature Chopin's attitudes toward formal process in the mazurkas. At some time no earlier than 1843, he entered four melodic ornaments in students' printed editions of mazurkas. Three of the four annotations were entered in op. 7 no. 2, the fourth was written in op. 24 no. 1. Now these are the only ornaments we are certain Chopin added to students' copies of mazurkas (he far more often inserted them in nocturnes, where they fit more appropriately with

---

[31] Gerald Abraham was one of the first to discuss this technique; see *Chopin's Musical Style* (London, 1939), 46–7.

the general thematic style).[32] For this reason, the decision to pen some melodic variants for some themes from early mazurkas seems especially significant. Surely this decision was motivated by the modifications that Chopin's conception of form in the genre had undergone. Increasingly disquieted by the uniformity of thematic repetition and return in the mazurkas, he must have viewed these annotations as a way of differentiating, if only slightly, the themes of these early pieces.[33]

What do Chopin's struggles with repetition and return in the mazurkas tell us? On a straightforward level, the revisions inform us text-critically, for in several instances, modern editions have transmitted schemes of repetition and return that Chopin expressly altered. At the same time, we learn from the revisions that not all texts may be so resolutely determined: given the inherent formal ambiguity in op. 7, the printed versions here cannot really exert any authority over the various manuscript versions.

Most significant, perhaps, are the insights gained into Chopin's conception of the genre. The revisions direct us to strategies for repetition at the onset of a mazurka, to the aura of dynamism that Chopin tried to instill through propulsive literal repeats. They lay bare the formal problems created by literal repetition and return in the interior and at the close of a mazurka. And just as important, since understanding a genre usually involves grasping how it gradually transforms itself, the revisions expose both how and why modified initial repetition, functional differentiation of successive statements of the same theme, and expansive codas came to be introduced. But the revisions also highlight that the changes were neither radical nor all-encompassing. Chopin did not depart entirely from the concepts he espoused in earlier mazurkas; they still underlie the formal processes instigated in mature mazurkas. That a modified

---

[32] I derive this information from Eigeldinger, *Chopin: Pianist and Teacher*, 148–9. Eigeldinger transcribes the annotations on p. 149; see also his facsimile edition of Chopin, *Oeuvres pour piano*, xxxii–xxxiv. The annotation in op. 7 no. 1, transcribed on p. xxxii, is not in Chopin's hand; nevertheless it functions similarly to those definitely conceived by him, and may reflect his wishes.

Mikuli reported that Chopin loved to improvise ornaments in the mazurkas, but this statement does not agree with the written record in annotated editions. See Eigeldinger, *Chopin: Pianist and Teacher*, 74.

[33] Amusing confirmation of the change in Chopin's attitudes toward literal repetition in the mazurkas comes in a letter to Julian Fontana of 8 August 1839 (see Fryderyk Chopin, *Korespondencja Fryderyka Chopina*, ed. Bronisław Sydow, 2 vols. (Warsaw, 1955), i, 353). Chopin poked fun at a pair of mazurkas he has received from one Alexander Moszczeński, Starosta (i.e., Mayor) of Brześć. Chopin wrote: 'Respectable mazurkas, quite like you may want to put out: "ram didiridi, ram didiridi, ram didiridi, rajda"' ('Mazurki, jak sobie wystawić możesz, szanowne: "ram didiridi, ram didiridi, ram didiridi, rajda"'). Though Chopin never penned such a baldly predictable theme, might not some of his scorn have resulted from his efforts to avoid such stark repetition in his mazurkas?

return gives rise to differentiated function depends to some degree on one's awareness of the lack of differentiation inherent in literal repetition and return.

Nothing could be simpler than to revise a literal restatement of a principal theme. A double bar here, a cut there: Chopin made most of the changes we have examined with an easy stroke of his quill. But this simplicity belies the compositional significance of the alterations. For bound up in this persistent issue are basic notions of structure, concepts that figure centrally in the understanding of form and closure. Chopin confronted again and again the problem of repetition and return because it looms large in our esthetic response to the genre.

Fryderyk Chopin's op. 57 – from *Variantes* to *Berceuse*

WOJCIECH NOWIK

Historical Outline

The *Berceuse* in Db major op. 57 occupies a special place in Chopin's creative output. It is a work of remarkable beauty and technical perfection and these qualities are valued by us all the more in that Chopin wrote only one essay in the genre.

Numerous general observations have been made about the *Berceuse* in Chopin biographies and there are more specialised studies looking at specific technical and stylistic features. Yet while these commentaries have enabled us to get a little closer to an understanding of the piece, they remain only the starting-point for a more thorough examination of its special problems.

The present essay will tackle questions which have not yet been studied or which have been relegated to the margins of previous research. My investigation is first and foremost concerned with elucidating the reasons for the change of title from *Variantes* to *Berceuse*. I will offer some analytical commentary on the original conception of the piece and will then go on to examine the nature and purpose of the modifications made to it in association with the change of title. I will also explore Chopin's own attitude to the work and the reasons it remains his sole composition of this type.

The arguments presented here will be based on Chopin's correspondence, on biographical data and on the autograph sources for the composition. These autographs enable us to examine the piece's original shape, to investigate its specific structural properties, and to trace the course of the alterations which decided the change of title – in short to discover how this masterpiece, the only one of its kind, was created.

Scholars disagree in their dating of the *Berceuse*, suggesting 1843,[1] 1844,[2] or 1843–4.[3] The available biographical information is insufficient to enable us unequivocally and precisely to fix the date of its composition. The first mention of the work appears in Bohdan Zaleski's[4] memoirs of 2 February 1844: 'It was snowing – just like one of our winter days. At 4 p.m. I went to Chopin's house, where I found Witwicki,[5] and a little later Mrs Hoffmanowa[6] arrived with Miss Takinowska and Mr and Mrs Tomaszewscy.[7] Chopin came up to us, wan, frail, but in a good mood and inspired; he greeted me warmly and seated himself at the pianoforte. It is impossible to describe what and how he played. For the first time in my life I felt the beauty of music so intensely that I burst into tears. I had caught in flight all the shades of the master's emotion and perfectly recall the motives and expression of each piece. He played first a magical prelude, then a cradle-song, then a mazurka, then the cradle-song again, prompting Mrs Hoffman to remark, "Surely this is how the angels sang in Bethlehem. . .".'[8] Zaleski's recollection is very important. It shows that a *Berceuse* had already taken shape and therefore dated from before that meeting. As evidenced by its repeat performance, the *Berceuse* met with great approval from the audience, in whom it produced a spontaneous reaction.

Before the piece was published the composer doubtless gave further performances of it to different audiences.[9] Yet no further light is cast upon its

---

[1] Zdzisław Jachimecki, *Chopin. Rys życia i twórczości* (Cracow, 1957), 309; Bronisław Sydow, *Bibliografia F.F. Chopina* (Warsaw, 1954), 11; Arthur Hedley, 'Chopin' in *Grove's Dictionary of Music and Musicians* (London, 1966), ii, 266; Igor Bełza, *Fryderyk F. Chopin* (Warsaw, 1969), 383; Adam Zamoyski, *Chopin* (London, 1975), 209.

[2] Ferdynand Hoesick, *Chopin. Życie i twórczość* (Cracow, 1967), ii, 419, 429; Leopold Binental, *Chopin. Życiorys twórcy i jego sztuka* (Warsaw, 1937), 6; Józef Chomiński, *Chopin* (Cracow, 1978), 166; Jan Ekier, *Wstęp do Wydania Narodowego Dzieł Fryderyka Chopina* (Cracow, 1974), 46 and appendix; Jim Samson, *The Music of Chopin* (London, 1985), 96.

[3] Maurice Brown, *Chopin. An Index of his Works in Chronological Order* (London, 1972), 157; Gastone Belotti, *Chopin* (Torino, 1984), 424; Mieczysław Tomaszewski, 'Chopin' in *Encyklopedia Muzyczna PWM* (Cracow, 1985), ii, 137.

[4] Józef Bohdan Zaleski (1802–86). Poet who took part in the November Uprising. From 1832 an émigré in France. Co-founder of and activist in the Slavonic Society; Young Poland; Polish Democratic Society (1835–7); Commission of Polish Emigration (1848) etc. Friend of the leading representatives of the Polish émigrés in Paris, including Mickiewicz and Chopin, who composed four songs to his texts. Zaleski's wife – Zofia Rozengardt-Zaleska – was a pupil of Chopin from 1843 to 1844.

[5] Stefan Witwicki (1801–47). Poet, from 1832 an émigré in Paris. Friend of Chopin. In 1830 he published the *Piosnki sielskie* which Chopin set to music (ten songs of op. 74).

[6] Klementyna Hoffmanowa z Tańskich (1798–1845). Writer, from 1831 an émigré in France. Pioneer of women's patriotic–civil education. Author of socio-historical novels, promoter of literature for children.

[7] Józef Tomaszewski. School-friend of Zaleski; Konstancja – his wife – a pianist.

[8] Franciszek German, 'Zofia i Bohdan Zalescy a Fryderyk Chopin', *Rocznik Chopinowski* xv (1983), 46

[9] This is indicated by Chopin's letter to his family of 18–20 July 1845 and of August 1845, *Korespondencja Fryderyka Chopina*, ed. Bronisław Sydow, 2 vols. (Warsaw 1955), ii, 138 and 145.

fortunes until Chopin's correspondence with his publishers and the press announcement of its publication. In a letter (probably of January 1844) to his publisher, Schlesinger, Chopin wrote: 'Ma Sonate ainsi que les variantes sont à votre disposition. Je veux pour les deux ouvrages douze cents francs.'[10] On 5 January 1845 Schlesinger hastened to inform readers of *La revue et gazette musicale de Paris* that: 'Chopin est de retour à Paris. Il rapporte une nouvelle Sonate et des variantes. Bientôt ces deux importants ouvrages seront publiés.'[11]

One can therefore assume that at that time the composer had decided to call the piece *Variantes*. Yet this assumption would appear to be wrong in view of a document dated 21 December 1844, in which Chopin sold his Leipzig publishers the author's rights to his recent compositions: 'Moi soussigné Fréd. Chopin demeurant à Paris rue St. Lazare place d'Orleans reconnais d'avoir vendu à Messieurs Breitkopf et Härtel à Leipsik la propriété des ouvrages ci-des-sous nommés de ma composition, Savoir: 1ᵃ *Sonate* (en si mineur) op. 57, 2° *La Berceuse*. . .58'.[12]

Data from the same period reveal Chopin's indecision about the title. It is difficult to believe that he intended to publish the piece in France under the title of *Variantes* and in Germany as a *Berceuse*. Neither Chopin's correspon-dence nor his biographers offer any information on the subject. All we know is that the piece was published in 1845 as the *Berceuse* op. 57.[13] It is worth then examining the autographs of the piece – a sketch, a fair copy and a copy – in the hope that these will help us to solve the problem.

Analysis of the sketch

The sketch of the *Berceuse* is one of Chopin's most unusual and intriguing manuscripts.[14] The musical text covers two pages of 12 staves each. The sketch-like character of the text is evidenced by its atypical spatial arrangement, by the numerous abbreviations of notation, the omissions from the text, the composer's idiosyncratic markings, crossings-out and corrections and his trying-out of the pen and ink (Example 1).

[10] Ibid., 384.

[11] Ignacy Blochman, 'Dwa autografy listów Chopina w Belgii', *Kwartalnik Muzyczny* xxvi–xxvii (1949), 46. Frederick Niecks (*Frederic Chopin as a Man and Musician*, 2 vols. (London, 1902), ii, 122) is uncertain about the title *Variantes* and even suspects a printing error.

[12] Jeffrey Kallberg, 'Chopin in the Marketplace', *Notes* xxxix (1983), 823–4. Chopin gave the wrong opus numbers of both compositions in this document.

[13] Dalila Turło: ('Problemy identyfikacji i chronologii pierwszych wydań Chopina', *Rocznik Chopinowski* xiv (1982), 52) also gives the month of publication of the *Berceuse* in London (April), Paris (June) and Leipzig (July).

[14] A detailed description of the autograph and its provenance appears in Krystyna Kobylańska, *Rękopisy Utworów Chopina, Katalog*, 2 vols. (Cracow, 1977), i, 311.

Example 1.

The *spatial arrangement* of the material on the page is unusual and without any equivalent in the composer's other autographs. Instead of notating the piece as a sequence of successive bars, Chopin wrote out virtually the whole piece in columns made up of four-bar segments. An exception is the final segment on the second page of the sketch marked by the number '14'; this comprises four four-bar sections.

As a result of the material's *segmentation*, the sketch precisely and extraordinarily clearly displays the different levels of construction, the function of the individual components and the underlying principle by which the piece is developed. A four-bar *model* serves as the basis for the piece's construction. Each bar of this model constitutes a *type* made up of characteristic material: a constant ostinato accompaniment and a variable melodic line. The material of the model is subjected to transformations produced by an assortment of variation techniques.[15] These transformations are contained within segments notated successively one below the other. In this way a kind of table depicting the piece's *structure* is built up. The type and its variants appear in the columns, whilst the model and the segments appear in the rows (Example 2). The mor-

Example 2. Tabular arrangement of the material of the sketch. In brackets ( ) incomplete types

Segments	Types				
1	A	B	C	D	Model
2	A	B	C	D	
3	A	B	C	D	
4	A	B	C	D	Variants
5	(A)		C	D	
6	A	B	(C)	D	
	etc.				

phological and positional connections of the types, variants, model and segments form functional categories which define the various levels of the piece's structure.

It should be stressed that the motivic relations which most strongly unite the type with the variant are gradually loosened and even obliterated throughout the course of the piece's composition. The variant then becomes integrated with the model by means of more general connections: melodic (e.g., a similar direction in the unfolding of the melody), harmonic and dynamic. If, however,

[15] A description of these techniques appears in Zofia Lissa, *Studia nad twórczością Fryderyka Chopina* (Cracow, 1970), 406–45.

their action is too weak and a structural analogy is not clear on the micro-architectural level, then the macro-architecture takes on the main integrating role. The composer's precise definition of the *position* of the variant in the segment dispels any typological doubts.

The contextual (syntagmatic) tie acts more strongly within the framework of the section than does the typological (paradigmatic) connection. For example, staff 3, bar 6 of the sketch (bar 41 in the piece) could be classified according to its morphological features as a variant of type C. Yet its contextual position demonstrates unequivocally that it is variant B of segment 11. Similar doubts may be aroused by the identical variants C and D of system 3, in different registers. However, the composer has specified their exact position and function in the context by means of 'insertion' marks i.e., lines linking the text to the place where it is to occur.[16] One can point to a similar situation in relation to the identical variants C and D of segment 10 (bars 41–2 in the piece).

The tabular formulation of the material in the sketch not only assisted its subsequent reproduction and transformation but also enabled the position and role of the individual segments within the whole to be defined, and the various architectural units to be integrated into a total form.

The material of the sketch is ordered in two different ways. The first results from the spontaneous generation of material in the form of segments. The sequence of these segments in columns probably corresponds to the order in which the ideas appeared in the composer's imagination during the first stage of the creative process. Then, during the process of verification, the material produced was restructured, resulting in changes to some of the variants (Example 3). The most important task for the composer was to fix the final sequence

Example 3. Texts crossed out by the composer

---

[16] The 'insertion' here links the text written on the fifth staff of the second page, marked 'X', with the third staff of the first page (right-hand side), marked with a connecting line and a similar 'X'. Beneath this sign the composer crossed out the motives analogous to segment 9B, while below, on the fourth staff, he crossed out motives belonging to segment 9C.

of segments. To this end he introduced another kind of ordering: *numeric* marking. This numbering underwent alterations which are now hard to reconstruct from an analysis of photographs of the sketch. The numbering of the first column (1–6) clearly provides superfluous information since it follows the original chronology. However, in the second column, where the sequence of segments was altered several times (segments 8, 9, 11), and on the second page (segments 12, 13, 14) – the numbering was essential.

The ordering by numbers was designed to *integrate the material into a form*, and to mark its principal *climax*. This occurs in segment 11 (bars 43–4 of the piece) and is expressed by an intensification of movement and by the unfolding of the melodic line over a significantly greater compass than in the other segments.[17] The climax that was initially planned (page 1, column 2, segment 2, according to the original chronology) came too early and undermined the effect of the conclusion. By altering the sequence of the segments the composer was able to prepare the conclusion more carefully, with a characteristic reduction of dynamics, and a gradual slowing-down and halting of the melodic flow.

The material's integration into a form involved the confirmation of existing connections, and the establishment of new connections, between segments. The segments constitute the architectural basis of the work and their form-giving role was made plain during Chopin's final fixing of the unfolding melodic line. Each segment constitutes an integral architectural unit but through their structural equivalence the composer was able to interchange individual segments. The ordering of the segments and the assignation of their functions gave rise to an unusually cohesive and homogeneous form.[18]

The tabular formulation of the material assisted the development of the form and played on important *operational* role. It also contributed to the *economical* (i.e., sparing, but at the same time transparent) notation of the material. The numerous omissions from the text and the various abbreviations become more legible and easier to reconstruct thanks to the material's segmentation and presentation in columns. Not surprisingly Chopin usually omitted the accompaniment's isomorphic material, noting only its very infrequent variants (segments 2, 7, 13, 14). In the melodic line he employed a much greater variety of abbreviation codes.

[17] Samson (*The Music of Chopin*, 96) also considers that the apex of the development of the piece's ornamentation occurs in bar 43.

[18] Hugo Leichtentritt (*Analyse von Chopinschen Klavierwerken*, 2 vols. (Berlin, 1921), ii, 280) on the material's homogeneity: 'Die Reihenfolge der einzelnen Variationen ist durchaus nicht gleichgültig, das Stück würde in dem wohltuenden Ausgleich seiner auf- und absteigenden Konturen verlieren, wenn man die einzelnen Variationen von der ihnen zugewiesenen Stelle anderswohin versetzen wollte.'

These appear as:

1 *Repetitions*, indicated by means of
   a) oblique strokes (their number corresponding to the rhythmic
      values of the notes ♪ ≡ ♪ ≈ ♪ ⌐) – segments 5C, 6C, 10C, D;
   b) vertical strokes – segment 8A;
2 *Abbreviations* of the unfolding of the melodic line in the form of a
   wavy line – segments 8B, 11A;
3 *Omissions* from the text – segments 5A, B;
4 A 'synthetic' formulation of the figuration – segments 5D, 10A, B, C.

All the omitted material can be reinstated from the context and from an understanding of the work's underlying principles of development. The most interesting of the abbreviation codes cited is the 'synthetic' formulation of figuration. Here Chopin *reduced* the motives to their fundamental (initial) notes,
producing a melodic skeleton of the basic structure of the line (segment 5D);
he also reduced the triplet motive to a sequence of dyads (segments 10A, B, C).

The reductive strategies seen here are a clear indication of Chopin's structuralist approach to the material of the piece. As a result the composer sowed
the seeds of 'polymelody',[19] even marking this in the text of the sketch (segment 5D – an unbroken line, joining the extra downstrokes to the top of the
first notes of the four-note motives), and later expanding them in the copy
(segment 10, bars 39–42 in the piece).

Chopin's very individual markings are supplemented by a written-out key
signature 'D♭ major' and by the aforementioned 'insertions' (segments 10 and
11). The inclusion of fingering in segment 14D is also of interest, for it is
extremely rare in the sketch (the same fingering occurs at the analogous place in
the copy). The fingering on the sketch demonstrates that the composer was
thinking in terms of performance and interpretation even at this early stage of
the creative process.

There are two final observations. One is struck by the fact that there are very
few crossings-out or alterations to the text, indicating not only Chopin's sure-
ness of invention but also his special feeling for variation form. And we should
note that the material of the sketch is both essential and sufficient for the full
expansion of the piece.

Analysis has shown the composer's structuralist approach to the special
problems associated with the composition of the *Berceuse*.[20] This approach

---

[19] The term 'polimelodyka' is used by Bronisława Wójcik-Keuprulian in *Melodyka Chopina* (Lwów,
   1930).

[20] The cradle-song is not the only – although certainly the most characteristic – example of a structuralist conception of the generation of form in Chopin. I have examined this question in
   relation to another piece in 'Chopinowski konstruktywizm w rękopisach Nokturnu c-moll
   (bez opusu)', *Rocznik Chopinowski* xiv (1982), 21–33.

reveals itself in the manner of notation and in the arrangement of the material on the page, thanks to which the following are clearly distinguished: the basic units of the micro- and macro-architecture; the underlying principle of development and the means by which the material is transformed; the role and function of the segments. The form of the piece, in short, has been marked out precisely. Moreover, the layout of the text contains operational features which facilitate the ordering of the material; it also provides data which help clarify the abbreviation codes, textual omissions etc.

The sketch reveals above all Chopin's preoccupation with structural problems. For here we have an innovative attempt to create an ostinato variation-form rather different from anything in his earlier music. The slight four-bar theme marks out the dimensions of the later variations. But its role extends beyond this. It supplies not only the basic melodic material but also qualities of 'substance'[21] and of structure, qualities which determine the cohesiveness of the ornamental melody and the concision of the overall form. The unchanging accompaniment[22] is the canvas upon which new kinds of figuration can be painted (chordal, harmonic, polyphonic and polymelodic), at times foreshadowing the novel tonal qualities of impressionism.[23] This tightly structured, closely unified composition, based upon ostinato variations, was given by Chopin the wholly appropriate title of *Variantes*.[24] With this word he captured its essential structural qualities, as revealed clearly in the pages of the sketch.

Analysis of the fair copy •

The fair copy of the piece was made on three pages of 12 staves each[25] (Example 4).

Here the material is expanded into a direct sequence of successive bars in accordance with the formal development indicated in the sketch. This, there-

---

[21] Lissa (*Studia nad twórczością Fryderyka Chopina*, 432) points out the unity of substance in the *Berceuse*.

[22] Ludwik Bronarski, 'Kilka uwag o basso ostinato w ogóle i u Chopina w szczególności', *Kwartalnik Muzyczny* xvi (1932). Bronarski made a detailed study of the accompaniment of the *Berceuse*, indicating hints of four-part writing in it (p. 712).

[23] Mieczysław Tomaszewski ('Chopin' in *Encyklopedia Muzyczna PWM*, ii, 147) detects a precursor of impressionism in the harmony of the piece.

[24] Ignacy Blochman ('Dwa autografy listów Chopina w Belgii', 47) notes 'the term *variantes* should be understood in the German sense of 'Veränderungen', as in Beethoven's op. 120'. However, the *33 Veränderungen über einen Walzer von Diabelli* are numbered variations, and represent a genre different from that of the *Berceuse*. Jan Ekier (*Wstęp*, 50) points out that the variations *Souvenir de Paganini*, published by J. Kleczyński in 1881, are labelled as *Warianty*, and makes an analogy between their construction and that of the *Berceuse*. This analogy is debatable, as is Chopin's authorship of *Souvenir de Paganini*.

[25] A detailed description of the autograph appears in Kobylańska, *Katalog*, i, 311.

Example 4.

Example 4. (*cont.*)

fore, is a traditional formulation. It is distinguished, however, by the tendency to notate bars in fours or multiples of four (except for page 3, staves 4–5, 7–8 in bars of six), reflecting perhaps the segmentation of the sketch's material. Another characteristic feature is the strictly applied '3-staff working unit', where the first and second staves are allotted to the melody and accompaniment, while the third is used for alterations and corrections.

The text of the fair copy is defined in full, without abbreviations or omissions. It contains several innovations in relation to the sketch: bar 36 – the division of the final group of seven: ♪♪ ♪♪♪ ♪♪ ; bars 52 and 57 – the melody as in the final version. There are also some minor inaccuracies: bar 30 – f‴ instead of e♭″, bar 31 – d♭‴ ♩ instead of ♪, bar 38 – g♭″ instead of g″, bar 49 – f′ ♩ instead of ♪, bar 59 – b♭′ without a tie. The only interpretative indication which the composer includes is the phrasing of the melody.

The fair copy confirms that the material of the sketch was sufficient for the complete expansion of the piece. It contains no data, however, which would lead us to suspect that Chopin intended to change the name from *Variantes*.

Analysis of the copy

A copy containing the composer's corrections was written out on three pages of 12 staves each[26] (Example 5). Like the fair copy, it contains the fully defined and developed text of the piece. However, none of the pages of the copy, made by an unknown hand, reflects the spatial layout of the material of the sketch.

Chopin added to the copy an assortment of interpretative markings: phrasing, pedalling, dynamics, expression and tempo. These are very important indications since they emphasise the basic character of the piece. They also show that the composer was giving much thought to the expressive qualities of the musical material at this stage of work on the piece. He highlighted through notation several features which had been barely indicated in the sketch (the polymelody in bars 38–42, for example, and the inverted pedal in bars 33–4). He also marked the fingering in bars 43, 49–50, 55–6, and made some small changes to the text, adding in bar 36 the chord ab″ – db‴ – gb‴. Insignificant errors crept in at this stage: in bar 38 there is no natural sign in the final group

Example 5.

---

[26] A description of the copy appears in Kobylańska, ibid., 312.

Example 5. (*cont.*)   Op. 57 – from *Variantes* to *Berceuse*   37

to cancel the g♭'', while in bar 49 – as in the fair copy – there is a crotchet instead of a quaver.

However, the composer made his most important changes at the end and – more crucially – at the beginning of the piece. He shortened the rhythmic value of the final chord to a crotchet, while at the beginning he inserted a two-bar ostinato accompaniment introduction. These changes are of great significance in relation to the form of the piece, our perception of it and its expressive qualities.

In the original version the form was made immediately obvious. The composer plunged *in medias res* into a chain of variations of the opening material, while the final bars, based on dominant and tonic harmony, allowed the sound to fade imperceptibly into silence. In the later version the form has an introduction which strengthens the role of the accompaniment as a means of integrating the entire musical material. Moreover the shorter final note has the effect of delimiting more clearly the boundary between the sound-structure of the piece and the silence which surrounds it.

The changes which Chopin implemented are equally important from the psychological standpoint. The listener's perceptual readiness as he comes to hear a piece of music gives away to cognitive uncertainty and anxiety from the moment the first bars sound, and the anxiety may frequently border upon disorientation if he does not know the composition. Right at the outset, after all, the listener must appraise many different aspects of the work, distinguishing between primary and secondary elements, defining the relationships between them, predicting the direction which the musical flow will take and so forth. Chopin's addition of an introduction is therefore of great psychological importance and embodies many different meanings. It facilitates the listener's comprehension, for it leads him gradually from simple structures (the accompaniment) to far more complex structures (the model, the variants). It also channels and focuses his perception, paving the way for the various associations which arise gradually and are subsequently intensified throughout the course of the piece's development.

Chopin's alterations are equally important from the expressive or 'semantic' perspective. The musical structures embody several features which designate more or less definite meanings. Certainly the accompaniment has enough clearly-defined features (the inverted pedal, the curved outline of its contour, the 'halting' of the movement, the dominant-tonic cadence) for the listener to connote their meanings (rocking, movement on the spot, repose etc). These meanings are fundamental to a grasp of the overall expressive quality of the music. The use of an introduction based on the accompaniment alone may well reflect the composer's desire to create an expressive–semantic determinant for the work as a whole.

Conclusion

The changes described here marked a turning-point in Chopin's appraisal of the piece's function. He no doubt appreciated the prevalent tendency among audiences to impose 'concrete' meanings on to their musical experience of this piece. The technical means were seen then not as conveying some undefined, abstract expressive world, but rather as provoking specific 'cradle-song' associations.[27] The composer tested this effect by playing the piece to different groups of people before publishing it. On certain occasions he even performed the piece twice – as at the musical gathering described by Zaleski. It may well be that Chopin wanted to check audience reaction to his new composition before and after they knew its title.

Elisa Gavard[28] credits herself as being the 'godmother' who supplied the name *Berceuse*. Unfortunately, she gives neither the date nor the circumstances surrounding the event. From the aforementioned correspondence which Chopin conducted concerning the piece's publication it transpires that he was uncertain about the title until very nearly the last minute. It seems that he took the final decision to entitle the composition *Berceuse* only when he added the introduction and the amended conclusion to the copy of the piece. The copy sent to Breitkopf and Härtel was preceded by a title-page with the inscription:

Berceuse
pour le Piano forte
dédiée à Mademoiselle Elise Gavard
par F. Chopin.[29]

No doubt Chopin's indecision was caused partly by his awareness of the dangers inherent in programmatic titles. Hitherto the piece's musical language alone had directed the listener's associations, whereas a title fixed the 'essence' of the perception, and did so even before the piece had begun. This weakened the power of the music to stir the listener to exercise his own imagination, and to develop his own associations.

The strength and beauty of the music of the *Berceuse* were very soon recognised, since almost the moment it was published it found exponents.[30] Moreover, Chopin himself numbered it among his favourite pieces. The *Berceuse* was an obligatory item on the programme of the concerts which he

[27] Zofia Lissa ('Rola kojarzeń w percepcji dzieł muzycznych' in *Szkice w estetyki muzycznej* (Cracow, 1965), 74–5) makes a detailed study of the conditioning of musical associations.

[28] Niecks, *Frederic Chopin as a Man and Musician*, ii, 339; 'I was one who helped to christen the *Berceuse*.'

[29] Kobylańska, *Katalog*, ii, 94 includes a reproduction of the title-page.

[30] *Korespondencja Fryderyka Chopina*, ii, 145. A letter of August 1845: 'Nowak(owski) is playing my *Berceuse*. I'm pleased to know this; I feel as if I can hear him from afar. Give him my love.'

gave in 1848 in Paris,[31] London,[32] Manchester,[33] Glasgow[34] and Edinburgh.[35]

The *Berceuse* remained Chopin's only composition of its kind. The original title, *Variations* together with the piece's technical methods link the *Berceuse* with the variations composed during Chopin's early period and with later pieces of other genres which employ variation technique (e.g., the Impromptu in F♯ major op. 36 which also uses the ostinato type of variation).

Because of the nature of its expressive world the *Berceuse* – known also as a nocturne – became part of Chopin's set of 'night-music' pieces, continuing the line traced by pieces such as the Nocturne in E♭ major op. 9 no. 2 and the Nocturne in D♭ major op. 27 no. 2.[36]

In the light of this analysis of the autographs and of the facts quoted above, it seems that Chopin's alteration of the title following a long period of indecision stemmed from his deep concern that his music should convey the clearest possible artistic meaning. It is evidence, too, of Chopin's respect for his public.

---

[31] Hoesick, *Chopin. Życie i twórczość*, iii, 122.
[32] Niecks, *Frederic Chopin as a Man and Musician*, ii, 285.
[33] Ibid., ii, 294.   [34] Ibid., ii, 296.   [35] Ibid., ii, 297.
[36] The programmes of Chopin's concerts of 1848 link the Nocturne in D♭ major with the *Berceuse*. Cf: *Chopin na obczyźnie* collected by M. Mirska and W. Hordyński, supplemented and edited by J. Ilnicka, (Cracow, 1965), 300 – reproduction of a concert poster from a concert hall in Manchester.

The composition-draft of the Polonaise-fantasy: the issue of tonality

JIM SAMSON

Introduction

The musical work is, or may be viewed as, many things. It is an autonomous structure; it is a document of social history; it is a mirror to changing tastes and attitudes; it is a creative act. These different perspectives will often intersect in unusual and interesting ways, lighting up the piece from different angles. An analysis of structure, for instance, may take on quite new dimensions when confronted by some knowledge of context, function, reception or intention. Its conclusions need not lose authority through any such collision of perspectives. Rather they will gain an enhancing surround. My purpose here is to juxtapose two perspectives on the Polonaise-fantasy op. 61. I will examine first the structure of the work, specifically its tonal structure; and secondly its genesis, referring to a surviving composition-draft of nine leaves.[1] This draft has already been the subject of extended analyses by Wojciech Nowik and Jeffrey Kallberg,[2] but it is easily rich enough to sustain further commentary, especially as my discussion will be confined to a single issue, and one which is not central to their arguments. Detailed discussion of genesis and structure in the Polonaise-fantasy will be preceded by some general observations on both these perspectives.

---

[1] Strictly speaking there are two drafts, one of eight leaves and the other a single leaf. They are listed in Krystyna Kobylańska, *Rękopisy Utworów Chopina. Katalog*, 2 vols. (Cracow, 1977), i, nos. 815 and 816.

[2] Wojciech Nowik, '*Proces twórczy Fryderyka Chopina w świetle jego autografów muzycznych*' (Diss., U. of Warsaw, 1978) and Jeffrey Kallberg, 'Chopin's Last Style', *Journal of the American Musicological Society* xxxviii (1985).

Genesis 1

The study of a composer's sketches will of course yield only a partial view of his compositional process. Musical composition is a rather specific kind of symbolic thought, whose mental processes are as yet little understood. In particular it is uncertain how far it can usefully respond to current psychological approaches to creativity, most of which have been verbally or visually based.[3] In their mode of existence, and often too in the manner of their organisation, musical sounds have more in common with words than with visual images, and the analogies have frequently suggested common analytical approaches to verbal and musical languages. The association may be as misleading as it is helpful. Quite apart from obvious instrumental and semantic differences, there are, it would seem, fundamental operational (neurological) differences in the ordering of sounds and the ordering of words. The evidence of physiological psychology suggests that thinking in sounds remains in large measure independent of thinking in concepts, though it is obvious that the latter must play a role in *any* type of intellectual operation.[4] As a facet of human thought, then, it seems likely that musical composition involves *both* thinking in sounds *and* thinking in concepts. Saul Novack refers to a 'mind–ear axis', with infinite variability in the positioning of a work along the axis.[5] Within the creative process the two streams of 'ear' and 'mind' are constantly mingling – influencing and even distracting one another. Yet the distinction is a real one, and it may be present right from the first thoughts about a piece.

This distinction is possibly related to, though it is certainly not congruent with, a more commonly drawn distinction concerning the working methods of composers. A contrast is often recognised between composers such as Beethoven, who work their way slowly through a succession of sketches to the finished manuscript, and composers such as Chopin, for whom the activity of writing is largely post-compositional. Beethoven scholars have rightly insisted on the need to qualify any over-simple categorisation of composers in this way,[6] but the generalisation remains.[7] Certainly it seems that in some works Chopin would begin with a sound, even before he had a clear view of its eventual context. And the sound – often an extended, relatively self-contained

---

[3] One attempt to investigate creative process as a dimension of psychology is John Sloboda's chapter 'Composition and Improvisation' in his *The Musical Mind: A Cognitive Psychology of Music* (Oxford, 1985).

[4] A useful bibliography of this subject can be found in Sloboda, ibid., chapter 7.

[5] Saul Novack, 'Aspects of the Creative Process in Music', *Current Musicology* xxxvi (1983), 137–50.

[6] See in particular Lewis Lockwood, 'Beethoven's Sketches for Sehnsucht (WoO 146)' in Alan Tyson, ed., *Beethoven Studies* (London, 1974), 97–122.

[7] Chopin comes closest to the 'Beethovenian' approach in his Cello Sonata op. 65, for which there are more than two hundred pages of sketches.

musical paragraph – would be conceived in an apparently spontaneous way. There is some evidence for this in the sketches, including those of the Polonaise-fantasy. As both Nowik and Kallberg have pointed out, the leaves of the Polonaise-fantasy sketch divide into two classes: (1) continuity-drafts where the flow is continuous, as with the sketch of the main theme, the central B major slow section and the reprise. It is clearly significant that these form the skeleton of the large-scale ternary form which underlies the work, despite Chopin's later strategies of concealment: (2) leaves comprising short segments from different parts of the work, in particular links and bridge passages which are worked and reworked constantly.[8]

We cannot be sure, of course, that there were no earlier sketches for the first of these categories, the more fluent continuity-drafts. Nor can we know how much earlier drafting took place at the piano. But the evidence of the sketch can be supplemented by written accounts of his creative practice from George Sand, Karl Filtsch and others: 'Invention came to his piano, sudden, complete, sublime' etc. Revisions to the continuity-drafts were largely a matter of refinements of detail; for the most part they were complete *in intellectu* before they were written down. In some ways this kind of spontaneous creativity is the most fascinating and at the same time the most intractable of all for the analyst. We know very little about the causal network between an existing store of musical knowledge and the intuitive generation of 'new' musical thoughts, about the mental processes by which conventional schemata are learnt, refined and transcended, about the pre-conscious habit-formation which turns recognition into initiation. Composition is in essence a *re*-structuring of existing systems, but it is clear that at times this process takes place at very high speed and in a manner which minimises the role of conscious manipulation. An obvious difficulty in analysis at this level is that thinking in sounds – almost by definition – cannot easily be translated into verbal language, the natural medium for thinking in concepts.

A great deal more can be said when we turn to the larger construction of a work, which in Chopin's case often meant linking together extended, already composed paragraphs. Here thinking in concepts begins to play a more prominent role, and the sketches are accordingly more instructive. In particular they enable us to witness something of the problem-solving dimension which becomes important in creative process at this level. Any form of creativity necessarily involves solving open constructional problems, problems with more than one possible solution.[9] In the case of musical composition the

[8] In general this distinction in the working methods of composers is echoed in the creative process both of writers and of mathematicians.

[9] Wojciech Nowik discusses this aspect of compositional process in his 'Chopinowski konstruktywizm w rekopisach *Nokturnu c-moll* (bez opusu)', *Rocznik Chopinowski* xiv (1982), 21–32.

terms and conditions of the problem are selected by the composer himself, but the selection usually makes close reference to conventional schemata. Something of the nature of this problem-solving process is often registered in sketches. It is self-evident that the unfolding of a work through successive compositional drafts embodies an informal hierarchy, expressed through elements which remain fixed in successive drafts and elements which are variable. We might think of the process as a feedback model where trial solutions attempt in different ways to supply the detail within provisionally unchanging frames, with the possibility that the frames may themselves change to deal with unexpected discoveries arising from the detail.[10] The parameters of the frames will be culture-determined in very large measure, as to medium, genre and language.

The main issues to be addressed later in this study will concern language frames, specifically relating to tonality, but it may be useful to conclude these remarks on creative process with a brief reference to medium and genre frames. For Chopin medium was more-or-less a constant, and certainly unlikely to be changed in the formative stages of a work. All the same it is worth noting that the cello-piano medium which he tackled at the end of his life evoked significant differences both in creative process and in musical style.[11] Genre is a much more complex issue in Chopin, and one which until recently received scant attention in the literature.[12] Stability is threatened in this area by a frequent interpenetration of genres, by a deliberate subversion of generic expectations[13] and by the composer's changing view of some genres as his musical language developed. This latter point is worth expanding briefly as it is symptomatic of more fundamental changes in Chopin's esthetic commitments. Documentation suggests, for instance, that in his early years he accepted prevailing views of the nocturne as a partially open text, which might be ornamented spontaneously in performance, whereas in later years he regarded it as a firmly closed text.[14] To oversimplify somewhat, the *composer-pianist* of

[10] The modelling techniques employed in artificial intelligence studies might eventually prove a fruitful way of approaching this subject, but the variables are such that results are at present almost certain to lack refinement. For an introduction to this field see Margaret Boden, *Artificial Intelligence and Natural Man* (Brighton and New York, 1977), especially the chapter on creativity.

[11] There is some evidence that Chopin may have been considering further departures from the piano medium at the end of his life. Among the sketches for the Cello Sonata there are some pages for violin and piano.

[12] See Jeffrey Kallberg, 'The Rhetoric of Genre: Chopin's Nocturne in G minor op. 15 no. 3' and my 'Chopin's F♯ Major Impromptu: Notes on Genre, Style and Structure' in *Chopin and Romanticism*, the proceedings of a Chopin conference held in Warsaw in October 1986 (forthcoming). See also Jean-Jacques Eigeldinger's contribution to the present volume.

[13] Kallberg, ibid.

[14] Eigeldinger cites the evidence for Chopin's 'alternative' ornamentation of op. 9 no. 2 in Jean-Jacques Eigeldinger, *Chopin: Pianist and Teacher* 3rd, English edn. (Cambridge, 1986). By con-

the early nocturnes has become the *composer* of the later nocturnes. Moreover this transformation has important consequences for the status of the musical text. The composer-pianist initiates a communication chain directed to a specific audience. In such a chain the written text is as much a social as a personal document and its authority as a fixed text is accordingly weakened. For the composer, on the other hand, there is no genuine communication chain. He constructs a text largely as a form of self-expression and that text goes its own way in the world. His concern is to create structures.

Structure 1

The development of music analysis as an independent discipline is clearly part of a wider movement in the history of ideas. This wider structuralist project responded to the scientific thrust of the second half of the nineteenth century by reviving rationalist assumptions that we may understand the world most completely through an observation of its structures and systems, its 'universal forms'. One effect of the structuralist project was a suppression of the subject in any explanation of reality, either because structures were taken to be independently classifiable or because their elements were perceived in such relative terms that the subject became itself a component. Until recently the former premise has dominated music analysis, at least in Anglo-American scholarship. The assumption has been widely made that there is *a* structure in the musical work, there to be discovered. Only in more recent years has music analysis responded to the more radical implications of French structuralism and semiology, particularly with the incorporation of structures into more fully-fledged *systems* which find a place for the author and listener as well as the work. Inevitably the location of structure within such systems is problematical.

Structure is clearly heavily influenced by authorial intention. Yet at the same time it remains independent of that intention.[15] Structure is also permeable and context-dependent in the sense that it is decoded anew in multiple individual perceptions. The text is a reservoir of potential relationships from which each listener makes his or her selection using particular interpretative codes. Structure then is not to be identified cleanly with either authorial intention or individual perception.[16] At the same time the taxonomic methods of

trast Jeffrey Kallberg demonstrates the scrupulous care exercised by the composer to restrain and limit the ornamentation of op. 62 no. 1 (*'The Chopin Sources: Variants and Versions in Later Manuscripts and Printed Editions'* (Diss., U. of Chicago, 1982), 248–75).

[15] The classic text here is Wimsatt and Beardsley, 'The Intentional Fallacy', originally published in *The Sewanee Review* in 1946. Phillip Gossett challenges its applicability to music – not entirely successfully – in 'Beethoven's Sixth Symphony: Sketches for the First Movement', *Journal of the American Musicological Society* xxvii (1974), 248–84. See especially pp. 260–1.

[16] The non-congruence of these outer poles of the work's history (what Molino and Nattiez call the poietic and esthesic domains) can be demonstrated from the sketch of the Polonaise-fantasy. For many music-lovers, especially in Poland, the work has been perceived at least partly in ideo-

Jean-Jacques Nattiez and others have demonstrated that if there is a neutral level of structure it is a heavily polluted one, that there can in fact be no objectively classifiable structure.[17] The most we can claim is that listeners with similar musical backgrounds will often impose *similar* structures and even similar semantic meanings on a work, suggesting that the work itself embodies constraints which make some codes appear more appropriate or profitable than others, and that there is a shared knowledge which facilitates the selection of these codes. Jan Broeckx refers to a 'residual layer of receptional insight'.[18]

The precise means by which this shared knowledge is transmitted remains uncertain (at least to me), raising questions concerning innateness and learning mechanisms which belong properly within the cognitive psychology of music. It is enough to make the rather obvious point that common features in a class of works inevitably facilitate the listener's task of decoding an individual work belonging to that class as he or she seeks coherent structures. The search for a formal theoretical basis for this largely intuitive process – especially tempting within the style system of classical tonality – is perhaps over-ambitious, even if the theory admits so-called 'preference rules' such as those proposed by Lerdahl and Jackendoff.[19] It is more realistic to recognise that prominence factors will create possible structures within which the listener may move around, so to speak. Within classical tonality some of these structures will be strictly hierarchical, some not.[20] It will be helpful to outline four main categories of structure, drawing some terms of reference from Lerdahl and Jackendoff.

(i) Associational structures. These, especially when based on motivic or thematic identity, are an important means of strengthening the cohesion of a work for many listeners. They can be regarded as hierarchical only within an unhelpfully general meaning of the term. From Schoenberg and Mersmann onwards, extravagant claims have been advanced for the unifying control of motivic association through relationship (often concealed) to an underlying

logical terms, in that it is grouped with the other late polonaises and the dance rhythm assumes powerfully symbolic values. Yet the sketch suggests that it was only at a rather late stage of the compositional process that Chopin thought of the piece as a polonaise at all, indicating that any such semantic meaning had little significance for *him*.

[17] Jean-Jacques Nattiez, *Fondements d'une semiologie de la musique* (Paris, 1975).
[18] Jan Broeckx, *Contemporary Views on Musical Style and Aesthetics* (Antwerp, 1979), 129.
[19] Fred Lerdahl and Ray Jackendoff, *A Generative Theory of Tonal Music* (Cambridge, Mass. and London, 1983).
[20] For a full discussion of hierarchy in tonal music see Eugene Narmour, 'Some Major Theoretical Problems Concerning the Concept of Hierarchy in the Analysis of Tonal Music', *Music Perception* i, no. 2 (1983–4), 129–99.

Grundgestalt.[21] Paul Hamburger for one has approached the Polonaise-fantasy from this viewpoint, and the present study will have nothing further to offer.[22]

(ii) Metrical structures. These act both as driving and as binding agents. They are the motor of tonal music, propelling the phrase and at the same time linking through their invariance materials which may be sharply contrasted in other respects. They are by definition hierarchical, but our capacity to perceive their hierarchies beyond a certain level is limited. Within these limits there is a constant 'fading' of earlier material as new material comes into view, so that as a *hierarchy* metrical structures remain a local phenomenon.[23]

(iii) Grouping structures. These are also hierarchical and may be perceived as such across the entire span of a work. Their importance is evident, yet even at low levels they are concerned with boundaries rather than territories, with landmarks rather than journeys, with form rather than process. I shall not deal with them in the Polonaise-fantasy beyond remarking that the higher levels of grouping structure in this work are strikingly innovative in relation to Chopin's normal practice. There is a new freedom in the sequence of ideas, a deliberate formal discontinuity which achieves on the large scale something of the fluidity and asymmetry of the themes themselves.[24]

(iv) Tonal structures. Like grouping structures these are hierarchical and their hierarchies may be registered at the highest structural level. At the same time they may account, in theory at least, for every detail of pitch organisation on low levels. For many, therefore, they offer the best hope of hearing a work as a unified totality, where the part is related organically to the whole. The interpretation of these hierarchies – in analytical terms the nature of the reductive process – is of course another matter and one which extends well beyond the scope of this study. In the discussion of tonal structure in the Polonaise-fantasy which follows, only a few of many possible codes are deployed.

Structure 2

A traditional approach to tonal structure, given its most refined expression in

---

[21] The concept of *Grundgestalt* is fully explored and its bibliography cited in David Epstein, *Beyond Orpheus: Studies in Musical Structure* (Cambridge, Mass. and London, 1979). Hans Mersmann's related concept of *Substanz* is less well-known in Anglo-American scholarship. See *Angewandte Musikästhetik* (Berlin, 1926) and other writings.

[22] Paul Hamburger, 'Mazurkas, Waltzes, Polonaises' in Alan Walker, ed., *Frédéric Chopin: Profiles of the Man and the Musician* (London, 1966), 73–113.

[23] Lerdahl and Jackendoff (*A Generative Theory of Tonal Music*) substantiate this conclusion.

[24] The compositional process as to grouping structure in the Polonaise-fantasy is discussed powerfully in Kallberg's 'Chopin's Last Style'.

Schoenberg's theory of monotonality, might identify the principal tonal regions of the Polonaise-fantasy as follows (Example 1). Such a presentation, suggesting a succession of closed regions, is crude at any time, but it is particularly crude in this work, where closure is often avoided and tonal clarifications more often than not give way to tonally unstable material. Nonetheless some useful generalisations can be drawn even from this analysis. We might note informally the distancing of the B major slow section from the flat regions of the outer sections, a gesture reminiscent of the F minor Fantasy. At the same time we would note the *integration* of this remote region into the tonal structure through an interlocking of minor thirds around G♯/A♭, dovetailing the slow section into the reprise (Example 1). The link is strengthened by the

Example 1.

$\downarrow$ = major

$\rfloor$ = minor

thematic parallelism of the G♯ minor and F minor sections. Even at this most basic level of tonal interpretation the importance of the minor third is clear.

Another approach to the work's tonal structure would adapt Robert Bailey's concept of 'double tonality'.[25] Here the integrative role of the minor third gains greater privilege, enabling us to express rather more fully the relationship of detail to whole. We would note that the first two chords of the piece are built on A♭ and C♭, presaging in a remarkable way the main tonal centres of the work as a whole (Example 2). The introduction then, with its continuing succession of minor third progressions, might be seen as establishing important harmonic and ultimately tonal premises. The point is strengthened when the interlocking relationship between the slow section and the reprise centres around an unexpected return of the introduction, beginning on B – the tonality of the slow section – and progressing to F minor by making the sequential pattern harmonically functional (Example 2). The tonal pairing is strengthened further when the A♭ of the reprise is deflected, albeit briefly, towards a parenthetical B major harmony. Stylistic sympathy would lend support to these minor third pairings, for the tandem of tonal 'relatives' is so prominent in Chopin as to constitute an element of style. We need only think of the Scherzo op. 31 or the Fantasy op. 49.

A third approach would avail itself of Heinrich Schenker's hugely influential theory of structural levels. Here tonal regions will not be viewed as static platforms, but rather as stages in dynamically unfolding voice-leading progressions

[25] Robert Bailey's theories have been publicised through the writings of Deborah Stein (*Hugo Wolf's Lieder and Extensions of Tonality* (Ann Arbor, 1985)) and William Kinderman (numerous articles and chapters, including his contribution to the present volume).

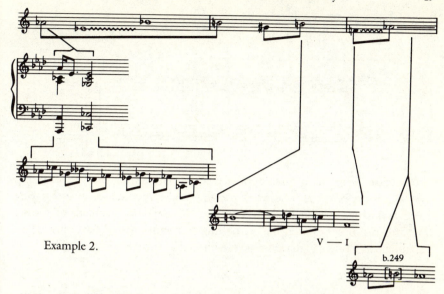

Example 2.

V — I

b.249

on several interactive hierarchical levels. Schenker-derived approaches to the Polonaise-fantasy strengthen further the points made about the minor third relationship. A middleground graph of the introduction, for example, indicates that the A♭ minor chord – the first chord of the piece – is composed out through enharmony in the voice-leading which follows (Example 3). More-

Example 3.

over the strongly integrative relationship of this introduction to the main body of the piece is shown clearly in a graph of the entire work (Example 4).[26] What emerges is that, despite the major mode of the piece, the A♭ *minor* triad unfolded in the introduction is duplicated at the highest structural level. The structural fifth of the fundamental line E♭/D♯ is an important pivot as the fifth of A♭ major/minor and the third of B major. Its eventual arrival at the end of the slow section following a lengthy anticipative Cx/D♮ is thus a crucial stage of the tonal argument.

[26] There are alternative ways of graphing this piece. For a discussion see John Rink 'Schenker and Improvisation' in *Chopin and Romanticism* (forthcoming). See also Nicholas Cook, *A Guide to Musical Analysis* (London and Melbourne, 1987), 340.

Example 4.

It is clear from these three approaches that the minor third relationship Ab–B/Cb is the essential cohesive factor on several structural levels, integrating detail and whole in a remarkably cogent way. It would be reasonable to assume that this major cohesive agent of the tonal structure would have formed an essential part of the language frame established in the genesis of the piece.

Genesis 2

The composition-draft of the Polonaise-fantasy is instructive as to many aspects of its structure. The present examination, however, will be concerned exclusively with the issue of tonality. The beginning of the draft (Example 5)

Example 5.

indicates three stages in the genesis of the opening bars, two successive approximations to the final form within certain fixed constraints. The constraints are the formal scheme – a two-part model and response – and the melodic substance. The variables are tempo, phrase structure and harmony, of which only the latter will concern us. Chopin's first draft has three flats in the key signature and begins with a C minor rather than an Ab minor chord. The draft continues a third higher until bar 6 at which point it realigns with the final version. A fourth flat in the key signature may be inferred from this point, and the draft proceeds more or less as the final form through to the presentation of the main theme.

Chopin remained dissatisfied with the harmonic setting of the opening, however. His second thought was to transpose it up a fourth and he indicated the new harmonic starting-point with an *F mol* (sic) designation at the opening. On a later page of the draft there is an alternative version of the opening in that key, and it is from here that the arpeggiation of the final version was taken. The F minor setting had certain advantages over the C minor, both in relation to the continuity of the introduction as a whole and also in the characteristic association of F minor and Ab major. Chopin remained dissatisfied, however, and his third attempt – the final version – was drafted on the third staff, the opening sketched in the treble clef and connected by a wavy line to bar 5 in an implied bass clef. This version is the strongest of the three, with model and response leaning respectively to tonic and dominant harmonies, while the overall structural line forms a single descending scalar motion (Example 6).

Example 6.

Draft (a)

Draft (b)

Draft (c)

Two things emerge from this examination of the opening bars of the sketch. First, it is clear that the duplication of the main tonal centres Ab and B in the opening bars was not part of Chopin's original intention. Secondly, in seeking the most advantageous route to the main theme and key Chopin was happy to shift a pre-composed paragraph from one tonal platform to another. The latter point is not particularly surprising, since the introduction functions harmonically as a tonal anacrusis, homing in on the main key only gradually. It is striking, however, that the same procedure may be observed on a much larger scale later in the work. To facilitate a discussion of this I will offer a crude synopsis of the grouping structure of the work.

Principal themes		Principal tonal regions
X	Introduction	〰〰
A	Polonaise theme	A♭ major
Y	Episode	
A¹	Transformations of Polonaise theme	[E♭ major] 〰〰
B	First nocturne	B♭ major
C	Slow section	B major
D	Second nocturne	[G♯ major]
C	Slow section resumed	B major
X	Introduction returns	〰〰
D	Second nocturne returns	F minor
A	Apotheosis of Polonaise theme	A♭ major
C	Apotheosis of slow section	A♭ major

Perhaps the most surprising feature of the composition-draft is that Chopin sketched the slow section not in B major, but in C major. Example 7 is the rele-

Example 7.

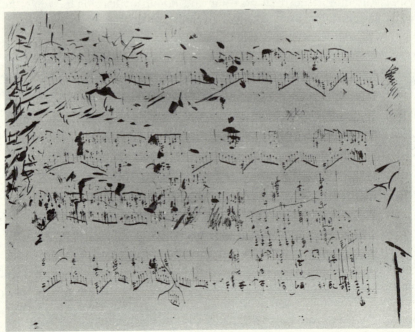

vant page of the draft, including the main body of the slow section, its brief introduction (bar 148) and its resumption after the second nocturne. It is worth remembering that this leaf is one of the continuity-drafts referred to earlier and that it forms the middle section of the ternary design which was almost certainly Chopin's starting-point. In view of that it is interesting that, as Jeffrey Kallberg points out,[27] some of his early departures from the first main section should have been directed towards a tonal centre of C. The *thematic* goal of these passages is not clear, but it is unlikely to have been the first nocturne. This was probably not part of Chopin's original formal conception, but rather one of several strategies he adopted at a later stage in order to blur the edges of the overall ternary design. The sketch of the first nocturne is on a separate leaf and, like the slow section, it is a semitone higher than in the final version i.e., B major rather than B♭ major. Moreover the second nocturne, enclosed within the slow section, was also sketched a semitone higher – in A minor – on a separate leaf. Before sketching this second nocturne Chopin had already drafted the resumption of the slow section a semitone higher in C major (Example 7).

As often in this composition-draft Chopin's difficulties came with links and bridges. He tried out several versions of the link between the second nocturne and the resumed slow section, a link which in its final form consists of a cadenza-like passage culminating in triple trills. It was in the course of drafting this link that Chopin rethought the entire tonal layout of the central sections of the work. Example 8 reproduces the relevant leaf and Example 9 transcribes the various stages of the compositional process at this point. Draft (a), corresponding to bar 193, is close to the final version for bars 193–4, though a semitone higher. Draft (b) adds two further elements present in the final version, the motive at bar 196 and an early form of the cadential trill, resolving to C major, presumably for the resumption of the slow section. Draft (c) expands the motive at bar 196 for a further two bars, exactly as in the final version, though a semitone higher. The trill is removed but bar 199 remains a cadential dominant preparation for C major. Drafts (d) and (e) represent an alternative continuation which is not retained in the final version. Draft (f) is the point at which the tonal scheme is altered, with a B major key signature implicit from bar 194. The 'X' at bar 196 refers to draft (c) (bars 196–8) and the beginning of the trills in their final form is at bar 199. The remaining five bars of trills are also sketched (Example 8), as is the beginning of the resumed slow section, already drafted in C major, now in its final B major setting. Since the first nocturne had already been sketched in B major, Chopin had to change its tonal setting also. He abbreviated the second transformation of the main theme and adjusted the

---

[27] 'Chopin's Last Style'.

Example 8.

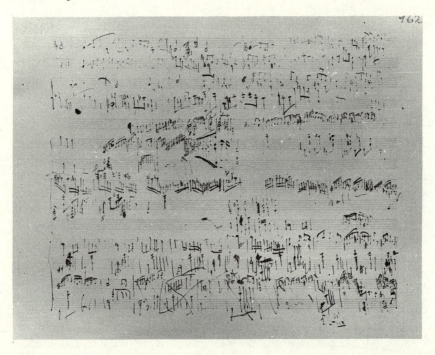

bridge so that the first nocturne could begin a semitone lower in B♭ major. Effectively, then, some ninety-eight bars of the piece as finally constituted, comprising several formally differentiated sections, were shifted down a semitone. The overall tonal frame was in Chopin's original conception very different indeed from the final form and the change operated not just at a foreground or even a middleground level of structure, but at a background level.

Any attempt to recreate Chopin's thinking at this vital stage of the compositional process must remain speculative. In particular we cannot be sure which of several possible factors initially suggested to him an alternative tonality for the slow section. Two factors of a rather informal character may be mentioned immediately. One concerns the connotative values of keys. By transferring the B major region from the first nocturne to the slow section, Chopin found a more appropriate setting for the associations of stillness and serenity which the key of B major carried for him. It is worth noting in this connection that the comparable slow section of the F minor Fantasy is also in B major. The other is an issue of piano technique, easily tested at the keyboard. In a B major region there is a much more congenial lie of the hand for the

Example 9.

Example 9. (*cont.*)

legato melody of the slow section, and we might note here that Chopin referred to B major as a more 'natural' hand shape than C major.[28]

It seems likely, however, that these advantages were by-products of a decision made on purely structural grounds. It may have been triggered either by a glance forwards or a glance backwards. If Chopin had already given his attention to the means by which he would effect a transition from the slow section to the Ab major reprise, he would have realised the advantages of bringing back the introduction X on B rather than C. This made possible the subtle harmonic relationships noted above and outlined in Example 10. Alternatively,

Example 10.

V — I

Chopin may have recognised after the event the potential of his opening chords as a means of signalling the larger tonal movement of the piece. He may indeed have noticed that this tonal pairing at the minor third was duplicated in the overall harmonic progression of the introduction. We cannot know for sure. But whatever the trigger, the effect of this single change to the background tonal frame was to enable many different aspects of the tonal scheme to fall neatly into place. Above all a cohesive element operating on several structural levels and coming into sharp focus at major junction points in the form emerged at this late stage of the creative process. It was not planned by the composer, but rather recognised as a possibility after the music had been in essence composed. This bisociation of several factors in a single moment of creative discovery is not unlike what Koestler calls the 'Eureka process'.[29]

Conclusion

By cleanly separating genesis and structure in this way we permit a confrontation not only between compositional strategies and perceptual structures, but also between two quite different, historically mediated, poetics – between Chopin's world and ours. Our world applies certain holistic codes in order to understand the musical work as a unified *Gestalt*. Of these codes Schenkerian reduction has proved among the most fruitful, and it is worth remarking that

[28] See Arthur Hedley, *Chopin* (London, 1947), 127.

[29] Arthur Koestler, *The Act of Creation* (London, 1969). The field of modern heuristics also seems germane to this resolution of numerous problems in a single creative discovery. Heuristic reasoning is in essence a willingness to entertain different mental representations of a problem, in marked contrast to Euclidian deductive reasoning. Within heuristics we may arrive not just (or at all) at a solution to the original problem, but also (or instead) at a redefinition of the problem. Much of the work in this area has concerned creativity in mathematics; see, for instance George Polya, *How to Solve It: A New Aspect of Mathematical Method* (Princeton, 1948), and Jacques Hadamard, *An Essay in the Psychology of Invention in the Mathematical Field* (Princeton, 1949).

Chopin has been one of the most frequently plundered of all composers by Schenker himself and by Schenkerians. None of their analytical insights is in the least compromised by any discoveries we may make about compositional process. A more sensitive issue, however, is the projection of such codified perceptual structures into the realm of compositional strategies, even if these are regarded as subliminal. Such a projection is explicit in Schenker himself and implicit in the work of many Schenkerians. At the very least it would be argued that Chopin proceeded from an *intuition* of the *Ursatz*.

This brings us from our world to Chopin's world. His musical language developed from the popular concert and salon music of early nineteenth-century pianist-composers, within which audience expectation was an important stylistic determinant. It was music addressed to a specific taste public, designed to be popular and ephemeral, accepting willingly its commodity status. The composer-pianist made a clear distinction between such 'public' music and 'private' or 'epic' music – sonatas, chamber works, symphonies – which was addressed to a quite different taste public and which had some pretensions to an atemporal status. Both esthetic and stylistic dimensions of early nineteenth-century pianism bear upon our argument. We may consider first the esthetic issue. The essential point here is that the frontiers of a work – especially a work in 'free' style[30] – were by no means rigidly determined. The borderline between composition and improvisation was blurred, and even the 'final' version of a work could remain conceptually incomplete. We turn now to the stylistic issue. Within the 'brilliant' style of early nineteenth-century pianism there is a dual impulse of display and sentiment – technically speaking, bravura figuration and ornamental melody. The result, in formal terms, was often a linked chain of relatively self-contained melodic or figurative paragraphs where tonal frames are clearly-defined. Both esthetically and stylistically Chopin transcended this musical world, enriching it with elements drawn from other worlds and transforming utterly the meaning and function of its components. One measure of this change is the ever-increasing self-criticism which we witness in Chopin, a self-criticism which reached a painful, harrowing point in his later years. In one sense the sketch of the Polonaise-fantasy stands as testament to that self-criticism. Yet in another sense – and in particular in relation to tonal strategy – it documents the continuing, if greatly emaciated, presence of those more popular styles which shaped his musical language in the first place and which he never completely disowned. The composition-draft tells us about structure and about creative process. It also tells us about history.

[30] The distinction between a piece in 'free' style and one in 'strict' or 'severe' style was recognised by numerous critics and commentators in the early nineteenth century, Fétis and Schilling to name but two.

Directional tonality in Chopin[1]

WILLIAM KINDERMAN

A familiar feature of tonal practice in the Classical style of Haydn, Mozart and Beethoven is the appearance at the outset of a work of the tonic key, against which a secondary tonality or tonalities is pitted and eventually resolved. Although the tonic tonality is sometimes initially obscured (as when Haydn begins in the 'wrong' key), or prefaced by a harmonic curtain (as in Beethoven's First Symphony), the first section of a movement in this style is almost invariably in the tonic.[2] For Beethoven, the tonic key of a movement normally provides both the initial and the final point of orientation.

There is, however, another logical possibility inherent in the tonal system, one that was exploited with increasing frequency during the nineteenth century, in the works of such composers as Wagner, Bruckner and Mahler. The tonic key may be treated not as an initial point of orientation, but as the goal of a directional process. In this case a piece will begin not in the tonic but in a secondary tonality, which in turn can be presented in such a way as to imply and prepare for the tonic key. Such a procedure has been described as 'progressive' or 'interlocking' tonality, but perhaps most aptly as directional tonality.[3]

[1] For helpful comments and criticism from the earliest stages of this study I am indebted to Professors Robert Bailey, Joseph Kerman, and especially Kevin Korsyn.

[2] An exceptional case is Beethoven's Piano Sonata op. 101, which opens on the dominant, and avoids a strong cadence in the tonic until the beginning of the final movement.

[3] The terms 'progressive' and 'interlocking' tonality have appeared in Dika Newlin, *Bruckner, Mahler, Schoenberg* (New York, 1947) and Graham George, *Tonality and Musical Structure* (New York and Washington, 1970), respectively. Of coure, if any analysis of tonal relations is to prove esthetically sound, it is important not to regard tonalities as abstract entities apart from the music, a danger to which George succumbed in his treatment of 'interlocking tonality'. The concept of 'directional tonality' and the related concept of 'tonal pairing' have been discussed and exemplified in several recent articles on the music of Wagner. See W. Kinderman, 'Dramatic

59

The present study examines three major works by Chopin that pioneer this tonal procedure: the Second Scherzo op. 31 (1837), the Second Ballade op. 38 (1836–9), and the Fantasy op. 49 (1841). These are the only large works by Chopin beginning with a section in a secondary tonality.[4] The following analyses will attempt to demonstrate how the modulatory structures of these works are integrated with the basic thematic material and reflected in harmonic and melodic detail. The works are discussed not in chronological sequence, but in order of complexity, with the most problematical example, the Second Ballade, treated last.

Scherzo no. 2, op. 31 (1837)

All of the Chopin scherzos contain two complexes of contrasting material: a tempestuous scherzo section, in presto tempo, and a trio of more subdued character. In the first and last scherzos, the trio material serves only the role of a contrasting section, whereas in the second and third these two sections are integrated with one another. In their overall form, these are the most complex of the scherzos.

The tonal structure of the Second Scherzo is characterised by a delayed arrival of the principal key of Db major. The opening music in Bb minor avoids a firm cadence in that key, and foreshadows the main tonality by going to Db in its second phrase. The opening key of Bb minor, then, is treated not as the principal tonality of the work, but as an offshoot of the true tonic of Db.[5] That Db, and not Bb minor, is the tonic key of the work as a whole can be demonstrated further by reviewing the overall key-relations of the scherzo. These have been shown in Figure 1. If Bb minor is regarded as the tonic key, the tonal plan of the piece appears rather puzzling. Not only would there be much more music in Db major and minor than in Bb minor, but the other tonalities, such as A and E, would be quite unrelated to the presumed tonic. Once the tonic is understood as Db, however, the tonal relations of the work become clear. They all lie in the circle of major thirds or circle of minor thirds from Db.

Recapitulation in Wagner's *Götterdämmerung*, *19th-Century Music* iv (1980), 101–12; 'Das "Geheimnis der Form"' in Wagners *Tristan und Isolde*, *Archiv für Musikwissenschaft* xl (1983), 174–88; 'Wagner's *Parsifal*: Musical Form and the Drama of Redemption', *The Journal of Musicology* (Fall, 1986), 431–46; and (Spring, 1987), 315–16.

[4] There are several smaller works that begin and end in different keys, such as the Prelude op. 28 no. 2 and the Waltz op. 70 no. 2, as well as other works beginning with a modulating or tonally ambiguous passage, such as the Bolero in A minor op. 19 or the Third Scherzo in C♯ minor op. 39.

[5] The role of Db as the central tonality has not gone unrecognised in the literature on this work, but the overall tonal framework based on descending thirds has not been closely examined. See, for instance, Heinrich Schenker, *Free Composition*, ed. and trans. Ernst Oster (New York and London, 1979), Figure 13 and Figure 102/6.

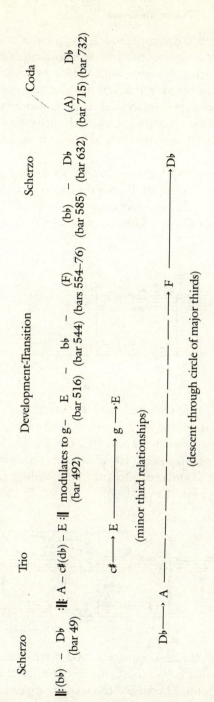

Figure 1. Scherzo, op. 31

The most basic structure is a descent through the circle of major thirds: Db–A–F–Db (A represents of course the enharmonic equivalent of Bbb, a major third below Db). Chopin makes this framework audible by highlighting the sonority of the major third to mark the arrival of these keys descending in thirds. Each of these passages represents an important moment in the musical organisation: the first firm assertion of the tonic key, the beginning of the trio, the climax of the development-transition, the recapitulation, and the final cadence.

The emphatic arrival of the Db tonality in bar 49, for instance, is stressed by the vast spacing of the major third Db–F, with the bass and treble separated by five octaves (Example 1). This distinctive spacing of the Db–F sonority returns repeatedly in the coda and also forms the final chord of the work.

Example 1.

At the beginning of the trio, on the other hand, the Db from the end of the scherzo section is reinterpreted as the third degree of A major, the new tonic, and the pitch C# is consistently sustained above the note A in the bass (Example 2). In the continuation of this passage, C# is further emphasised by a series of repetitive motives circling around this pitch, and by the following elaborate ornamentation closing the phrase (bars 281–4).

Example 2.

After repetition of the trio the development section begins with a series of sequences. Harmonically, this is the most unstable part of the work, as thematic material from both the scherzo and trio sections appears in new key areas. The goal of this development section, however, is reached only after the cadence in B♭ minor, marked *sempre con fuoco* (bar 544). In the following passage, the dominant chord of B♭ minor, F major, is repeated ten consecutive times in the same high register and wide spacing, always with the major third, A, in the highest voice (Example 3). The music thus pauses and hovers on F,

Example 3.

not merely as a means of establishing the dominant of B♭ minor (B♭ had already been firmly established by the preceding cadence), but as a means of articulating the pitch level of F major as the next structural point within the circle of major thirds from D♭. This overall framework of descending major thirds is shown in Figure 2.

Figure 2.

Scherzo section   Trio section   Development-Transition   Scherzo section

In the coda, finally, Chopin recalls both the A major and F major tonalities. The beginning of the coda is marked by an abrupt modulation from D♭ major to A major, whereas its final bars recall the emphasis on F from the end of the development. The peculiar pathos of the final recall of F derives from its harmonic support to the crucial pitch A, common to the A major and F major triads; the central harmonic relationship of the piece is thus reaffirmed at the last possible moment, before being resolved into the cadence in D♭.

A tension between D♭ and A lies at the heart of this work, as we have seen. It even overflows, as it were, into the texture of the scherzo section near the beginning of the work, as is shown by the persistent melodic emphasis on B♭♭ – the enharmonic equivalent of A – in both treble and bass (Example 4).

Example 4.

The most pervasive emphasis on the semitone B♭♭–A♭ is evident at the end of the recapitulation and beginning of the coda. The only alteration of the scherzo section in the recapitulation is an extension that takes the final melodic phrase before the cadence to B♭♭ (bar 707). This high octave on B♭♭ is left hanging and unresolved, until the last recall of A major is realised in an explosion (Example 5).

Example 5.

From this moment the crucial semitone, whether written as A–A♭ or B♭♭–A♭, is incessantly repeated and resolved to the tonic triad. Most extraordinary, however, is the manner in which the opening progression of the scherzo is reinterpreted in the coda. The opening of the scherzo in B♭ minor had treated A as leading-note to B♭ in its first and third phrases. When this thematic material is transformed in the coda, the A is carried downward to A♭ as part of a larger linear progression, while the silent fourth bar of the theme, which was originally occupied by rests, is filled in by a third triplet configuration. Chopin thus provides simultaneously a tonal and rhythmic resolution of the opening theme (Example 6). The continuation of the theme rises from the low octave A♭ to an emphatic high chord with uppermost pitch A♭, and the progression is then broadened through a series of chromatically rising sequences leading to the climactic cadential resolution in D♭ in bar 756, which is marked by the distinctive spacing of the D♭–F sonority as discussed above. The registral discontinuities present in every previous appearance of this material are eliminated here, in this powerful, and seemingly inevitable, progression to the cadence.

This passage seems to have been overlooked by commentators such as Rawsthorne,[6] and Abraham,[7] who assert that the scherzo ends in the relative major. When even the thematic material originally in B♭ minor has been resolved to D♭ major, it is hardly correct to refer here to a close in the 'relative' major. If tonal analysis is to have any power of illumination, its terms must

[6] Alan Rawsthorne, 'Ballades, Fantasy, and Scherzos', in Alan Walker, ed., *Frederic Chopin. Profiles of the Man and the Musician* (London, 1966), 68.
[7] Gerald Abraham, *Chopin's Musical Style* (London, 1939), 58.

Example 6.

coincide with the actual compositional plan of the work at hand. In this case, the work begins with a passage of somewhat developmental character outside of the tonic key, a passage that is accordingly resolved, in logical and essentially classical fashion, in the coda. This technique of the delayed resolution of an unstable opening to a work was to assume increasing importance in the nineteenth century, in such works as Wagner's *Tristan* and *Parsifal*.[8]

In the D♭ major Scherzo, Chopin achieves a form of directional tonality without any consequent weakening of the tonic key center. In the words of Herbert Weinstock, this scherzo by itself 'refutes the often parroted judgement that Chopin remained an architectural fumbler who could create firm units of nothing more complex than simple song or dance forms'.[9]

[8] For a detailed discussion of this technique in Wagner, see the studies of *Tristan* and *Parsifal* cited in n. 2 above.

[9] Herbert Weinstock, *Chopin: The Man and His Music* (New York, 1949), 231.

Fantasy, op. 49 (1841)

The Fantasy begins in F minor and closes in Ab major, exploiting the same tonal relationship of a minor third as in the Second Scherzo. There, however, the similarity ends; the basic structural plan of this piece consists of a chain of ascending thirds extending through two octaves from F to Ab (Figure 3).

The main body of the work consists of a sonata-like framework containing an exposition of four thematic subjects in the ascending key-sequence F minor–Ab major–C minor–Eb major, a developmental section based primarily on this material and centred in Gb major, and a recapitulation of the four subjects from the exposition in the tonal-sequence Bb minor–Db major–F minor–Ab major.[10] The exposition is prefaced by an extended introductory march in F minor.

Immediately following the march, Chopin introduces a passage in arpeggios that prefigures the tonal structure of the entire work. An ascending series of arpeggiated chords presents the triads of F minor and Ab major, each set off by a fermata, followed by C minor and Eb major; and, when the passage is restated, by the triads of Eb minor, Gb major, Bb minor, and Db major. This is precisely the modulatory plan of the Fantasy as a whole (the beginning of this passage containing the first ascent of a third from F to Ab, is shown in Example 7).

Example 7.

This gesture outlining the rising third from F minor to Ab major strongly foreshadows the beginning of the Polonaise-fantasy op. 61, from 1845–6. The initial chords of the Polonaise-fantasy present an ascending third from Ab minor to Cb major, with the Cb triad elaborated in a rising spiral of arpeggios analogous to those in the Fantasy. As in the earlier work, the harmonic gesture in op. 61 signals the tonal structure of the music to follow, which is largely based on the polar tonalities of Ab and B, the enharmonic equivalent of Cb. In the Fantasy, unlike the Polonaise-fantasy, however, the directional quality of

---

[10] Abraham (*Chopin's Musical Style*, 109) points out this key-sequence in the exposition and recapitulation, but does not mention that the development section, by its stress on Gb, continues the chain of thirds.

Figure 3. Fantasy, op. 49

	Introduction – 'March'	Exposition	'Development'	Recapitulation	Coda
f (Ab)	(E) f (f) (Ab) etc. (bars 43ff.)	I II III IV f Ab c Eb (bar 68 – 143)	(c) (Gb) (Eb) Gb B (bar 199)	I II III IV bb Db f Ab (bar 235 – 310)	Ab
		f→ Ab → c → Eb ⟶ Gb ⟶ [B] → (chain of ascending thirds)		bb→Db→f → Ab	

the rising harmonic progression is embodied in the overall tonal progression of the entire work, which does not close in the key in which it begins.

The role of A♭ major as the central key of the Fantasy as a whole is affirmed by cadential passages at the end of the exposition and recapitulation, in E♭ and A♭, respectively. These passages consist of two parts: a majestic section in double octaves ending in an authentic cadence (bars 127, 294) and a strictly diatonic passage with a rapidly-moving bass line. The contrast between this diatonic writing and the chromatic sections surrounding it further heightens the importance of A♭ major as the stable key centre of the overall tonal structure based on ascending thirds.

The only fifth-related modulation in the work occurs at the end of the development section, in the Lento sostenuto, in B major. This section represents a tonal parenthesis in the overall structure, and this emphasises its contrasting expressive character. There is a particular sense of repose, serenity, even flatness in its twenty-four bars.[11] This effect is produced not only from the thematic material itself and from the change in metre to 3/4, but from its tonal context; it lies outside the scheme of ascending thirds that generates the other tonalities of the piece.

The march-like introduction in F minor is a complete binary form in itself and ends with a series of cadences in F major. The thematic material of this introduction does not recur in the Fantasy, though subtle tonal relationships nevertheless link the introduction with later passages of the work. Its second phrase is stated in the relative major, A♭, foreshadowing the tonal scheme of rising thirds, whereas the fourth phrase modulates to the remote key of E major in bar 17. An abrupt return to F minor occurs two bars later, when a seventh-chord on F♭ is interpreted as a German sixth, resolving to an A♭ major sonority. In the coda, when Chopin recalls the Lento sostenuto in the tonic A♭ major, he introduces the restatement with the same harmonic progression involving a German sixth on F♭ (Example 8, bars 317–20). The reminiscence of the Lento can thus be heard at the same time in relationship to this earlier passage from the introduction in the sharp key of E major, a passage similarly unrelated to the central chain of thirds.

The third relations in the work are clearly reflected in the basic thematic material, which is often conspicuously based on thirds and sixths. The diatonic cadential theme from the end of the exposition encompasses the sixth B♭–G, both ascending and descending, whereas the theme of the Lento spans the sixth from D♯ to B. In other passages, such as the end of the coda, and the parallel passage in G♭ major in the development, the juxtaposition of third-related keys is reflected harmonically by the addition of a sixth to the major

---

[11] Rawsthorne ('Ballades, Fantasy, and Scherzos', 61–2) writes that it sounds like 'A genuine trio section and not an episode'.

Example 8.

triad. The music of the final Assai allegro develops the ascending arpeggiated texture so characteristic of the Fantasy, while stressing F as the uppermost pitch adjoined to the Ab major triad in the highest register. This is precisely the same thematic material as was heard earlier, in a slower tempo, in the passage first presenting the chain of ascending thirds.

The Fantasy is a highly integrated work, in which the central idea of ascending thirds is projected simultaneously in harmonic detail and in the controlling tonal architecture. The sonata-like structure of the Fantasy is not undermined by the overall tonal scheme of the piece, since the entire recapitulation is stated a fifth below the exposition. Thus, in the main body of the work, Ab major is clearly the central tonality. It is surprising that the extended introduction should remain so firmly in the tonality of F. Yet this itself is testimony to its introductory character; it stands outside the principal action of the work.

Ballade no. 2, op. 38 (1836–9)

In the Fantasy and Second Scherzo, Chopin placed his first section in the relative minor of the eventual tonic key, whereas in the Second Ballade the opening passage is in the more remote bVI relation to the tonic. The Ballade is based on two strongly contrasting sections: a serene, pastoral Andantino in F major, and a turbulent Presto con fuoco in A minor. These two subjects are treated in a manner suggesting sonata procedure: the exposition is followed by a developmental section based on the material from the Andantino, and passing through various keys, and a recapitulation of the Presto follows. The exposition of this ballade may be regarded as analogous to an inverted sonata exposition, in which the material in the secondary tonality is stated before the material in the tonic key. A full recapitulation of the opening Andantino in F major does not occur in this work, however. Instead, it is the function of the development section to prepare this material so that its subsequent appearances in A minor will be musically convincing. Chopin's treatment of this thematic material, and the overall form of the work are shown in Figure 4.

This work is reminiscent of the second and third scherzos in that it is concerned with the gradual integration of thematic material that is initially dissociated. The Second Ballade is the most extreme case of this kind in Chopin. Its sonata-like structure demands more profound integration than is necessary in the scherzos, in which the trio forms a naturally contrasting section. The striking contrasts and unusual tonal plan of this work may have been associated with a literary programme. According to Robert Schumann, Chopin once stated that his ballades were based on poems by his compatriot Mickiewicz.[12] The poem apparently associated with the Second Ballade is *The Switez*, which tells the story of maidens from a Polish village besieged by Russian soldiers: to escape capture, the maidens pray to be swallowed by the earth; when their wish is granted, they return transformed as flowers that thereafter adorn the site of the village.[13] If this connection with the poem is valid, the F major Andantino is doubtless associated with the maidens, whose music is juxtaposed with and ultimately overshadowed by the passages in Presto tempo, in the basic tonality of A minor. The tragic perspective inherent in this compositional plan and programme is reminiscent of the works of Schubert, whose music so frequently exploits the expressive contrast between lyrical and dramatic music in the major and minor modes, respectively.[14]

Analysis of Chopin's treatment of the Adantino material will reveal how it is gradually integrated into the overall tonal plan centred in A minor. The

[12] In 1841 Schumann reviewed the Second Ballade along with the Nocturnes op. 37 and the Waltze op. 42 in the *Neue Zeitschrift für Musik*. In the same review he recalled having heard Chopin play it in a version ending in F major instead of A minor. Leon Plantinga suggests that Chopin must have played the work for Schumann during his second trip to Leipzig five years earlier, in 1836 (see Plantinga, *Schumann as Critic* (New Haven and London, 1967), 230–1). From this account we may conclude that Chopin extensively reworked the piece after his trip to Leipzig – unless Schumann was mistaken, and had heard (or remembered hearing) only the first section of the ballade.

[13] See the discussion of this poetic association in Harald Krebs, 'Alternatives to Monotonality in Early Nineteenth-Century Music', *Journal of Music Theory* xxv (1981), 14–15. The connection between *The Switez* and the Second Ballade appears in Alfred Cortot, Introduction to his *Student's Edition of Chopin's Ballades* (New York, 1931), 2; cited by Krebs, ibid., 16.

[14] For a discussion of this practice in vocal and instrumental works of Schubert, see W. Kinderman, 'Schubert's Tragic Perspective', in W. Frisch, ed., *Schubert: Critical and Analytical Studies*, (Lincoln and London, 1986), 68–83.

Figure 4. Ballade, op. 38

Section	Exposition		Recall of B	'Development' of B	Recapitulation of A	Coda; final recall of A and B
	B	A				
Key	F	a (bar 47)	F (a) (bar 83)	(Gb) E C (F)	(d) (bar 141)	a (bar 169)
	E♭ (bar 71)		F		a	a

F ——————————— F ————————→ E → C ——————→ a ————————— a

(resolution of opening B section)

Note: B = Andantino material originally in F major
A = Presto con fuoco material originally in A minor

opening Andantino section contains two phrases that go to A minor, in bars 18–21, and bars 35–8. When Chopin recalls this section (bars 83–94) before the development, he implies the move toward A minor by quoting only the first phrase of the theme, and, after a pause, the phrase in A minor from bars 35 to 38 (Example 9).

Example 9.

The development section that follows is entirely based on the Andantino theme, which is treated in a sparse, uneventful texture before the *stretto più mosso*.[15] The following passage builds to a climax in octaves, and culminates in three obvious parallel fifths, which seem to be used for intensity of effect. At this point the first phrase of the Andantino theme is stated again, first in E major, then in C major. The goal of the development is this restatement of the opening theme on pitch levels that are triadic degrees of the eventual tonic, A minor (Example 10).

The following recapitulation of the Presto continues to strengthen our perception of A minor as the basic tonal centre of the work. In the exposition of the Presto the second phrase of eight bars was heard in the remote key of G minor, but in the recapitulation the tonic is approached instead through its subdominant and the music then remains in A minor. Under a series of slow trills and a sustained tonic pedal, the head of the opening Andantino theme appears once again, now for the first time in A minor.

The ballade has gained increasing rhythmic momentum up to the beginning

[15] These octaves in the bass foreshadow the statement of the Andantino theme in A minor just before the coda (bars 157–64).

Example 10.

Example 11.

of the coda, which represents the first strong tonic downbeat in the piece.[16] Much of the power of this coda is derived from its synthesis, in an A minor context, of musical elements drawn from earlier passages of the work. Even the unusual tonal plan of the ballade seems to resonate in the fierce motivic emphasis, from the opening bars of the coda, on the upper and lower leading-notes to E, the dominant note of A minor.[17] In the second bar, these two semitones, D♯–E and F–E, appear in the treble (Example 11). During the final

restatement of the Presto theme these semitones appear in the bass. Chopin even changed the first version of his manuscript so as to emphasise further the F–E semitone in bars 189 and 190.[18] Near the end of the coda, the last chord

[16] The beginning of the first Presto does not sound like the tonic, since it directly follows the F major Andantino.

[17] Unlike the coda of the Second Scherzo, with its emphasis on B♭♭–A♭, both semitone relationships to the dominant note are prominently stressed here.

[18] See Oswald Jonas, 'On the Study of Chopin's Manuscripts', *Chopin Jahrbuch* i (1956), 149.

before the Tempo I section is a 'French' augmented sixth, a significant chord in this context, since it brings together both F and D♯. Chopin's pedal indication ensures that these two pitches are resolved to E in bar 199, in the final transfigured reminiscence of the original Andantino theme in A minor.

The most intense form of the F–E semitone occurs at the moment of elaborated restatement of the Presto theme, when it is stressed by a two-octave downward leap in octaves in the bass. An allusion to the parallel fifths from the development comes with a vengeance in the treble. These are the technical means by which Chopin marks the climax of the coda (Example 12).

Example 12.

A review of the overall tonal scheme of this ballade will reveal that this emphasis on the semitones D♯–E and F–E reflects larger structural events in the music. The opening theme, as we have seen, is first stated in F major, and reappears in the development section on the pitch level of E. It is notable that the other secondary key area of the exposition is E♭ (D♯) major, which is stressed by a decorated pedal point in the passage before the first restatement of the opening theme (Example 13). The emphasis on the upper and lower semitones to

Example 13.

E in the coda corresponds then to the large tonal areas of F major and E♭ (D♯) major in the exposition.

It is significant in this regard that thematic material from the passage on E♭ also returns in the coda. At the end of the exposition, for instance, the E♭ section leads into a restatement of the opening theme in F. This modulatory passage contains a chromatically descending bass line from A♭ to E. In the coda, it is this same descending bass line, twice repeated, that prepares cadences in A minor. Here again, disparate and even enigmatic elements from the body of the work find unity in the powerful synthesis of the coda.[19]

The Second Ballade is the most extreme example of directional tonality in Chopin's works. Here the establishment of a firm tonal foundation is postponed until the coda, while directional relationships are set up from two different key areas of the exposition. The length of the opening section in F major, the tonal instability of the exposition of the Presto in A minor, and the following, seemingly inexplicable hovering on E♭, all contribute to an impression of a fragmentary succession of parts. In view of these sharp contrasts, it is amazing to what extent the recapitulation and coda succeed in unifying the work.

One suspects that the unusual structural tensions of the ballade may have been connected with Chopin's difficulties in arriving at a final version of the piece. He returned to it repeatedly during the years 1836–9.[20] Virtually no other opus except the studies and preludes took him so long to complete. The Second Scherzo and the Fantasy are less problematic than the Second Ballade, for in each of them a tonal scheme based on thirds pervades the whole, integrating the opening key with the tonic key a minor third above. Nor, in the Scherzo and in the Fantasy after its introduction, is there as much emphasis on the opening key, which foregoes a strong cadence and passes directly into the eventual tonic tonality.

It is widely accepted that the 'dew pond' of Chopin's chromatic harmony, transmitted by Liszt to Wagner, influenced the course of later music.[21] Yet the possible influence of Chopin's formal innovations has remained largely unexplored. In these three pieces, and especially in the Second Ballade, Chopin seems to be feeling his way toward new forms based on a new conception of tonality.

---

[19] In his generally excellent book *Chopin's Musical Style*, Gerald Abraham writes (56–7) that instead of this coda, Chopin might have simply restated the first subject in full and in F major. Nothing could be more mistaken.

[20] See Rawsthorne, 'Ballades, Fantasy, and Scherzos', 50.

[21] D.F. Tovey, 'The Main Stream of Music', in *The Main Stream of Music and Other Essays* (New York, 1959; first published 1949), 345.

Melodic structuring of harmonic dissonance: a method for analysing Chopin's contribution to the development of harmony

EUGENE NARMOUR

Introduction

Chopin's importance in the development of tonal harmony has received wide acclaim in the field of musicology. His bifocal use of seventh chords, his local and remote mixtures of modal and chromatic harmony, his rapid, tonicising chromatic sequences, his planing of unresolved seventh chords, his extended pedal points creating a sense of harmonic stasis, his non-cadential endings, his vague tonal beginnings, his modulations to remote keys, his occasional experiments in non-tonality – all these have captured the attention of scholars.[1]

Chopin's prolongational treatment of dissonance has been celebrated as well. The article in *The New Grove*, for instance, observes that ordinary appoggiaturas are not 'incidental details' in Chopin's style but are often 'dwelt on' for the purposes of 'expressive significance'.[2] In this study, I will argue that Chopin's use of dissonance, as exemplified in the mazurkas and nocturnes, goes beyond that. Contradicting the conventional view, which states that the types of chords found in Chopin's harmonic style are 'simple and comparatively few in number',[3] I will demonstrate by means of a new theoretical method that, in

---

[1] For a survey of studies in harmony concerning the music of Chopin, see Zofia Helman, 'Chopin's Harmonic Devices in 20th-Century Theoretical Thought' in *Studies in Chopin* (Warsaw, 1973), 49–61.

[2] Nicholas Temperley, 'Chopin, Fryderyk Franciszek', *The New Grove Dictionary of Music and Musicians* (London, 1980), iv, 302.

[3] Remarks made by Gerald Abraham in *Chopin's Musical Style* (London, 1939), 78–9. Abraham goes on to say that the overlay of dissonance in Chopin's music often makes 'unrecognisable' what he regards as the basic chord types. And therein lies the contradiction: when an assumed simplicity is unrecognisable, it is usually the result of a permanent and complex *structural* change

addition to the usual structural dissonances found in the style of this period, certain melodic patterns in his music generate a rather large pool of dissonant sonorities that actually come to function structurally, though not necessarily transformationally, on some level. I will, moreover, attempt to show through the numerous examples that this rather large vocabulary of sonorities, some of which challenge our traditional tonal nomenclature, forms an integral part of Chopin's language as a harmonist – a language which all concede contributed unmistakably to the revolution in dissonant harmonic thinking that came to characterise so much of the music of the nineteenth century.

Probably the most important analytical idea acquired in music theory in the past thirty years is the recognition that harmonic structure is as dependent on voice-leading – on the emergence of 'horizontal' structure in the melodic parts – as it is on 'vertical' intervallic relationships existing among the members of the chord.[4]

Consider the following instance (Example 1) from Chopin's Mazurka op. 24 no. 3.[5] Here the diminished seventh chord on the second beat of bar 2 (marked with an 'x' in parentheses) would be analysed in terms of voice-leading as a point of harmonic structure because, although dissonant, its outside voices function in retrospect to initiate linear melodic patterns that terminate on the C minor chord in the next bar (see the analysis above the staff).

In contrast, a roman-numeral analysis of that bar, attending to the resolution of the diminished seventh chord and the tonicisation of each triad, would make the consonant chord on Ab (bar 2) the point of structure. In other words, a roman-numeral analysis would deal with the progression in bar 2 prospectively, as if it were highly similar to the two tonicisations preceding it, while the voice-leading analysis would ignore the chord-pair tonicisation and retrospectively treat the Ab consonant chord as nothing more than a transitory

in the material. Moreover, if Chopin's vocabulary of chords were simple and few in number, then an analysis of his chord types would be statistically little different from those of, say, Bach – an argument which has actually been made. For a good discussion of the problems of this reasoning in the harmonic practice of Chopin, see Jim Samson, *The Music of Chopin* (London, 1985), 147–8.

[4] For this we are indebted to Schenkerian theory, a great improvement in harmonic analysis over the traditional use of roman numerals which, as is well known, tends to emphasise vertical chordal relationships to the detriment of melodic–contrapuntal motion. Schenkerian theory, however, does not make roman-numeral analysis obsolete. For roman-numeral symbols often capture important low-level harmonic relationships that would tend to be overlooked when viewed exclusively in terms of a Schenkerian voice-leading assimilation. In the analyses below I employ roman numerals not because I am fond of the theory behind them or because I think they are unproblematic – the symbology is often clumsy and cumbersome, for instance – but because they offer a quick and economical way to give the reader the general harmonic context without expensively having to reproduce in the numerous examples the whole excerpt.

[5] In addition to opus numbers in the captions for the examples used in this article, I will use the italicized capital *M* to refer to mazurka and *N* to refer to nocturne followed, of course, by the usual opus numbers.

Example 1. *M* op. 24 no. 3, bars 25–8

passing note (PN). Both analyses are partially correct, the one analysing prospectively from the chord-to-chord relationship and the other looking back from the voice-leading pattern that emerges from the vantage of the C minor chord in bar 3. Indeed, Chopin's phrasing proves the validity and necessity of both analyses, the right-hand phrasing in bar 2 differing from that of the left hand, an important performing detail for any sensitive pianist.[6]

Although the noncongruence between 'horizontal' melody and 'vertical' harmony in the above example is really noncongruence between prospective and retrospective meanings, the example reminds us that music is actually made up of independent parameters. For our purposes, what is important to recognise is that melody need not be congruent with harmony – in fact, if we define harmony narrowly as merely the temporal succession of verticalities, it is clear that the direction melody takes and the structure it achieves may often be 'at odds' with harmony, or with any other parameter for that matter. It is also important to recognise how powerful certain kinds of melodic structures are in the establishment of structure: they can make a consonant, tonicised chord sound like a passing note (e.g., the A♭ chord); and, when initiating a voice-leading pattern, they can make a dissonant chord function as a structural event (e.g., the VII[7] over G in bar 2).[7]

---

[6] I have checked a microfilm copy of the manuscript which confirms the different phrasing in each voice.

[7] Those familiar with Schenkerian analysis will come to see in this paper that the melodic–harmonic structures I derive are on the whole significantly different from those of Schenkerian theory. With the exception of the *Stufen*, Schenkerian theory argues that contrapuntal voice-leading creates harmonic structure. One problem, in my view, is that Schenker made the mis-

In this respect, Chopin is truly a fascinating composer. That he is one of the world's great melodists goes without saying, as does the statement that he is among the most significant figures in the development of harmony. In what follows, we will explore in considerable detail the relationship between Chopin's melodic structures and his treatment of dissonance. To maintain focus, we will concentrate on four types of melodic structures, and in addition, we will carefully examine specific durational and metrical contexts as they affect both the emergence of melodic structures and the preparatory-resolutional functions of dissonance. Since to conceptualise and treat parameters separately requires straining their elements through a rather fine analytical net, and since when finished we must have some means for restoring these interrelationships into an integrated musical whole, I will begin by laying out a modest programmatic methodology and a rather simple symbology in order to effect a modicum of logical consistency in the arguments and conclusions based on the analyses.

A methodology for analysing Chopin's music

Melody. – In the theoretical model employed below, there are four basic kinds of melodic structures to consider: process, reversal, processive reversal, and registral return.[8] A *process* is any melodic pattern of three or more pitches of similarly-sized intervals moving in the same registral direction. Patterns like ascending or descending scales, for instance, are processes because their intervals – major and minor seconds – are sufficiently alike. A melodic triad (e.g., C–E–G or C–F–A) also fits the definition of a process as do patterns like C–D–F or C–E–F. So long as the difference between any two intervals in the same direction does not exceed a minor third, we may say that a process has been created.[9] In the analyses which follow, I shall outline the pattern with

take of not allowing melody, as opposed to voice-leading models, to interfere with, or even prevent, if necessary, the emergence of the *Ursatz* and *Ursatz*-like structures on every level. Another problem is that melody in Schenkerian analysis is always reduced to voice-leading models. But if one truly believes in the importance of counterpoint in the structuring of harmony, then one must also believe in the independence of voices. It thus follows that a single voice by itself, which is to say, melody, can irrevocably influence the shape of harmony. Schenkerian theory compromises the power of melody in harmonic structuring and, moreover, by reducing most dissonant notes out of the analytical picture, does not live up to its contrapuntal conviction. My argument will be that melodic structuring can make certain dissonances structural – rather than just prolongational – in either the formational or transformational sense.

[8] A fifth – two-element groupings – need not concern us here. There are also other combinations and variations of the patterns discussed above that the theory generates, but they are not necessary to the argument in this article.

[9] An ascending pattern like C–G–A, for example, is not a process because the difference between the perfect fifth and the major second is a perfect fourth. More formally, processes in the

brackets and symbolise process with the capital letter P (see Example 2 below). Three or more repeated pitches – iteration – I call 'duplicative' and symbolise their patterns with the letter D (see, for instance, the three Fs in Example 2c, second level).

A *reversal* is a melodic structure in which one (usually large) interval is followed by a smaller one. Reversal has separate registral and intervallic aspects.[10] For instance, an ascending pattern of highly differentiated intervals like C–G–A exemplifies a reversal pattern in terms of interval, whereas an up-down pattern of small intervals like C–E–D exemplifies reversal in terms of register. (The same would be true of patterns ending on a unison, e.g., C–E–E). More commonly, reversal structures combine both aspects, as in the up-down pattern of C–A–G where the change from large interval to small is emphasised simultaneously by a change in register. I shall symbolise reversal patterns in the analyses by the letter R (see the analysis below, Examples 2a, 2d and 2e).

Processive reversal, as the name implies, combines the emergence of process in one registral direction with that of registral reversal in another. An ascending processive pattern like C–E–G followed by a descending step to F in the opposite direction, for instance, is a typical processive reversal structure, as is the

Example 2. (a) *M* op. 59 no. 1, bars 1–4 (b) *M* op. 50 no. 1, bars 1–4 (c) *M* op. 17 no. 1, bars 1–3 (d) *M* op. 67 no. 4, bars 1–4 (e) *M* op. 30 no. 2, bars 1–2

parameter of melody are A + A relationships where, between any two adjacent melodic intervals, A – A = m3 or less. This rule of intervallic similarity changes when dissonance contributes differentiation to the melodic patterning. For example, the ascending melodic pattern of C–E–F lies at the extreme of the A + A boundary (M3 – m2 = m3); thus, if F were moderately dissonant, the three pitches would not be grouped as a process. Of course, degree of dissonance – weak, moderate, or strong, defined later in the text – would affect the rule of similarity somewhat differently.

[10] Intervallically, reversal may be formally expressed as an A + B relationship where B – A = M3 or more; since registral change itself, however, is a form of differentiation, its occurrence alters this intervallic rule somewhat. For reasons of space I cannot discuss this complication here. Since the analyses are largely self-explanatory, the reader should have little trouble understanding my analytical ascriptions of reversal.

Example 2. (*cont.*)

up-up-down melodic pattern of C–D–E–D or C–F–A–F.[11] I shall symbolise processive reversal in the analyses with the letters PR (see the analyses above, Examples 2b and 2c).

The last kind of melodic structure to concern us is that of *registral return*. Unlike process, reversal, and processive reversal, registral return refers to a discontiguous relationship involving three notes with a change in registral direction where the third pitch is the same, or nearly the same, as the pitch initiating the pattern. The definition of 'nearly the same' is a difference of a major second or less between the first and third pitches.[12] Thus, an up-down pattern like C–D–C signifies exact registral return because the difference between the first pitch and the third one is none. An up-down pattern like C–D–B or C–D–C♯ exemplifies near registral return because the difference between the first note and the third note is a minor second.[13] I shall symbolise registral return in the analyses with the small letters of aba or aba', depending on whether the return is exact or nearly exact (for aba, see Examples 2c, 2d, and 2e; for aba', see Example 6a).[14]

As mentioned, I shall place in the analyses brackets spanning the initial note and the terminal note of the analytical structures of P, R, and PR because in the parameter of melody, *melodic structural notes are found at points of initiation and termination*.[15] In terms of perception, a point of initiation becomes structural because the listener construes a function of *primacy*, whereas a point of termination becomes structural because the listener perceives a function in *closure*.[16]

---

[11] Formally, the letters A+A. . .+B typify these kinds of structures – A+A for the process and B for the reversal.

[12] Formally: A – A ≦ M2.

[13] In contrast, an up-down pattern like C–E–A does not create a sense of registral return because the distance between the first and last note is too large (a minor third).

[14] The concept of registral return in melodic analysis is, of course, not new. Neighbour notes, for instance, create patterns of exact registral return; 'escape notes' typify patterns of near return. The advantage of the concept of registral return is that it draws attention to structural similarities among all kinds of melodic patterns previously conceived as belonging to different classes. For example, a down-up pattern of C–G–C is not a neighbour note; but it is a pattern of exact registral return and, because of that, can be organised under the same principle of registral return governing neighbour notes and escape notes.

[15] As will be seen, certain notes can belong to two different kinds of melodic structures simultaneously. For instance, the last 'a' of an aba-structure can belong medially to a process (see Examples 4b, 4c, 5a, and 13a).

[16] The theory I am outlining looks at music from a perceptual point of view and as such is based upon certain psychological principles of pattern perception. For instance, process is a case of the Gestalt law of continuation operating under the perceptual rules of similarity and proximity. Reversal is governed by principles of differentiation. Registral return is a function of the general psychological concept of return. Because the model I am sketching is based largely on psychological principles of pattern perception, it is heavily oriented in analysis toward viewing musical matters from the listener's perspective. Thus, the listener's expectations – or what in objective terms of the music I call implications – form an integral part of the analytical explanation. In the full-blown implication–realisation model, I symbologically distinguish prospective from

To return for a moment to Example 2, since the initial and terminal notes in all these cases create points of melodic structure, it follows as a result of the hierarchical transformations of those low-level structural notes that the same general kinds of melodic structures – processes, reversals, and so forth – will be found on higher levels as well. In Example 2a, for instance, the structural notes E–C of bar 1 belong to an E–C–A process reversed on the B of bar 2; thus, on the second level, E–C–A–B create a processive reversal (PR). By the same reasoning, the initial F♯ of bar 3 goes on to make with the C and the E of bar 4 an ascending process (P).[17] Note that even higher levels than this may occur. In Example 2b, for instance, two foreground processes create a reversal (R) on level 2 (D–A–C) which itself goes on to cause the emergence of another reversal pattern (R) on level 3 (D–C–B) – melodically integrating the end of bar 2 into the start of bar 3. In contrast, the low-level structures of Example 2c create structural notes making a sequence of iteration (D), process (P), and reversal (R) on level 2, whereas the iterations and reversals of Example 2d produce a process (E–C–A) on a third level (underlined by the A+A form).[18]

The analyses and comments above deal exclusively with structures belonging to the parameter of melody. But since the 'interference' of consonance and dissonance in the emergence of melodic structure is central to the harmonic style of Chopin, it is thus beneficial at this point to hypothesise a rudimentary but convenient nomenclature as well as a practicable symbology to deal with

retrospective implication in the structures of process, reversal, and registral return. Owing to considerations of space and the aims of this paper, however, these refinements in analytical explanation, important as they are, will not concern us here.

[17] The A on the second beat of bar 3 is omitted from level 2 because it is dissonant. Nevertheless, its durational cumulation, about which more later, makes it quite articulative as a melodic event despite its dissonance. Observe as well in this example that the pacing of structural notes on the next level – another important aspect of melodic motion that can be tracked effectively through these symbological representations – is regular in bars 1–2 (two notes every bar in the mazurka rhythm of ♩ ♩ | ♩ ♩), and slightly less regular in bars 3–4 (♩ ♩ ♩ | ♩ ♩). Finally, it should be noted on level 2 that the B to the E in bar 2 forms a dyadic (two-group) relationship, the subject of which, for want of space, will not be discussed in this article; the connection between B–E (bar 2) and the F♯ of bar 3 is thus not a reversal. Bar 2 is connected to bar 3 at a much higher level in the hierarchy, on a level not shown here.

[18] In other words, certain of the rules of the theoretical method outlined so far are recursive. But in a real hierarchical system, the *interpretations* of implicative meaning cannot be recursive. In Example 2a, for instance, the higher-level C–E in bar 4 is different in pitch from any of the other intervals in the F♯–C–E pattern because it emerges from the lower level through a C–F–E reversal structure; F♯–C in contrast is underpinned by a process. Durationally, each structural note is approached differently on the lower level as well: the quaver C follows two crotchets, the E two quavers, and so forth, which also affects implicative meanings on the higher levels. In other words, because of what is embedded individually in each note, the higher-level F♯–C–E pattern is only superficially like a process on the note-to-note level. For more on the true nature of hierarchies in music, see my article, 'Some Major Theoretical Problems Concerning the Concept of Hierarchy in the Analysis of Tonal Music', *Music Perception* i (1983–4), 129–99.

such parametric interactions. Basically, we want to identify the most general kinds of consonance-dissonance patterns there are, and we want to be able to pinpoint their function with respect to melodic structuring. Since ultimately I intend to demonstrate that Chopin's melodic patterning brings about structural dissonances that are transformed on to new hierarchical levels, I shall invoke a symbology to keep track of the effects of duration and metre on melody as well. Let us therefore continue our quest to construct a methodology by considering dissonance.

Dissonance. – The kind of symbols I will use to keep track of consonance-dissonance relationships – 'x' in various formats – has already been seen in Example 2 above. There, the 'x' with parentheses – (x) – stood for melodic dissonances that were 'integrated' into the diatonic-triadic chords belonging to a key. The parentheses denote that these kinds of melodic dissonances are relatively weak, as for example, the tritone in diminished or diminished-seventh chords (bar 2, Example 2b), the minor seventh in dominant or secondary seventh chords (bar 4, Example 2b; bar 3, Example 2c; and bar 2, Example 2d), or the major or minor ninth in dominant (or subdominant) ninth chords (bar 2, Example 2e). Dissonant melodic notes that form part of a fuller chord over a pedal point – the case of the A in bar 3 of Example 2a – are also symbolised with (x).

The 'plain x' (without parentheses) represents a somewhat stronger melodic dissonance, one that still belongs diatonically to a key but is not integrated triadically into the harmonic texture, as for instance, the lone diatonic passing or neighbour notes over single pedals (bar 3, Example 2c; bars 1–4, Example 2d; and bar 1, Example 2e).

Finally, dissonances in the melody that are both out of the key and not integrated into what seems to be the implied chord – what I will call *contramodal dissonances* – are symbolised with an '⊗' to denote a stronger degree of dissonance (bar 1 of Examples 2c and 2d).[19]

Although the study of harmony is obviously much more complicated than these rudimentary 'vertical' symbols suggest – the sheer number of dissonances in a chord, the number of common notes between any two chords, the motion in the bass, the position of the soprano and the bass with reference to chord member, the part-writing, spacing, prospective and retrospective contexts, and so forth all have to be considered – the usefulness of (x), x, and ⊗ for our

---

[19] That a melodic note can be intervallically consonant yet contramodal is also a possibility – for instance, a sudden shift from major to parallel minor back to major. I will symbolise such cases with a plain 'x' to represent the instability present even though such melodic notes are not in fact harmonically dissonant but, rather, discordant in terms of what is perceived to be the prevailing mode.

purposes is that they will enable us economically to pinpoint various degrees of dissonance in a given melodic line. Equally important, they will also allow us to keep track of various degrees of resolution since, for instance, a consonance following an (x) is weaker than one following an x or an ⊗.[20]

In structural terms, within the parameter of harmony (as narrowly defined on p. 79), dissonances resolving to consonances create various degrees of *closure*.[21] The function of closure thus pertains not only to how melodic structures come to end, as we saw in our discussion of process (P), processive reversal (PR), reversal (R), and exact or nearly exact return (aba, aba′), but is also pertinent to the termination of harmonic implication – in the form of a dissonance moving to a consonance. This, as we shortly shall see, is crucial in understanding not only the interplay between melody and harmony but also the interrelationship between harmony and duration. And nowhere do we find the interaction among various parametric closures treated more subtly than in the music of Chopin.

Duration. – The topic of closure is equally relevant to conceptualising the parameter of duration.[22] For, like dissonance moving to consonance, short notes that move to long notes, which is to say cumulative patterns, also create closure and thus structure on the terminal note. Long notes moving to short ones (counter-cumulative) produce structure only on the initial note, while the terminal note in such cases is nonclosural and ongoing. Additive patterns – sequences of three or more repeated durations of the same length – display structural 'nodes' at both the initial and the terminal points.[23]

All durational patterns exemplify one of these three types of temporal configurations. Moreover, as in the case with the parameter of harmony, we can measure the extent of durational closure or nonclosure by attending to the degree of cumulation (cum.) or counter-cumulation (c/c.). For example, a cumulative pattern of a quaver moving to a crotchet (♪ ♩ ; ratio 1:2) is less

---

[20] The importance of prospective and retrospective meaning in harmonic analysis can hardly be overemphasised even though our current analytical symbols are wholly inadequate to deal with it. For instance, in Example 2a the downbeat F♯ of bar 3 over the rest is not literally consonant or dissonant with anything (and thus I have not marked it with an 'x'), yet in retrospect to the V⁷ of the preceding bar a good case could be made for its being heard as 'contextually' discordant. Similarly, the F in bar 4 of this same example is not literally dissonant (it is a consonant sixth over a bald A in the bass), yet our expectation from both the V⁷ preceding it and the A in the bass under the C in the soprano that the downbeat chord is a tonic makes this F sound somewhat unstable. Thus, though it is not, strictly speaking, a dissonance, it is nevertheless not as contextually 'neutral' as the absence of an 'x' in the analysis makes it out to be.

[21] Note, however, that closure is not synonymous with transformation. Closure can cause low-level structuring without the notes involved giving rise to the creation of a new level.

[22] As the reader may surmise, the theory I am cursorily outlining here invokes the same set of principles for treating all the primary parameters of melody, harmony, and duration.

[23] As mentioned earlier, additive patterns, duplicative and iterative, are symbolised by the letter D.

closed than quaver moving to a dotted crotchet (♪♩. ; 1:3); conversely, a counter-cumulative pattern of a minim moving to a crotchet (♩ ♩ ; 2:1) is less unclosed than a minim moving to a quaver (♩ ♪ ; 4:1). Additive patterns (♩ ♩ ; 1:1), once initiated and until terminated, are also implicative and on-going – though less nonclosural than counter-cumulative patterns.[24]

When relevant, I shall symbolise durational patterns in the analyses as follows:

cum. = cumulation;
c/c. = counter-cumulation;
add. = additive;

and, when examining in detail the interrelationship between harmony and duration, I shall sometimes show the ratio between the durational elements making up the pattern. The importance of doing this is that, with considerable precision, we capture the problem of defining parametric noncongruence – of comparing the degree of nonclosure in harmony with the degree of closure (or nonclosure) in duration. And in turn we can evaluate the degree of non-congruence in the light of the structuring in the melody.

For instance, in Example 2d earlier, the dissonant neighbour note F in bar 1 is weakened because it is introduced counter-cumulatively (♩♩. ♪ =5:1); the dissonant neighbour note D♯ in the same bar, despite its contramodal property (⊗), is neither strengthened nor weakened by the duration since, as a medial note, its setting is additive. (I am assuming the mordent on the E is played before the beat; of course, metrical placement – both dissonances are off the beat – increases the instability of both of these notes, about which more in a moment.) By contrast, in bar 2, the moderately strong dissonant C is dura-tionally cumulative (♪♩ =1:2); moreover, the reversal structure in the melody (E–B–C) is congruent with this durational closure (not to mention occurring on the beat), *making the dissonant C structural*, without which no registral return (aba) between the C of bar 2 and the C of bar 3 would emerge. This C–D–C pattern also serves as the model for the sequential repetition of that

---

[24] There is obviously more to all this than I have room to explain here. A question arises, for instance, about rests. A quaver followed by a quaver rest followed by a crotchet (♪𝄾♩) is, it is true, cumulative to the extent of 1:2, but it is cumulative within an additive temporal length of one crotchet followed by one crotchet (♩ ♩ or 1:1). Cumulative, counter-cumulative, or addi-tive patterns thus take up time, but their durational elements also occupy temporal positions. Because of this, rests cause apparently cumulative or counter-cumulative patterns to function as subsets of additive patterns, and when this happens, the inherent degree of closure is affected. For example, the pattern mentioned above (♪𝄾♩), a subset of additive patterns (1:1), is not as closed as a quaver going directly to a crotchet (♪♩) even though on the surface both display a 1:2 duration. Of course, the cumulative pattern with the rest belonging to the additive class will be more closed than a purely additive sequence of two plain crotchets.

figure – A–B–A – in bars 4–5.[25] Melody and duration, in other words, prevent
the C in bar 2 from functioning as a mere passing note to the seventh of the
dominant seventh on beat three.

This is the kind of structural dissonance intrinsic to Chopin's style; and the
method outlined here, which keeps track of parameters separately, will allow us
to discover more such interesting relationships in the pages which follow.

Metre. – Like duration and harmony, we mentioned in connection with Example 2d that metre exercised an important influence over the degree of structure brought about by initial and terminal melodic functions. Simply put,
structural melodic notes congruent with beats are structurally stronger, all
other things being equal, than structural notes off beats. The 'all other things
being equal' is an important proviso, however, since obviously other parametric 'interference' – for example, appoggiaturas in harmony – can alter the
structuring or weakening metrical effects of beats and off-beats.

As already seen in Examples 2c, 2d and 2e, I shall, in the traditional way,
symbolise beats in the analyses with accents (–) and off-beats with nonaccents
(⌣). This will allow us to attend in detail to the interrelationship between
metre and the other primary parameters of melody, harmony, and duration.[26]

At this point, a summary of all the main analytical symbols and their functions is in order:

P = process   (x) = weak dissonance
R = reversal   x = moderate dissonance
PR = processive reversal   ⊗ = strong dissonance
D = duplicative (iteration)   – = on the beat (accent)
aba = exact registral return   ⌣ = off the beat (nonaccent)
aba' = near registral return

Exact registral return (the neighbour note)

In order to discuss Chopin's contribution to the development of harmony,
it is first necessary to see how all the parametric hypotheses discussed so far
operate together. This in turn will help us to understand more fully how the

---

[25] It is largely the closural reversal in the melody that makes this dissonant C structural. This is in
contrast to the cumulative dissonant A of bar 3 in Example 2a; there, the ongoing melodic
process makes the cumulative dissonant note function as a point of strong articulation rather
than as a point of structural transformation.

[26] I make no distinction between the kinds of beats; in this theory, beat one in 4/4 metre is not
necessarily stronger than any of the other beats, nor is beat three stronger than beats two and
four. I do not in general deny the importance of downbeats or the possibility of differentiation
among the various beats in a given metre – only that I prefer to deal with beats interpretively in
the written text (the 'natural language') rather than give them their own analytical symbols.

later analyses, and thus the stylistic conclusions which follow from them, are derived. Although music is composed of separate parameters – and because of that the method advocated here conceptualises them separately – analytical ambiguity nevertheless can arise since any one parameter can, and often does, interfere with the apparent function of another. For this reason, we must first understand some of the norms of parametric interaction. Most especially, we must understand the methodological principles of parametric interplay that determine the *grouping* of melodic pitches in order to analyse correctly melodic structuring and its effect on dissonance in the examples. During this discussion, we will observe some interesting features about Chopin's handling of melody, harmony, metre and duration.

One potential problem is that of confusing the 'digression' of a registral return (the 'b' of aba) with the initiation of process (P) since at that point both process and return often involve the same intervals of similarity defining each separate melodic function (Example 3a). By emphasising either the function of return or the function of process, however, metre and harmony often make clear the dominant melodic patterning, such that processes often emerge after the completion of the aba, as the norms displayed in Examples 3b (P) and 3c (the first PR) show.[27]

Example 3. (a) synthetic (b) *N* op. 72 no. 1, bars 32–3 (c) *N* op. 15 no. 2, bars 1–2

[27] Note in the trill of Example 3b, which is really executed as a mordent, the embedded aba structures.

Example 3c is interesting because the registral return (aba), which initiates the descending processive reversal (PR) on the downbeat, is durationally cumulative, lying noncongruent against the harmonic instability (a six-(three)) quickly resolving to a five-(three). Note that the harmonic instability of the six on the beat does not prevent the melodic process of A♯–G♯–E♯–C♯ from arising; indeed, it is the registral return and the cumulative rhythm that causes the descending melodic process to emerge and makes the harmonically non-congruent A♯ structural. One finds a good deal of such noncongruence in the music of Chopin, and, as we shall see, such patterns often involve striking dissonances that cannot be rightly reduced to any patent preordained harmonic scheme.[28]

Chopin is also fond of metrically distorting the beginning or end note of the normal aba scheme. For instance, in example 4a the dissonant, counter-cumulative, neighbour b-part of the first aba occurs on the beat with the result that, on the exact registral return off the beat, the ensuing process (P) is initiated metrically somewhat weakly.

Example 4. (a) *M* op. 59 no. 3, bars 33–4 (b) *M* op. 6 no. 1, bars 1–2
(c) *N* op. 9 no. 2, bar 1 (d) *M* op. 68 no. 4, bars 9–10

---

[28] Those wishing to compare this analysis of the melody with Schenker's may consult *Der Freie Satz* (Vienna, 1956), ii, 71.

Example 4. (*cont.*)

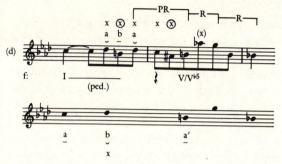

Because triplet figures are metrically weak dactyls (– ⌣ ⌣), a melodic registral return set that way affords a special opportunity for capitalising on the ambiguity mentioned earlier between the similarity of the intervals making up both the aba pattern and the processive structuring (recall Example 3a). For instance, in the triplet figure of Example 4b, whose beginning and ending notes are deformed because the 'empty' harmony (F♯ over C♯) momentarily seems to imply a four suspension, what begins as a neighbour note aba actually becomes part of a descending process (P); this eventuates in the emergence of a dominant chord, which goes on to a tonic on the downbeat of bar 2. Starting on a six or four (realised or implied) is, of course, a favourite device of Chopin (recall Example 3c or the A major Prelude op. 28 no. 7). In Example 4b it is not that the process (P) takes precedence over the aba but that Chopin has built in the melodic ambiguity so that both types of melodic structures are heard, the registral return albeit fleetingly.

If the ambiguity between process and registral return can be turned to esthetic advantage, then a double neighbour-note pattern (abab) offers a double possibility of exploiting further the deforming effects of harmony on these kinds of structures since either the a- or the b-part or both can function as a model for registral return. The famous opening of the early E♭ nocturne (Example 4c) is a case in point. The pedal on E♭ raises the possibility on beat two that the unaccented quaver G ending the triplet is a return of the opening G since, though lying dissonant against the diminished seventh (VII⁷) over the pedal, it is nevertheless a consonant third with the tonic (E♭) pedal point itself. But if, on the other hand, the G as a dissonant note is regarded as a point of registral return, then it would seem some small measure of registral return must also be accorded the downbeat dissonant F on beat three since the unaccented, somewhat harmonically stable quaver F on the second beat, clearly a chord member of the diminished seventh, can also function as the initial note of a pattern of return. Moreover, the dissonant F on the third beat is moderately cumulative (1:3). (Even when the dissonant F moves to the E♭

on the fourth beat, a new dissonance occurs as the pedal in the bass moves from Eb to D).

In short, although both metre and harmony strongly favour the G–F–G as a neighbour-note pattern, harmony, at least at the start, and duration somewhat favour F–G–F as well. The point is, as before, that melodic ambiguity on the note-to-note level is an inherent part of the structure, and it would do Chopin's music an injustice to reduce simplistically either the first F or the second G to an either-or analytical solution of one aba-neighbour note or to view the second F only as a mere appoggiatura.[29]

Chopin's pedal points, as we shall see later, create particularly instructive contexts for studying interrelationships among melodic, metrical, harmonic, and durational structures since they offer the opportunity for the simultaneous existence of different, independent harmonies, with harmonically clashing chord members. The opening of Example 4d, no ordinary set of changing notes, appears to imply through its melodic aba an augmented-sixth chord concurrent with the tonic (in the left-hand part); this results in a particularly striking dissonance. All the notes of the aba are quite dissonant, and the discordant contramodal Bɭ occurs on the beat. Observe that because the down-beat C over the rest in bar 2 is in retrospect an implied appoggiatura, the end note of the aba initiates a melodic process, reversing on the B of beat two of bar 2 (PR). On the next level, the end note of the aba pattern makes an aba' (C–Db–B). This kind of complexity of registral return on two levels is a hallmark of Chopin's appoggiatural style.

Near registral return and the escape note

In the theory outlined here, traditional passing notes function as medial parts of processes. Neighbour notes on the other hand, are classified under the rubric of exact registral return; changing notes also fit as well into this latter scheme. Appoggiaturas have been dealt with in light of registral return as well, and we have examined in some detail how Chopin alters their ordinary scheme by either deforming the first and last note (or both) or by making the dissonant note articulative through the use of durational cumulation and metrical accentuation.

Traditional escape notes also exemplify melodic structures of near registral return (aba').[30] But as we shall see, Chopin often begins a process on the dissonant escaping note itself, giving that note a melodic function of initiation

---

[29] My criticism is directed against Schenker's 3–2–1 analysis of this phrase in *Der Freie Satz*, ii, 42. The same remarks apply to Felix Salzer's analysis in *Structural Hearing* (New York, 1962), ii, 117.

[30] Schenkerian theory calls these 'incomplete neighbour notes'. The trouble with this term is that there is nothing incomplete about escape notes: they form patterns of near registral return.

and thus making a structural note out of what would ordinarily be simply a dissonant 'ornamental' note. As in registral return, the factor of durational patterning often enters into the analytical equation, strengthening the structural function of processive initiation on such dissonant escape notes. Let us look at the contextual norm for escape notes in Chopin's music first.

Example 5a is typical. Near registral return (aba'), that is to say, an escape note pattern, creates a linear pattern in the melody on the next level (C–Bb, making an Eb–D–C–Bb process). Such 'non-harmonic notes' occur commonly over root-position chords. And often the dissonant pitches involved belong to the chord to follow, so that the escape notes appear 'out-of-sync' with the general progression, a kind of 'anticipation by leap', as in Example 5a. Chopin likes to exploit the notion of melody being dissonantly 'out-of-phase' with consonant harmony.

Example 5. (a) *N* op. 9 no. 2, bar 12 (b) *M* op. 63 no. 3, bars 1–4 (c) *N* op. 37, bars 13–14

The dissonant escape note, however, can be made to function structurally, though not necessarily transformationally. Commonly in patterns of near registral return in the music of Chopin, the interval from the b-part to the a′-part is filled in, and thus what in terms of derivation was a plain escape note comes to function as the initial note of a melodic process. We should not confuse the initial and terminal functions of dissonance in these melodically processive types of examples with the escape note norms that we have just seen.

Points of processive initiality are melodically structural even though harmonically dissonant, and they affect harmony analytically, from creating dissonant chords that are merely articulative to creating those that cause new hierarchical levels. Conceptualised historically, such dissonant chords can function *formationally*, staying on the low level and thus still remaining relatively 'close' to their escape note roots, or *transformationally*, thus belonging to the next level of syntactic relationships which may change the style. In other words, we conceive formation as a structur*ing* function and transformation as a structur*al* function. Regardless of level, we must recognise the role initiation and termination of melodic process plays in contributing to musical structure.

Example 5b is a case of such structuring which is weakly formational and thus only articulative owing to its counter-cumulative and metrical setting (off the beat). Were it not for the interpolation of an accented passing note C♯ on the downbeat of bar 2, for example, the dissonant quaver D♯, anticipating the dominant of bar 2, would appear as a typical counter-cumulative escape note. As it happens, however, despite its counter-cumulation, the process of additive note values initiated by the dissonant, 'escape note', quaver D♯ creates some, albeit weak, sense of formation and structuring on the low level. The same is true of the anticipatory, 'out-of-sync' E in bar 3.

Durational patterning, however, can conspire to make the initial note of a melodic process begun dissonantly function more strongly as a structural note – to the extent that a new level emerges. When, for example, the initial and terminal notes of a process are concurrently also set as the initial and terminal notes of a closural durational pattern, then transformation of dissonance must be considered as a possible consequence. Consider, for instance, Example 5c. Here, the initial structural notes (G and E♭) of every other process in the melody (G–F–E♭; E♭–D–C) appear completely out-of-phase with the chords of the harmony. Yet we cannot dismiss the 'strange' sonorities created by these dissonances as mere escape notes because the durational patterning (dotted quaver, semiquaver, crotchet; 3:1:4) is congruent with the initiation and termination of melodic process, thereby ensuring the stability of the dissonant notes on the crotchet level. Observe that Chopin even writes grace notes to increase the rhythmic cumulation on the E♭ in bar 2.

Of course, we know where these dissonant structural notes 'originate' from: they belong to the chords that follow them (G belongs to the E♭ chord; E♭ to the C chord) and thus are 'anticipations by leap', as it were. But it would be an analytical mistake in Example 5c to align the dissonant notes with the consonant chords following them just to get a typical roman-numeral analysis or to see the initiation of these processes merely as ornamentations of escape notes – even though on level 2 'escape notes' via near-registral return (aba′) seem clearly present.[31]

What is musically out-of-phase must remain analytically out-of-phase if we are to understand the essence of Chopin's harmonic art. If we recognise that it is often voice leading which determines the direction of harmony (recall Example 1), and if we admit that the initial and terminal notes of melodic processes influence the harmonic structuring of consonance and dissonance, then it follows that we must allow patterns such as Example 5c to stand analytically for what they really are: *structurally transformed dissonances* which, being out-of-phase, do not neatly fit into our traditional preconceptions about tonal harmony. Such structural dissonance is one of Chopin's most important contributions to the development of harmonic language, a development which eventually came to revolutionise the way Western composers conceived harmony.

Seventh, ninth, and 'thirteenth' chords

Before looking at other unusual harmonic transformations, let us briefly examine the effect durational cumulation and melodic process have in 'attaching' dissonance on to the normal consonant triads found in Chopin's style. Weak or moderately strong dissonances (symbolised by (x) and x, respectively) become inherent properties of chords largely in three ways: (1) when, through the congruent initial and terminal structural functions of melody and duration, the dissonant note is made structurally formational or transformational; (2) when the resolution of the dissonance on the low level is so deformed by melody or duration (or both) that some next-level closural function must serve as the resolution; or (3) when no resolution is present on any level.[32]

[31] I say 'seem' because in a true hierarchical analysis the 'escape notes' on the next level are not like escape notes on low levels at all since embedded within the high-level escape notes are the primacy functions of initiating the melodic process and the durational patterning on the low levels (♩. ♩ ♩). Hence, in a very real sense the high-level 'escape notes' here are *more* stable than the next-level analysis shows. This is, of course, the point about their being transformational. For more on this, see Narmour, ibid.

[32] Sometimes, of course, resolution of dissonance is completely prevented when one dissonant chord goes to another that is even more dissonant; but that is more common later in the nineteenth century than in the music of Chopin.

Consider first a few settings for dissonant sevenths, seventh chords, and tritones. Aside from such chords resulting from the usual transitory appoggiaturas, passing notes, escape notes, or suspensions, the dissonant note also emerges structurally in the music of Chopin through the initiation of melodic processes (Example 6a, a major seventh over a triad; and Example 6b, the third process of which emphasises a minor seventh). Observe in Example 6b how the durational patterning (♪♩ ♩ ; c/c.-cum.) underlines each melodic process in contrast to Example 6a, whose process is set additively. And note in Example 6b how the counter-cumulation on the D in bar 3 (3:1) weakens the sense of a normal stepwise resolution of the seventh; as the initial note of a process, the dissonance moves past the semiquaver D to the downbeat C♯ in the next bar over the six-three chord. (The same kinds of observations could be

Example 6. (a) *N* op. 27 no. 2, bar 70 (b) *M* op. 59 no. 1, bars 37–40
(c) *N* op. 48, bars 7–8

made about the 'resolution' of the major ninth on the E in the first bar of the example.) The processive and counter-cumulative envelopment of the 'normal' stepwise resolution adds to the structural function of the dissonances in these examples.

Often in Chopin's music, one cumulative dissonance is followed by another such that the first dissonance gets no resolution at all. Because of that, it must be regarded even more strongly as part of a structural chord. Example 6c is a particularly interesting case. Left hanging as the initial note of a reversal structure (R) on two different levels, the highly cumulative minor ninth (E♭) over the dominant (♪ ♩.. =1:7) goes unresolved because it is followed by an almost equally cumulative major seventh cadential 'retardation' (♪♩.♪ = 2:13) on the downbeat F♯ (which harmonically connects a reversal pattern on the next level to the crotchet G on the third beat, the demisemiquaver consonant G being much too counter-cumulative – 13:1 – and metrically weak to qualify for the resolution).

Chords of the 'added sixth', mild dissonances which Chopin seems particularly fond of in connection with tonic pedals, can, of course, be made more stable by a cumulative patterning – as with the use of grace notes to create the chord (Example 7a). At other times, processive structuring in the melody brings about the sonority. For instance, the G♯ over the tonic B chord in Example 7b terminates a process of D♯–F♯–G♯; the stable, structuring effect of G♯ thus cannot be reduced to a simplistic neighbour note above the F♯, as, for example, a typical Schenkerian verticalisation would have it.

Example 7. (a) *M* op. 24 no. 3, bars 1–2 (b) *M* op. 33 no. 1, bars 23–4

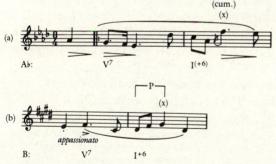

Much in the same way as the sevenths we have seen, Chopin stabilises the dissonances of ninth chords by introducing them processively and by employing durational cumulation. A small sample of processive structuring of major and minor ninths over both major and minor chords is shown in Examples 8a, 8b (both metrically strong), and 8c (terminating cumulatively on the dissonance). Even ninths functioning medially in processes (that is, as 'passing

Example 8. (a) *N* op. 9 no. 2, bar 8 (b) *M* op. 6 no. 1, bars 14–16 (c) *M* op. 7 no. 5, bars 6–7

notes') are often delayed by cumulative durational patterning (Examples 9a, bar 1, and 9b, bar 3). It should be mentioned as well that Chopin also uses the initiation and termination of melodic reversal patterns (R) to create structural dissonances (Example 9c). Here the dissonant minim G♯ both durationally cumulates and terminates a melodic reversal (R); moreover, while still dissonant, this note initiates a process going to the third bar. There is no satisfactory immediate resolution of this ninth; only with the remote F♯ on the third beat in bar 3 can it be said that the cumulative reversing ninth on the minim G♯ or the processively initiating quaver G♯ of bar 2 resolves to a note of any structural substance.

Finally, let us turn our attention to the so-called thirteenth chord, one of Chopin's favourite sonorities.[33] This chord arises ornamentally in his music

---

[33] I say 'so-called' because historically it does not appear that this chord came about from a stacking of thirds but rather from independent contrapuntal melodic lines that resulted in dissonance. Moreover, the 'thirteenth chord' is often missing the fifth, the ninth, and the eleventh – with which it sounds more like a polychord than a single sonority – so it is somewhat implausible that its origins are triadic. (It should be mentioned, however, that plenty of chordal examples exist in the music of Chopin when both the fifth and the 'thirteenth' are present; see, for example, the dense chord eight bars from the end of the Mazurka op. 41 no. 2). It would be more accurate to refer to this chord as a seven–six–three sonority – figured from the bass. But be that as it may, we seem to be stuck for better or worse with the name 'thirteenth'.

Because of the lack of the ninth and eleventh, the note given the name of the thirteenth (the dissonance between the seven and the six above the bass) does not sound 'integrated' into the root, third, and seventh of the chord; I shall thus symbolise the rather pungent quality of its dissonance with a plain 'x'.

Example 9. (a) *M* op. 7 no. 1, bars 1–2 (b) *M* op. 59 no. 2, bars 1–4 (c) *M* op. 59 no. 1, bars 42–4

from escape notes, neighbour notes, suspension figures, and passing notes. But the establishment of melodic process can also play an important part in making the note of the 'thirteenth' structural, whether occurring from the introduction of appoggiaturas by leap which are approached cumulatively (Example 10a); from suspensions of the sixth of six-four chords into the dominant seventh (Example 10b, the thirteenth of which is a kind of V^7 plus an added sixth); from durationally 'frozen' incomplete neighbour notes turned into processes (Example 10c, whose thirteenth, uncharacteristically, also has the ninth); or from *both* closural reversal (R) and the initiation of process (Example 10d; note the 1:6 cumulation on the dissonant note; recall also the reversal structure on the dissonance in Example 2d earlier).

Example 10. (a) *M* op. 50 no. 1, bars 11–13 (b) *N* op. 55 no. 1, bar 15 (c) *M* op. 30 no. 1 bar 19 (d) *M* op. 59 no. 1, bar 71

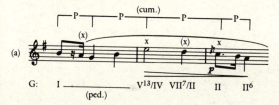

Example 10. (*cont.*)

(b)

f: I_4^6 V^{13} V^7 I

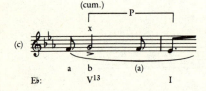

(c)

E♭: V^{13} I

B: V^7 V^{13} VI

Example 10 amply demonstrates that Chopin is treating the thirteenth chord as a stable structural sonority in its own right. Chopin ordinarily omits the fifth, ninth, and eleventh in this chord because their presence with the thirteenth, even when carefully deployed in the texture, tends to generate the kind of confusing, ambiguous dissonances associated with 'polychordal' sonorities.[34] Unambiguous 'polychordal' sonorities frequently occur when Chopin writes extended single or double pedal points, resulting in some very striking structural harmonic subtleties, to which we shall now turn.

---

[34] One difficulty with traditional harmonic theory is that if we admit chords of ninths, elevenths, and thirteenths and at the same time do not require such chords to have thirds, fifths, or sevenths, we can give a nonsensical triadic name to any kind of dissonant sonority. For example, all the notes of a major scale (C–D–E–F–G–A–B) make up a complete thirteenth chord (C, E, G, B, D, F, A); C–D–E–F–G–A is a thirteenth without the eleventh (C, E, G, B, D, A); C–D–E–F–G, an eleventh without the seventh (C, E, G, D, F); C–D–E–F, an eleventh without a fifth or a seventh (C, E, D, F); C–D–E, a ninth without a fifth or a seventh (C, E, D). On the surface, these ascriptions seem absurd, but they can be found throughout textbooks on harmony which attempt to apply roman numerals to the harmonic complexities of nineteenth-century music. The textural deployment of chord notes is obviously important in positing any triadic generation to such dissonances, but more importantly, what counts is whether such notes are actually made structural by the parameter of melody.

Pedal points

A pedal point is not so much the result of various voices occurring 'out-of-phase', as in some of the examples we looked at earlier, but rather that motion in one voice is temporarily suspended, either by the voice being literally held, or by its being prolonged through repetition over some noticeable span of time. Seen retrospectively, a pedal is thus a note within which other melodic and harmonic activity occurs. As we shall see in Chopin's music, when several simultaneous pedal points of different lengths exist, one harmonic motion can become embedded in another, which itself can be nested in still another.

Even though we ordinarily refer to pedals in terms of their scale-step (tonic, dominant etc.), a pedal point often signals an implied chord held above it as well – particularly if one or more of the implied chord members of the pedal are common with the notes of another chord actually present. As a result, harmonic patterns of great interest and considerable complexity arise. For the composer, pedal points are thus a prime source for harmonic experimentation; hence, for the analyst–historian they are a fertile field to explore in connection with the development of harmony.

There is no instrument on which a pedal point sounds better than the piano (with its ready-made damper mechanism), and, safe to say, no composer more fond of harmonic pedals than Chopin. Single pedal points are numerous in his music, but so are double and triple ones. In the mazurkas, for instance, double pedal points, doubtless representing drones transplanted from a folk tradition, figure heavily in op. 6 (nos. 2 and 3), op. 56 (no. 2), and op. 67 (no. 1); op. 17 no. 4 and op. 68 no. 2 have extensive single and double pedals as well.[35] Occasionally, 'exotic' dissonances occur as a result of double pedals, as in the major sevenths and tritones brought about by the descending melodic processes of Example 11a (bars 1–2; note the cumulative duration bringing out the medial dissonances; the mordented, dissonant C in bar 1 embeds an aba structure as well). There is no reducing such melodic structures involving dissonances to mere prolongations of the Gb tonic-pedal chord.

Of course, what looks like a double pedal may not be one inasmuch as any given note may belong simultaneously to two different chords, the most typical case being that of a dominant chord over a tonic pedal, the root of a dominant also being the fifth of an implied tonic chord. But in Chopin there are many cases in which it is clear that the first degree and the fifth degree are generating double pedals of both implied tonic and realised dominant chords,

---

[35] Many scholars have attributed Chopin's unique use of pedals to the influence of folk music. See, for instance, Zofia Lissa's article 'Die Chopinische Harmonik aus der Perspektive der Klangtechnik des 20. Jahrhunderts' in *Deutsches Jahrbuch der Musikwissenschaft* iii (1958), 74–91.

Example 11. (a) *M* op. 7 no. 1, bars 45–7 (b) *M* op. 7 no. 4, bars 25–6
(c) *N* op. 27 no. 2, bar 14 (d) *N* op. 15 no. 1, bar 3 (e) *N* op. 15 no. 2,
bars 6–8

Example 11. (*cont.*)

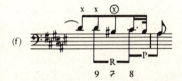

as in bar 1 of Example 11b, where processive melodic structuring brings out the seventh and fifth of the dominant chord, and where the root, third, and seventh recur in the inner parts as well. (Exact and near registral return help create the dissonant chords of bar 2.)

In other instances using double pedals, the degree of dissonance is more pronounced, owing to the structuring that takes place in the melody. On beat two in Example 11c, for instance, the melody, via registral return and ascending-descending processes in both top voices of the right hand, brings out the E♭ minor chord which goes with the tonic pedal; at the same time in the inside voices of the left hand a full dominant-seventh chord emerges. The result of having the notes of the E♭ minor chord simultaneously structured in the melody *against* the dominant seventh makes for a considerably more dissonant effect than the double pedal points discussed earlier. There, the two pedal points were registrally segregated – the tonic in the bass and the dominant (or supertonic) in the treble – with the colliding effect kept to a minimum. Here, melodic structuring in both upper parts of the right hand brings about a clash significantly contributing to the passion of the passage.

Example 11d is similarly structured (though completely different in esthetic effect). In this case, durational cumulation and melodic structuring in the soprano increase the sense of a dissonant simultaneity: a II–VII–V–I progression appears normally over a tonic pedal, but in the soprano the melodic processes are consonant with the bass (D–E–F; F–G–A), the initial and terminal F supporting the tonic on beat two. The net effect of this melodic and durational structuring, where for a moment the outside tonic Fs bracket the VII⁶, results in a considerably heightened dissonance such that the ordinary analytical description of 'tonic pedal' is quite inadequate.

As a last example of Chopin's original use of melody in structuring dissonances over pedals, consider Example 11e. Highly striking as an instance of dense harmonic dissonance for the style of this period, this example illustrates the theoretical phenomenon of embedding or nesting mentioned earlier. The figured-bass analysis shows the basic voice-leading patterning. Over the C♯ (dominant) pedal, the melody in the top part in bar 2 exhibits what would normally be called ornamental changing notes around the sixth above the bass (A♯–B–G♯–A♯; 6–7–5–6 on each beat). This, however, does not do justice to the melody, for the A♯ terminates a process, the B initiates one, and the G♯ ends one. Moreover, the return to the A♯ on beat four (the 6) – what, following roman numeral analysis, we earlier called the thirteenth – is quite cumulative (roughly 1:6) coming after the trill on G♯; indeed, the trill ending itself exemplifies exact registral return ending on a mini-process (F× –G♯–A♯) terminating on the fourth beat. Thus, as dissonances, the A♯–B–G♯–A♯ notes in the soprano are no mere changing notes.

The alto in bar 2 would typically be described as a 9–8 suspension (D♯–C♯) with an ornamental appoggiatura (raised 7 on the contramodal B♯); however, the dissonant D♯–B♯ to consonant C♯ creates a melodic structure of reversal (R) whose initial note emphasises the dissonant suspension on the 9 (the D♯; see Example 11f). Even the melody of the tenor in bar 2 of Example 11e (G♯–F♯–E♯) – as a fifth above the bass lying dissonant against the sixth in the soprano and resolving to the fourth above the bass before going to the third of the dominant chord – creates a process reversing on the VI chord at the beginning of the next bar (PR; see Example 11g).

All of these melodic structures are enveloped by the C♯ in the bass, the main pedal point. But we might also see in bar 2 the F♯ on the second beat in the tenor as a secondary pedal assimilating the alto and soprano on beats two and three; and finally the D♯ in the alto on beat two could be imagined as a pedal spanning the B–A♯ in the soprano. Each melodic structure in each part could thus be envisioned as having its own temporal configuration in the counterpoint: each at some point suspends motion; each upper part is contrapuntally embedded in another; and through the parameter of melody, each uniquely contributes structurally to Chopin's subtle kaleidoscopic motion of dissonantal change.

Contramodal dissonance and the structuring of melody

Chopin's use of melodic notes lying outside the key – e.g., ♭2, ♯4, ♭7, ♭6, etc. – and his mixing of major and minor modes in the selection of chords have long been recognised as among the hallmarks of his personal style. It also happens that the melodic notes of such conflicting modalities are often set as dissonances.

As defined earlier, a contramodal dissonance is simply one that lies outside the prevailing key; thus, the same interval – a minor seventh, for example – will sound more unstable if its dissonant pitch is 'chromatic' rather than diatonic. Even what are in fact harmonic consonances will sound unstable if the melodic pitches involved lie outside the predominant mode.[36]

To be sure, many typical cases exist in the music of Chopin where chromatic melodic tones are purely transitory – those, for instance, that function as medial notes of processes – what traditionally we call passing notes or neighbour notes, as the norms of bar 3 of Example 9c showed. But we should not overlook in the music of Chopin that, through durational cumulation, dissonant, contramodal medial notes are often made to function as strong articulations. In Example 12a, for instance, because of its 2:3 cumulation (counting the rest) and its placement on the downbeat, the contramodal C♯ of bar 2 is not just a simple appoggiatura on its way to a half-cadence. The same could be said about the passing G♮ in Example 12b, which is even stronger as a 1:4

Example 12. (a) *M* op. 33 no. 3, bars 7–8 (b) *M* op. 30 no. 3, bars 9–10

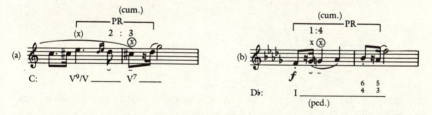

---

[36] I invoke the term 'contramodal' rather than chromatic in reference to such dissonance because I believe current harmonic theory tends to conceptualise most chromatic dissonances as transitory phenomena, governed by the presumption of an all-assimilating, always ultimately stable tonality. I regard such treatment as mistaken and misleading because, in my view, melodic structuring often forces such harmonic dissonances themselves to function structurally on some nonreductive level. With respect to dissonance, the use of the term contramodal in connection with the initiation and termination (or reversal) of melodic processes and the closural phenomenon of registral return (aba) will, it is hoped, allow us to see the inherent instability and the gradual dissolution of tonality in a new light.

cumulation. The durational cumulation on the contramodal notes of both of these examples adds significantly to the rhythmic structuring of the melody and, as a 'conflict' between durational closure and harmonic nonclosure, is an important source for the esthetic stress felt by the listener upon the appearance of the articulated chromaticism.

As with normal dissonances in a key, Chopin employs melodic structuring – often in congruence with cumulative durational patterning and metrical stress – to stabilise contramodal dissonances. Depending on the degree of dissonance, contramodal notes appearing at the initiation or termination of process (or both) can either be articulatively formational on the level of their occurrence or hierarchically transformational, thus creating a new level.

Example 13a (the continuation of Example 5c) is a particularly interesting case, owing to the degree of dissonance of the B♮ over the first-inversion IV-chord.[37] The grace notes, once again illustrating the importance of or-

Example 13. (a) *N* op. 37 no. 1, bars 15–16 (b) *M* op. 33 no. 4, bars 129–30

namentation in the music of Chopin, cumulate on the contramodally dissonant B♮ which in turn initiates a rising process. Although at the same time a pattern of exact registral return vies for attention, the additive grouping of the semiquavers along with the cumulation prevents the metrically weak neighbour note of C–B–C from dominating the melody and suppressing the ascending process: curiously, we hear *both* return on the C *and* a rising line initiated on the B. Because of this and because the stridency of the dissonance together with the contramodality of the B♮, this note is prevented from be-

---

[37] The key is moving to G minor, and C minor is not tonicised; thus the B is genuinely contramodal at this point.

coming hierarchically transformed. Nevertheless, as a 'formational' phenomenon, it functions structurally on the note-to-note level of the actual music. We
shall return to this example toward the end of the article to see how such
formation can be analytically represented.

Another of Chopin's favourite strategies – and among his major contributions to the development of a dissonant harmonic style – is structurally to
strengthen contramodal dissonance by weakening its resolution through both
the parameters of duration and metre. Example 13b demonstrates the technique at the end of a process; the metrically weak counter-cumulation on the
resolution is 3:1.

What if a metrically weak resolution also functioned in retrospect as a medial
note of a process initiated on the dissonance itself? Though this kind of non-
congruent structure is not something that can easily be captured through
traditional reductive analysis and its symbology, it should not deter us from
trying to understand what is indubitably an essential property of Chopin's
style. As will be seen, a function of formation or transformation on a processively structured contramodal dissonance followed by a metrical deformation
of its resolution produces, in an esthetic sense, a highly 'affective' harmonic
pattern.

For instance, the melodic-harmonic pattern of Example 14a – almost a cliché
of his keyboard style – is in terms of the theory espoused here *one* processive
reversal (PR: Cx –D♯–E–D♯, omitting the grace note) rather than two appog-

Example 14. (a) *N* op. 32 no. 1, bar 29 (b) *N* op. 55 no. 2, bar 25

giaturas of two notes apiece (Cx –D♯, E–D♯). Because of the pungent contramodal dissonance, the Cx here remains articulative and formational, portending another structural level, as it were, but never reaching it. Note also that the dissonant E on the beat, ending the process, is made more esthetically effective by an embedded cumulation via the grace note; ornamentation is never structurally gratuitous in Chopin. Significantly, the reversal note, which also initiates the process following the metrically deformed resolution on the processive reversal (on the second D♯), is also dissonant and 'out-of-sync', so that, taken as a whole, Example 14a is harmonically and melodically striking in almost every way.

Even more noteworthy is Example 14b, whose melodic shape is somewhat similar to the preceding example. The contramodal A♮, initiating both an ascending process (A–B♭–C♭) and a counter-cumulative durational pattern (2:1), is wildly dissonant, even 'contemporary' in sonority: a somewhat unprepared triple pedal point on B♭, E♭, and A♭ – a kind of 'quartal' sonority – occurs with the melodic A♮ appearing over the A♭ in the left hand. Moreover, the counter-cumulative B♭ in the melody is itself dissonant so that not even a potential resolution is present. Furthermore, the contramodal C♭ terminating the process is metrically strong and actually intervallically consonant. The momentary sound of an implied G major chord – though the spelling tells us that Chopin conceived the harmony on the third beat as a minor dominant ninth – is surely a momentary jolt to the listener. Nevertheless, owing to the lack of dissonance on the third beat and the function of C♭ in terminating the melodic process, this chord must be considered structural *and* transformational, at least on some analytical level.

Example 15a is one other instance of a structurally transformed contramodal consonance. The contramodal dissonance (E♯, bar 2) terminates a process cumulatively and metrically strong, on the beat; further, there can be no question here about the structural transformation of this dissonant chromaticism, without which one gets no structurally descending line (F♯–E♯–E–D♯) to go with the chords on the dotted crotchet level (bottom staff).[38] Finally, example

Example 15. (a) *N* op. 9 no. 3, bars 2–4 (b) *M* op. 17 no. 1, bars 9–10 (c) *N* op. 62 no. 2, bar 11 (d) *N* op. 9 no. 2, bar 10

---

[38] Moreover, both the metre and Chopin's phrasing (note the articulation of stress) tell us that the melody in bar 2 is a G♯–F♯–E♯ process rather than a G♯–F♯–E♯–F♯ processive reversal.

Example 15. (*cont.*)

15b illustrates contramodal dissonance (F♯, bar 2) that both initiates and terminates metrically strong processes, producing a dominant chord with two kinds of conflicting fifths (both natural five and sharp four on the F♯ are present in the actual music) which, once again, must be considered structural on some level of analytical representation. (Note as well the processively strong thirteenths on beats two in bars 2 and 3.)

Conclusion I: Chopin's contribution

Traditional harmonic theory prejudices us toward accepting certain kinds of dissonant chords as structural while rejecting others outright; the result is that we find it difficult to write the history of harmonic development – to bridge the gap between tonal and atonal harmony. We have no trouble, for instance, seeing the structural note D initiating the melodic process in Example 15c creating with the dissonant cumulative F on the beat a D–F–A♭–C♭ chord which would easily mingle with the notes of the minor subdominant pedal (A♭–C♭–E♭). But how many theorists would allow the initial note of the D♯–E–F♯ melodic process in Example 15d to create a structural chord of an 'added ninth' (no seventh) on the second beat above the VI, the C♯ minor chord? Yet if melody contributes to the structuring of dissonance in one place

(Example 15c), why not the other (Example 15d)? I do not pretend, of course, that Examples 15c and 15d are alike – only that an appoggiatura or neighbour note analysis in both is insufficient and that melodic structuring draws attention to the issue of dissonance formation in the study of harmony.

Such formation is, I believe, the key toward understanding Chopin's contribution to the development of harmony. Let us then at this point sum up both the normal and 'strange' kinds of sonorities we have seen brought about via the parametric structuring of melody in the nocturnes and mazurkas of Chopin (Example 16).

Example 16. Summary of structural chords

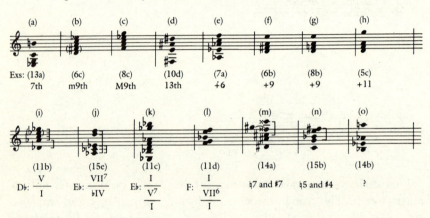

Examples 16a through o, extracted from earlier examples (the numbers of which are placed in parentheses below each chord), are a sampling of some of the kinds of dissonant chords that we have seen brought about by melodic structuring in the music of Chopin. Everyone recognises that most of these chords make up the 'materials' of Chopin's harmonic style; and everyone recognises that Chopin likes to 'prolong' dissonance. What is argued here is that these chords are more than harmonic materials and more than prolongational dissonances – that instead they function as inherent structural entities in his style.

In addition to normal dominant sevenths, major sevenths, and minor seventh chords, we thus have the somewhat odd, inverted major seventh chord of Example 16a. Minor ninths and major ninths are common (16b and c), as are thirteenth chords (16d), and chords with added sixths, added ninths, and added elevenths (16e, f, g, and h), these last three types being more dissonant than integrated triadic stacks because they lack one or more of the 'normal' chord members (e.g., sevenths or ninths). Melody was also found to cause the emergence of structural dissonance over normal pedal points (16i), over pedals where the coexisting chords shared tones symbiotically, as it were (16j), and over pedals where the textural setting of the notes of the two chords involved produced relatively independent, unintegrated, somewhat incompatible, functionally competitive sonorities (16k and l). Finally, we encountered melodically structured dissonant chords that simultaneously embraced both natural and altered notes operating on the same chord member, the chord function of which was usually clear (16m and n), and melodically generated chords that occasionally created a sonority of such dissonance, modernity, and peculiarity that we have no convenient name for it in tonal theory (16o). Given this sampling of harmonies in Example 16, it can fairly be said that Chopin's music *structurally* prefigures much of the harmonic language of the rest of the nineteenth century. The variety of such dissonances made articulative, formational, or transformational in his music truly foreshadows Brahms, Wagner, Strauss, Mahler, some Debussy, even early Berg.[39]

Conclusion II: the lesson for music theory

All of these chords, of course, can be given conventional analytical explanations as to derivation, function, voice-leading configuration, and so forth – and resolutions of some sort can doubtless be conjured up in the music for all of them. Moreover, as types, many of them commonly appear throughout the music of this period and are thus obviously not unique to Chopin's personal style. Melodically generated thirteenth chords, for example, can easily be found in the piano music of Mozart and Beethoven.

But to make these statements, or to analyse the dissonant chords of Example 16 conventionally, is to miss the point entirely. For what is unique about Chopin's handling of these dissonant sonorities is the extent to which he lavishes durational, metrical, and melodic care to ensure their *structural* stability. It cannot possibly be the case that all dissonances in tonal music are to be routinely reduced to consonant chords on the next level. Nor can it be true in a hierarchical sense that remote resolutions satisfy the same harmonic functions as proximate ones. Our knowledge of the gradual evolution of dissonance as a structural phenomenon in the history of music tells us that this is so.

Still, we are left with a difficult theoretical problem. For how in the symbology of our analytical reductions are we to square what seems harmonically con-

---

[39] I am, of course, far from the first to make this observation. See Lissa's article cited earlier, for example. Or see Jacques Chailley's article 'L'Importance de Chopin dans l'evolution du langage harmonique' in Zofia Lissa, ed., *The Book of the First International Musicological Congress Devoted to the Works of Frederick Chopin* (Warsaw, 1963), 30–43. Chailley discusses chords of the added sixth and the thirteenth as well as the subject of weak resolutions.

ventional with what seems harmonically unique? How can the simultaneous attributes of structuring formation and structural transformation within a given harmonic pattern be displayed? How can we show that a given melodic note simultaneously participates as a chord member in a known extra-opus style structure and as a chord member in an intra-opus style structure as well as a chord member of an idiostructural (unique) relationship?[40]

The three-dimensional display of Example 17, based on Example 13a earlier (q.v.), offers one possibility. The actual phrase (melody on the middle staff) obviously belongs to a well-known, extra-opus, voice-leading style structure (bottom staff) – that of I–IV⁶–V in a linear configuration – and a typical analysis would reduce the melody to this harmonic pattern (e.g., in Schenkerian theory), the structural notes being derived in part according to the projections suggested by the lower dashed lines.

Example 17. Three-dimensional graph of Example 13a

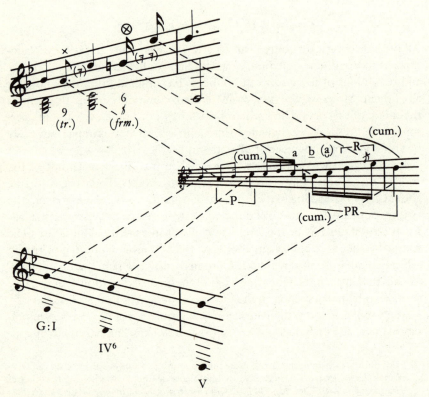

[40] For more on the concept of idiostructure, see my book, *Beyond Schenkerism: The Need for Alternatives in Music Analysis* (Chicago, 1977), chapter 11.

The top staff, however, by showing what notes have been omitted on the bottom one, illustrates how distorting the extra-opus style reduction of the bottom staff is: the dissonant and transformational (*tr.*) A, brought about as an initial note of the A–Bb–C process (P, middle staff), and the dissonant and formational (*frm.*) B, a result of the establishment of a processive reversal (PR, middle staff), as well as the consonant Eb, a consequence of an embedded reversal structure (R) within this process, are left out of the analytical voice-leading picture of the bottom staff – which is to say, Chopin's intra-opus style of both structuring (i.e., formational) and structural (i.e., transformational) dissonance is disregarded: the I chord has a ninth added to it; and the IV⁶ becomes momentarily a first-inversion seventh chord with a raised fifth (see the figured bass of the top staff).

As to the intra-opus style, it must be further stressed that the dissonant A and the contramodally dissonant B are not in reality simply incomplete neighbour notes or escape notes (as conventional linear reductive interpretations in harmonic theory would have it) since embodied hierarchically within each note are the functions of the melodic processes on the lower levels (trace the middle-staff analysis to the top-staff structural notes via the projections of the upper dashed lines).

So much for the extra- and intra-opus style structures. What of the idio-structure, that is, what of Chopin's unique creation in these bars of the Nocturne op. 37 no. 1? Here, all three staves together could be imagined as forming a composite that approximated the idiostructure of this phrase. The effect of the initiation of durational cumulation on the dissonant A, the cumulation on the B as a result of the three grace notes, which ensures its stability as a note-initiating process, and the cumulation of the single grace note on the Eb would all have to be taken into account in any analytical evaluation of the idiostructure.

For the six pitches of the melodic pattern on beat four are not heard as two separate motives. That is, the pitches B–C do not make one group according to the style-structural, neighbour note resolution (shown by the aba), with the pitches C–D–(F)–Eb making up another group contained within the IV⁶ (as a Schenkerian *Terz-zug* would have it). Rather, the pattern B–C–D–(F)–Eb–D is heard as *one* thing (a processive reversal). And in idiostructural terms the effect of the melody (middle staff) on the harmony could not be reduced to either the extra-opus voice-leading style structure of the bottom staff or to the intra-opus style structure of the top staff. *Melody is not a reducible aspect of voice-leading.* Although voice-leading can create structural dissonances, as in the conventional case we saw in Example 1 at the start of this article, voice-leading comes out of melody. Thus, we have to admit the effect of melodic structuring on harmony in the 'unconventional' cases of dissonance treatment as well.

In this article, I have sketched out a programmatic theory of melody in the hopes of our learning something about dissonance treatment in the music of Chopin. But as the last example attempts to demonstrate, Chopin's music, because it is so pivotally important to the nineteenth century as a whole, can also teach theorists much about what needs working on in revising current analytical practices with respect to the study of harmony. We are very much in the same position as physicists who must simultaneously conceive light as both particle and wave. Dissonance can simultaneously function structurally because of melodic patterning (as the top staff of Example 17 shows) and non-structurally in terms of traditional voice-leading patterns (as the bottom staff illustrates). And just as envisioning light as only particle or wave results in a distortion of the truth, so conceptualising dissonance in only one way – as always serving the claims of a preordained, extra-opus stylistic resolution – will not lead us to an understanding of musical artworks.

Can the study of a composer's style, or the writing of the history of harmony, or the analysis of idiostructural relationships in Chopin's works – or the analysis of any other humanistic endeavour – be less complicated than the scientist's study of the physical world? Can we continue to imagine the analysis of process in real pieces as a delimited, two-dimensional subject?

Phrase rhythm in Chopin's nocturnes and mazurkas

WILLIAM ROTHSTEIN

In this essay I will discuss certain aspects of phrase rhythm in the nocturnes and mazurkas of Chopin.[1] These two genres were chosen in part for their brevity and formal simplicity, but also because they aptly illustrate a more general issue which pertains to much nineteenth-century music. That issue, which I call the Rhythm Problem, was recognised in a well-known essay by Edward T. Cone;[2] it is, simply, the so-called 'tyranny of the four-bar phrase' which permeates so much music especially of the early nineteenth century.

In order to address the issue properly, it will first be necessary to define a number of terms. After that we will proceed to a series of analyses, through which we will form some conclusions concerning the distinctive nature of Chopin's rhythmic style. In addition, we will advance a few notions regarding Chopin's stylistic evolution in the years from 1830 to 1846.

We begin with the term *hypermetre*, a derivative of Cone's *hypermeasure*. A hypermeasure is a metrical unit consisting of two or more notated bars; within the hypermeasure, the individual bars function almost exactly like the individual beats within a single bar. Hypermetre is the metrical pattern established by a succession of equal-sized hypermeasures. Thus we will speak, for example, of 'four-bar hypermetre'.

A hypermeasure is not the same thing as a *phrase*. A hypermeasure is purely a metrical unit; a phrase is a complete musical thought based, in tonal music, largely on harmonic and linear motion. Therefore a phrase will end with some sort of cadence (usually authentic or half, more rarely plagal or deceptive).

[1] The present study is adapted from my forthcoming book *Phrase Rhythm in Tonal Music*.
[2] Edward T. Cone, 'The Picture Gallery: Form and Style' in his *Musical Form and Musical Performance* (New York, 1968), 57–87.

115

It will also include some definite linear motion, such as a linear progression or a large-scale neighbouring figure. In evaluating whether a given segment of music is a complete phrase or not, we will use the analytical techniques of Heinrich Schenker to determine its tonal – i.e., harmonic and linear – contents.[3]

A brief segment of music which forms a distinct group (usually on the basis of its rhythmic profile), but which is not a complete phrase in the sense defined above, is called a *sub-phrase*. Most phrases are divisible into two or more sub-phrases. Note that the concepts of phrase and sub-phrase closely parallel levels of grouping structure as described by Fred Lerdahl and Ray Jackendoff.[4] I prefer, however, to retain the traditional term 'phrase' (and terms related to it) in order to emphasise the tonal component in grouping structure.

A convenient example of the distinction between phrase, sub-phrase, and hypermeasure is the 'Blue Danube Waltz' of Johann Strauss, Jr (see Example 1). The four-bar melodic segments under the square brackets are sub-

Example 1.

[3] For Schenkerian terminology, I follow the usage established by Ernst Oster in his English edition of Schenker's *Der freie Satz* (*Free Composition* (New York, 1979)).
[4] See their book *A Generative Theory of Tonal Music* (Cambridge, Mass. and London, 1983), 13–67.

phrases, because each one contains little or no harmonic motion (until the last eight bars, which are shown as a single sub-phrase). The hypermeasures are also four bars long, but a different four bars: the long notes in the melody, which usually coincide with changes of harmony, provide the accents necessary to establish a four-bar hypermetre. (In the example, the hypermeasures are separated by double barlines.) Thus each sub-phrase begins with an upbeat of either a bar or a bar plus a crotchet.[5]

The shortest segments in Example 1 that may be counted as complete phrases are the two sixteen-bar halves of the waltz melody, on the basis of the authentic cadences at the end of each half.[6] (See the curved braces below the example.) These two phrases clearly go together to form a single, larger musical thought, and this larger unit is called (traditionally) a *period*. Within the period, the two phrases are termed *fore-phrase* and *after-phrase* (translations, introduced by Ebenezer Prout, of the German terms *Vordersatz* and *Nachsatz*).[7] A period is itself a phrase, but a phrase composed of two or more complete, smaller phrases.

A special type of period is the familiar *parallel period*, in which the two phrases making up the period begin in the same way, or very nearly the same. If, in addition, the first of these phrases ends in a half cadence, I use the terms *antecedent* and *consequent* to denote the two phrases. Note that this is a more restrictive definition of these latter terms than is usual; for the more general case of phrase pairing, however, the terms 'fore-phrase' and 'after-phrase' remain available.

If the final melodic note (or notes) of one phrase functions simultaneously as the first melodic note (or notes) of the next, the phenomenon is termed a *phrase overlap*. A phrase overlap may or may not affect the hypermetre; in the Chopin examples we will analyse below, the hypermetre is usually unaffected. Note that sub-phrases may also overlap, and do so frequently – more often than phrases.

If, between the end of one phrase and the beginning of the next, there is a short connecting passage – usually just a few notes – this connective is termed a *lead-in*. Like phrase overlaps, lead-ins effect a smoother melodic connection between phrases, but they do not result in any notes being shared between the

[5] Note that the four-bar hypermetre continues throughout Example 1, despite the lack of a long note in bar 30. Like regular metre, a hypermetre once established can continue for a considerable time with little or no external reinforcement. Only a strongly contradictory accentual pattern will affect it.

[6] The V–I progression in bars 26–9 does not conclude a phrase – in fact, does not constitute a cadence – because the melodic motion accompanying it strongly contradicts any sense of closure.

[7] Ebenezer Prout, *Musical Form* (London, 1893), 23. Note that I am only borrowing these terms from Prout; I am not adopting his conceptual framework (which derives from Hugo Riemann), nor his terminology as a whole.

phrases involved. Usually a lead-in has the metrical position and character of an upbeat.

If, by means of phrase overlaps and lead-ins (or by any other means), overt melodic punctuations between phrases are reduced to a minimum or effaced altogether, the melodic rhythm has attained the condition of *endless melody*. This term, of course, is taken from Richard Wagner, although the meaning I am giving to it here is exclusively a technical one (whereas Wagner's meaning includes an affectual and even a philosophical component).[8]

This list of definitions is not complete, but it will suffice for the present. A few additional terms will be introduced and defined in the course of discussion.

The character piece for piano was already well established by the time Chopin began composing them in the late 1820s. For the nocturnes, of course, there was the example of John Field, while the short dance piece for keyboard had a much longer history. The vocal, Italianate origin of the nocturne and the dance heritage of the mazurka both encouraged a phrase organisation in duple lengths – four, eight, sixteen, and thirty-two bars. In the character pieces of lesser composers, such duple organisation frequently led to difficulties – what I have called the Rhythm Problem. Even in the music of Field, who must be counted among the better composers of the second rank, one finds passages in which the phrase rhythm is too symmetrical, too uniform, and too highly articulated, hence tedious. (See, for example, the first sixteen bars of Field's 'Pastorale' in A major, originally composed for piano quintet but often included, as a solo piece, among the nocturnes.)

Throughout the nineteenth century, the Rhythm Problem was faced by every composer of character pieces. Each of the greatest composers solved the problem somewhat differently on the whole, and naturally their solutions differed subtly from one piece to the next. Chopin's solutions are unlike those of, say, Schumann or Brahms; as we shall see, Chopin's rhythmic peculiarities at times seem to anticipate the rhythmic innovations of Wagner.

In 1830, with the E♭ major Nocturne op. 9 no. 2 (see Example 2), Wagner is still very far off, but Field is quite close at hand. (Compare Field's first nocturne, in the same key (1812).) The form of Chopin's piece is a simple ABA' plus coda; the A and BA' sections are each repeated with their figuration slightly altered. Each letter of this scheme stands for a four-bar phrase (also a four-bar hypermeasure). While the form may seem rigid stated thus, it is remarkable how much rhythmic variety Chopin manages to create within a very conventional framework. In order fully to appreciate his ingenuity,

---

[8] See Wagner, 'Zukunftsmusik', in *Gesammelte Schriften*, vii, 121–80. A richly suggestive discussion of endless melody in Wagner's music is contained in Ernst Kurth's *Romantische Harmonik und ihre Krise in Wagners Tristan* (Berlin, 1919), 444–571.

Example 2.

Example 3.

we must have recourse to a Schenkerian analysis of the opening phrase (see Example 3).

This voice-leading graph, which is an edited version of an analysis by Oswald Jonas,[9] is given in two levels of detail. The first level (at a) shows the underlying third-progressions of the melody, which themselves divide into two structural levels, the over-arching third g″–f″–eb″ and the smaller offshoots that descend from g″ and f″. The second level (at b) adds some elaborations to this skeletal structure, including two new third-progressions which belong to the foreground (Eb–D–C in the bass and ab″–g″–f″ in the melody). All of the third-progressions in the example are descending ones, but the two just named – the two that have least to do with the underlying structure – play a special role as carriers of rhythmic continuity.

[9] See Oswald Jonas, *Introduction to the Theory of Heinrich Schenker: The Nature of the Musical Work of Art*, trans. John Rothgeb (New York, 1982), 65–6.

We can observe this special role more closely if we recompose the passage in a less ornate way, keeping the underlying structure and the basic melodic motives intact. This might give us the uninspired results shown in Example 4 (in which the left hand is given only as a bass line; the middle voices can be imagined).

Example 4.

Among other things, this pedestrian version brings us even closer to the style of Field. But how little of Chopin has been changed! This proves how much of the genius of this nocturne resides precisely in its foreground elaboration rather than in its middleground structure, however impressive the nested third-progressions of the latter (Example 3) may appear.

The sub-phrase organisation of Example 4 follows the common pattern 1+1+2 (in bars), a pattern that we will term (after Arnold Schoenberg) a *sentence*.[10] The durational pattern of each bar is identical, except that bar 4 lacks a quaver upbeat, thus reinforcing the unity of the two-bar segment (bars 3–4). In bar 2, Chopin's high note c''' has been changed to f'' (lower neighbour to g''), and a similar change has been made at the second beat of bar 3 (g'' changed to eb''). These changes serve to avoid the outlining of awkward melodic intervals – a ninth bb'–c''' in bars 1–2, a seventh ab'–g'' in bars 2–3.[11] They also cause the melody to hew more closely – i.e., less imaginatively – to the skeletal structure shown in Example 3b: ab'' is now more clearly an in-complete upper neighbour to g'' (bar 2), and the descending third-progression in bars 3–4 also stands out more clearly. Finally, the change in bar 2 eliminates an apparent third-progression, c'''–bb''–ab'', which prepares the connective

[10] See Arnold Schoenberg, *Fundamentals of Musical Composition*, ed. Gerald Strang and Leonard Stein (New York, 1967), 20–2 and 58–9. Note that I put more stress on the exact proportions of a sentence (normally 1:1:2) than does Schoenberg. Also, I do not use other terms, particu-larly 'phrase', in the same way he does.

[11] Melodic considerations such as this one – the avoidance of awkward (dissonant) intervals formed by the boundary points of a unidirectional melodic motion – are throughly discussed in Schenker's *Kontrapunkt*, i (Vienna, 1910). Note that the leap of a seventh in bar 4 of Example 4 is not awkward because the interval (bb'–ab'') belongs to the supporting harmony, V[7].

third-progression ab″–g″–f″ (connecting the upper neighbour ab″ to the more structural f″ of bar 3).[12]

Comparing Example 4 with Example 3a, it becomes clear that the phrase as Chopin wrote it likewise shows a 'sentence' type of sub-phrase organisation, 1+1+2, but that the boundaries of the sub-phrases are covered over by the two connective third-progressions eliminated from Example 4 (and from Example 3a). In bar 1 the end of the first sub-phrase, eb″, coincides with the passing note D of the bass third-progression. In bars 2–3, a connective third-progression between two sub-phrases substitutes for an upbeat beginning to the latter sub-phrase (compare Example 4). Chopin's slur in bar 2 pointedly emphasises the connection by *not* ending at ab″; this is a simple example of his utterly individual manner of slurring – in this case, the use of a legato slur to disguise a sub-phrase boundary. By contrast, the separate articulation of f″ in bar 3 helps the listener to connect this note with g″ in bar 1.

Other details of melodic elaboration also help to sustain rhythmic interest throughout the phrase. The detour upwards in bar 2, with the ensuing illusion of a fifth-progression from the cover note c‴ down to f″, provides a running start for the motion past the sub-phrase boundary (ab″) and into bar 3. The analogous detour in bar 4 – the two are obviously related – is more cadenza-like, foreshadowing the increasingly elaborate cadenzas to come later in the piece and leading to the *ascending* third c″–d″–eb″ (which connects to bb′ at the beginning of the bar).[13] In the voice-leading of bar 4, d‴ is cast in an ethereal half-light by virtue of its clash with the suspended eb′ in the left hand; the suspension robs d‴ of any middleground function, since it points to the note of resolution – d′ in the left hand and d″ in the right – as the 'real' D, the goal of the third-progression f″–eb″–d″ (bars 3–4). This dissonant clash must be treated delicately but lingeringly in performance, though probably less lingeringly here than on its elaborated return in bars 16 and 24.[14]

Even this early example – a relatively simple one, for Chopin – points in the direction that was to occupy him throughout his life. The use of lead-ins (in this case connective third-progressions) is but one way to avoid a stark division between successive melodic segments. Chopin often went to much greater lengths to avoid such divisions, becoming bolder and more original as he progressed.

[12] The third c‴–bb″–ab″ is not a true third-progression because bb″ is essentially a suspension, prepared in the left hand and transferred upwards. (This detail of voice-leading is not clearly evident in Example 3.) On illusory linear progressions in general, see Schenker, *Free Composition*, 74–5 and Figure 83.

[13] Chopin's *forte* at this point should not be taken too literally. It implies a contrast to the immediately preceding 'detour' – both a stronger and more declamatory expression and a resumption of strict tempo.

[14] In bar 16 the proper rubato is suggested by Chopin's fingering, which is reproduced in the Henle edition.

An unusually complex example for this early period is the middle section of
the Ab major Mazurka op. 17 no. 3 (1832–3). Here, too, the basic technique
employed is the lead-in between sub-phrases, with phrase overlap used
between complete phrases. An excellent voice-leading graph of this piece
appears in Schenker's *Free Composition*; it is reproduced below as Example 5.

Example 5.

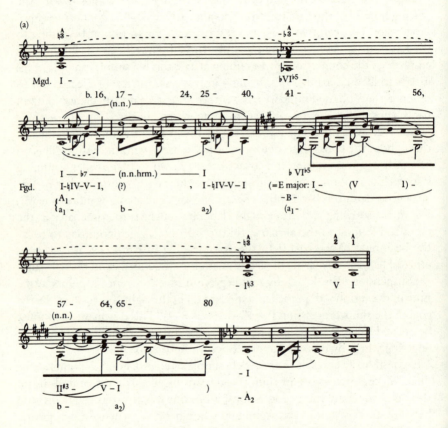

Schenker's portrayal of bars 41–56 requires some explanation. First, his
graph in effect shows only the consequent phrase, which starts at bar 49. The
antecedent is the same, except that the concluding fifth-progression shown in
the graph is interrupted at f♯' (2̂) over the dominant harmony; the consequent, as usual, provides the complete descent. Analogous interruptions in
the two outer sections are also not shown by Schenker, and the final section
(A') is given in abbreviated form – all of this done, no doubt, to save space.[15]

---

[15] Schenker alludes to the interruptions in his text (*Free Composition*, 75).

Secondly, Schenker's analysis of the sequence in bars 41–6 – three times two bars – may not be immediately convincing to the reader; I believe it to be correct, however. A more detailed analysis (my own) of the antecedent phrase is given below (Example 6); it emphasises the counterpoint between the melody and the upper notes of the left hand.

Example 6.

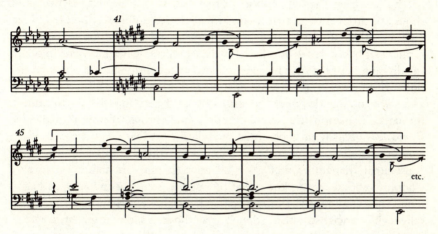

As this reduction shows, there is a pattern of parallel sixths between the upper voice and the tenor, although this is somewhat concealed by rhythmic displacements. The sixths in bars 42 and 44 do not actually appear until the second beats of their respective bars. The first sixth in bar 43 is merely implied, since by the second beat (when d♯' is sounded) the melody has already moved on from b' to a♯'. The sixth in bar 46 (also b'/d♯') is similarly implied.

Example 6 shows descending three-note motives where Schenker (Example 5) shows two-note motives. But the first note of each descending third is in fact a suspension, either prepared in the soprano (bar 41) or transferred upwards from the tenor (bars 43 and 45). Therefore Schenker is correct to show the two-note motive, beginning with the suspension's resolution, as basic;[16] the main melodic tone in each bar throughout bars 41–5 thus falls on the second beat. Significantly, this explanation of the voice-leading also serves to explain why the sub-phrases end on the second beats, not the downbeats, of bars 42 and 44 – despite the semiquaver rests in those bars, and despite the continuing slur in bar 44. (Note the brackets in Example 6.) Chopin frequently uses the rhythm ♪♪ as a sprightlier variant of ♪.♩ , especially in the mazurkas,

---

[16] Those familiar with Schenkerian theory will recognise these motives as typical 'reaching-over' motives, which in this case form themselves into an ascending arpeggiation, 'e'–g♯'–b'. See *Free Composition*, 47–9, including Ernst Oster's editorial comment.

without any implication of a break in the phrase or sub-phrase. Analysts who use rests as phrase indicators, rather than voice-leading and harmony, are often led astray by such rests. In Chopin, at least, they are elements of articulation (indicating a kind of staccato), not indicators of phrase structure.

If Chopin's rests are potentially confusing, his slurs are an analytical minefield. No composer so frequently slurred *against* the phrase structure of his music, rather than in support of that structure. Chopin's practice alone should be proof enough that legato articulation and phrase structure ('phrasing') are inherently different aspects of music, related only in so far as the former *may* be used to delineate the latter. This passage is a good case in point: the division between the antecedent and consequent phrases is obscured not only rhythmically, by the continuing quaver motion into bar 49 and the lack of a bass note on that downbeat; it is also obscured harmonically (V^7 continues), through articulation (the slur continues), and through Chopin's mandated *smorzando*.[17] Finally, it is obscured melodically, in that f♯' at the end of the antecedent (see Example 6, bar 48) is linked to f♯' at the beginning of the consequent (remember that g♯' is an appoggiatura). It almost seems as if Chopin wishes us not to know that one phrase is ending and another beginning. This is more than a simple phrase overlap; it is an attempt, within a basically regular phrase structure, to melt away the seams in that very structure.

The sequence which begins each phrase shows a similar conflict between the simplicity of the underlying structure and the complex continuity of the surface. The lead-ins between sub-phrases consist of ascending four-note arpeggiations in the melody, spanning an octave in each case (b–b' in bars 42–3, d♯'–d♯'' in bars 44–5). As Example 6 shows, each lead-in overlaps the end of one sub-phrase and leads to the first note of the next.[18] It also retraces the path of the immediately preceding *descending* arpeggiation, shown in unstemmed noteheads in Example 6. The resulting down-and-up motion within each triad joins the sub-phrase to the lead-in and thence to the next sub-phrase. The total effect is to de-emphasise the points of juncture almost completely.

Once again Chopin finishes the job with his seemingly capricious articulation. The first lead-in (bars 42–3) is played mostly *non legato* but with pedal. The second and fourth lead-ins (bars 44–5 and 52–3) are slurred into the following sub-phrases. The third lead-in (bars 50–1) is articulated in yet another way, emphasising the end of the consequent's first sub-phrase and thus

[17] One factor, however, subtly strengthens the downbeat of bar 49 – the hemiola pattern (3×4 quavers) of the preceding two bars. When two bars in triple metre are combined in a hemiola, the downbeat *following* the hemiola always receives added emphasis as a metrical goal. In this case Chopin deliberately takes away from bar 49 the emphasis that the hemiola and the hypermetre have given it, delaying a prominent bass note and a return to the dotted rhythm until the metrically weak bar 50. (The *smorzando* is probably meant to end at this point.)

[18] See n. 16.

the end of the ambiguous passage surrounding the phrase overlap. (In the otherwise literal reprise of the parallel period, bars 65–80, the articulation is again different!)

From the standpoint of phrase rhythm, the curious thing about this middle section is the disparity between the regular, sixteen-bar parallel period – with its two eight-bar phrases divided into sub-phrases of 2, 2, and 4 bars – and the apparent striving for seamless melodic continuity – the latter evident from the use of lead-ins, phrase overlap, and slurring against the phrase structure. Even the passage following this one begins with an upbeat (to bar 57) that mimics the original lead-in of bars 42–3. One might well ask: if Chopin sought to transcend points of articulation (division) between melodic segments, why did he employ phrase structures which by their very nature are highly articulated? In a mazurka, of course, such structures probably derive from the heritage of the dance, with its innate bias in favour of duple hypermetre and symmetrical phrase structures. But these structures are by no means restricted to Chopin's mazurkas.

In his character pieces from the middle and later 1830s, Chopin continues to develop the means of rhythmic continuity already present in his earlier music. There is, however, a trend toward ever greater refinement of rhythmic technique. It is in this period, too, that Chopin seems most addicted to peculiarities of articulation as a means of transcending phrase and sub-phrase boundaries.[19] In his later style – after about 1840 – the idiosyncratic and sometimes frankly puzzling slurs recede somewhat in importance, to be largely replaced by more organic compositional procedures.

A comparison of the early Eb major Nocturne (Example 2) with the B major Nocturne op. 32 no. 1 (1836–7) reveals some of the subtle changes that have taken place in Chopin's rhythm in little more than five years. The two pieces make an especially good comparison because they are both dominated by the motive of a stepwise, descending third. To make the comparison easier, Example 7 gives a bar voice-leading analysis of bars 1–8 of op. 32 no. 1, corresponding to Example 3. The same eight-bar phrase is then recomposed (Example 8) in a manner similar to Example 4 – this time with even more dreadful results.

Like the first phrase of the Eb major Nocturne, the opening phrase of op. 32 no. 1 has a 'sentence' type of sub-phrase structure, 2+2+4 bars. (It was 1+1+2 in the earlier nocturne.) The unity of the final and longest segment is slightly concealed by the rhetorical pause at the end of bar 6, but the harmonic and linear continuity over this break is very clear. (In Example 8 the pause is omitted, but the retention of the principal rhythmic motive in bars 7–8 still obscures the unity of the four-bar segment slightly.)

[19] See, for example, the Mazurkas op. 24 no. 1 (G minor) and op. 33 no. 1 (G♯ minor). Both works are cited for their peculiar articulation by Schenker in *Free Composition* (Figure 128).

Example 7.

I   II   V   I

Example 8.

(III   II⁶   V⁶₄   =   ₃⁷   ·I)

The first two sub-phrases in the B major Nocturne are run together – and run into the third sub-phrase – in a way reminiscent of op. 9 no. 2. There the three segments of the phrase were linked by connective third-progressions, first in the bass and then in the upper voice (see Example 3). Here they are linked in part by an apparent third-progression, f♯″–e″–d♯″, which obviously imitates the descending third of bars 1–2. Chopin's articulation emphasises this linking function, especially over the barline separating bars 2 and 3. (Compare the music with Example 8, where the links are omitted.)

But in the B major Nocturne there is an important inner-voice motion, shown in Example 7, which makes the tonal and rhythmic situation more complex than that in op. 9 no. 2. As the voice-leading reduction indicates, an exchange of voices takes place between the melody and the inner voice, in two-note groups (C♯–B, E–D♯). Partly as a consequence of this, the descending third in bars 1–2 sounds less complete than the corresponding third in the E♭ major Nocturne (bar 1),[20] and the linking motive f♯″–e″–d♯″ becomes something more than a mere lead-in tacked on to preserve the rhythmic flow. Thus, although the underlying sub-phrase structure may seem to be adequately expressed by Example 8, in fact *the voice-leading itself* naturally creates an

[20] The slightly ambiguous ⁶₄ position of the harmony supporting b′ also contributes to the feeling of incompleteness in bar 2.

overlapping of sub-phrases at the downbeats of bars 3 and 5. This is an example of the use of counterpoint as an aid in achieving rhythmic continuity, a resource on which Chopin was to draw increasingly in his later music.

Other sources of continuity in op. 32 no. 1 are more readily apparent. The sudden entrance of a dissonant chord on the second beat of bar 8 does not obscure the preceding cadence, but it does propel the motion forward – especially since its entrance *in tempo* necessarily sounds a bit rushed after the *poco ritenuto* of the cadence. (The repeated and syncopated $\hat{3}$ [d#''] just before the cadence is a virtual cliché of the *bel canto* style; the second d#'' demands to be rushed toward and then drawn out somewhat.)

The linking passage over the dominant pedal, bars 8–12, first seems to aim toward the half cadences in bars 10 and 12. A lead-in, c#''–d#''–c#''–c×'''–d#'', then appears to overlap the beginning of the next phrase (downbeat of bar 13). But since d#'' in bar 13 is also the resolution, on a larger scale, of the dominant seventh e'' in bars 9 and 11, this overlap, too, is grounded in the voice-leading and is thus 'organic'. (See the reduction in Example 9.)[21] In fact, basing a phrase on a large-scale neighbour note virtually guarantees an overlap when the neighbour note finally resolves, since the resolution will generally coincide with the beginning of the next phrase. Such is the case here: bars 8–12 constitute a large prolongation of V^7, with e'' as upper neighbour to the primary note d#''; the resolution of e'' to d#'' in bar 13 also marks the beginning of a reprise of bars 1–8. The broad arpeggiation of the chord in bar 13 is the perfect expression of the overlap; it highlights the resolution in the lower register (d#') and its transfer to the higher one. The local upper neighbour which follows, e'' in bar 13, should be played with special poignancy, as it sums up the entire preceding passage in its relation to d#'' (the primary note).

Example 9.

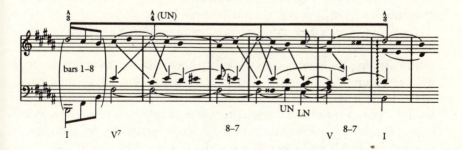

I V^7 8–7   V   8–7   I

---

[21] Chopin marks e'' for the listener's attention by means of the intensifying diminished seventh chord preceding it (fourth beat of bars 8 and 10) and by the appoggiatura f#'' which, in effect, accents e''. Note also the exchange of voices shown in Example 9.

One qualification should be made to our analysis of bars 8–12. Since we have determined that the entire passage prolongs a single dominant seventh harmony, it is not quite proper to call this a phrase according to our definition. It would be more accurate to say that these five bars form an extended link between two phrases (bars 1–8 and 13–20). Such linking passages involving the dominant seventh are not uncommon in Chopin; another example occurs in the E major Study op. 10 no. 3 (bars 6–8). The entire middle section of the F♯ major Nocturne op. 15 no. 2, can be understood as a fantastically expanded link of this sort; Schenker's analysis of the piece implies precisely that.[22]

The later works of Chopin – those composed after 1840 – are known for their often dense chromaticism, which has sometimes been said to anticipate Wagner's chromatic harmony. This is not the only sense in which Chopin's name might be linked with Wagner's, however. During the decade of the 1840s, both composers were moving towards an increasingly seamless style of melodic writing, which in Wagner's case has become famous under the name of 'endless melody.'

In the works of Chopin examined thus far, we have observed a tendency to minimise the articulation of divisions between phrases, and between sub-phrases. This tendency is so strong and so consistent that it must have been intentional on Chopin's part. In some of the late works, there seems to be an attempt to transcend phrase boundaries altogether, so that the melody flows unbroken throughout a long section of music or even through an entire piece. This trend in Chopin's music has not been sufficiently recognised. If 'endless melody' is the term used to describe roughly similar phenomena in Wagner's music, then the same term can with justice be applied to Chopin – at least to some of his late compositions in which complete melodic seamlessness is very nearly attained. It would not even be too far-fetched to imagine that Chopin may have influenced Wagner in this area, as he apparently did in the area of chromaticism (partly through the mediation of Liszt).

Not all of Chopin's later music achieves, or even strives for, endless melody. Some works show the tendency more than others, and some genres more than others. Among the shorter pieces, the late nocturnes and mazurkas are the most adventurous in this regard. The three late waltzes (op. 64) are more conservative, as the waltzes are generally. Among the larger works, the Polonaise-fantasy (op. 61) is the most radical in this as in other respects; the middle section of the Largo movement from the B minor Sonata (op. 58) also comes to mind, as does – to a lesser degree – the E major Scherzo (op. 54). The

[22] For a discussion of the E major Study, see the chapter on Chopin in my book *Phrase Rhythm in Tonal Music* (forthcoming). For the F♯ major Nocturne, see Schenker, *Das Meisterwerk in der Musik, Jahrbuch II* (Munich, 1926), 41–2 and (especially) Figure 33.

Berceuse (op. 57), while essentially a set of variations, can also be regarded as a virtual exercise in endless melody, since the four-bar variations – while still distinct – overlap continuously until the coda, largely avoiding perfect cadences along the way.

The means by which Chopin pursues endless melody in his music after 1840 are for the most part extensions of those techniques which he used throughout his career. Overlaps and lead-ins remain the favoured devices; but these devices are now used so lavishly that, in some pieces, few melodic segments remain unaffected by them. Two additional elements in this late music are an increased use of counterpoint – partly to aid in fostering rhythmic continuity – and, in certain pieces, an avoidance of expected full or half cadences. This latter element, the avoidance of cadences, is the one most directly reminiscent of Wagner's practice in his music dramas (all of which, of course, were composed after Chopin's death).[23]

An instance of a phrase overlap accomplished by contrapuntal means is shown in Example 10. It comes from one of the most complicated of the late mazurkas, op. 59 no. 1 in A minor (1845).

Example 10.

[23] For a somewhat different view of Chopin's late works (particularly the Polonaise-fantasy op. 61), see Jeffrey Kallberg, 'Chopin's Last Style', *Journal of the American Musicological Society* xxxviii (1985), 264–315. Kallberg's discussion is generally less technical than mine, although our conclusions are not dissimilar.

This is the beginning of the mazurka's middle section. The first phrase is six bars long and ends with a perfect cadence in bar 42; the cadence can be seen in the lower of the two voices on the treble staff. But a second and higher voice is added just before the cadence, obscuring the end of the first phrase and beginning a new one. The added upper voice recaptures the original melodic register of the mazurka, which was abandoned at the beginning of the middle section; it also re-establishes the primary melodic note, e'' (5̂). The cadence has a distinctive melodic rhythm, ♫ ♩ (derived from the first section of the piece), which identifies it at each occurrence. These occurrences are several, because – until the final two bars (see Example 11) – a higher voice always interposes to force the motion onwards.[24] Even in Example 11, the higher octave of the cadential note, a'', is added.

Example 11.

cadential
motive

The six-bar length of the first phrase in Example 10 is unusual for a mazurka, as it would be for any dance piece. This mazurka, like all of Chopin's, is not really meant for dancing, but it is one of only a few in which the duple standard for phrase lengths is largely abandoned. (Another is the B major Mazurka op. 56 no. 1.) The opening period of the first section, for example (see Example 12), is twelve bars long, consisting of three four-bar hypermeasures, each of which can also be considered a small phrase. This twelve-bar length is formed by giving one four-bar hypermeasure to each of three main harmonies – I, III, and V – each of which is preceded by its own dominant. The third and last hypermeasure also includes a IV–V–I cadence in the tonic.

In order to describe adequately the phrase rhythm of bars 13–26, which constitute the middle period of this section, it is necessary first to define the technique of *phrase expansion*. This is a familiar concept, having been described by theorists as diverse as Heinrich Koch, Hugo Riemann, and Heinrich Schenker, not to mention a number of contemporary writers.[25] Stated simply,

[24] See, in addition to Examples 10 and 11, bars 49–50, 117–8, and 121–2.

[25] For Koch, see his *Introductory Essay on Composition: The Mechanical Rules of Melody*, trans. Nancy Kovaleff Baker from vols. 2 and 3 of *Versuch einer Anleitung zur Composition* (New Haven, 1983). For Riemann, see his *System der musikalischen Rhythmik und Metrik* (Leipzig, 1903), especially

Example 12.

part 2, chapter 5 ('Erweiterungen der Sätze durch Anhänge und Einschaltungen'). For Schenker, see *Free Composition*, 124–5 and Figure 148; see also the present author's 'Rhythm and the Theory of Structural Levels' (Diss., Yale University, 1981), chapter 7.

phrase expansion is a type of rhythmic transformation which lengthens a given phrase, usually in one of the following ways: by elongating individual tones or harmonies beyond their normal or expected length; by interpolating extra, non-essential material; by extending the phrase's cadence or repeating the cadence; by repeating some other part of the phrase; or by some combination of these devices.

As the above definition suggests, to posit a phrase expansion is to separate a phrase into essential and non-essential components. This is often difficult, and heavily dependent on musical intuition; but contextual elements of musical patterning – including the precedents established by previous phrases – can guide us in making analytical decisions.

To complete our definition of expansion, the hypothetical 'normal' version of an expanded phrase will be called its *prototype*.[26] In metrical terms, a prototype is almost always more regular (i.e., more strictly hypermetrical) than its expanded counterpart. This may seem like circular reasoning – since, in practice, regularity of hypermetre is often a criterion for determining prototypes – but the prevailing hypermetrical patterns of a piece usually offer ample justification, in the form of precedent, for the construction of metrically regular prototypes. The comparison of a given prototype with its expanded version is the means by which the correctness of the rhythmic analysis may be judged; as always in analysis, the intellect has its say, but the ear has the final word.

Bars 1–12 of the A minor Mazurka do not form an expanded phrase, because the pattern of assigning one hypermeasure to each main harmony (as described above) is strictly maintained; if anything, the squeezing of the final cadence into the third hypermeasure might suggest a contraction. But the middle period is different. Like the first period, it is constructed sequentially; in this sequence, too, each of three triads is preceded by its own (applied) dominant seventh chord – E major, E♭ major, and D major, a chromatic descent.[27] The last V⁷–I progression, in D major, is prolonged tonally and expanded rhythmically by the interpolation of four bars over an A pedal (V of D major). These bars, placed in parentheses in Example 12, delay the arrival of the expected sixth bar of the period, which now appears as bar 22. The twelve-bar unit between the first period and the return of the theme – i.e., bars 13–24 – can therefore be heard as an expanded eight bars (unlike the twelve-bar first period, which is irreducible).

But the true rhythmic situation is even more complex than this. The harmonic goal of the middle period is not IV♯ (D major) but V♯ (E major), as the

---

[26] The term is Schenker's. In my dissertation ('Rhythm and the Theory of Structural Levels') I describe several categories of prototypes.

[27] A D major triad is implied on the downbeat of bar 22. (Thus c♯' in bar 21 implicitly resolves to d', before c♮' enters on the second beat of bar 22.)

diminished seventh chord on d# in bars 23–4 makes clear. The harmonic skeleton of the period is thus V#–IV#–V#, a large neighbour motion about the dominant, with the initial sequence serving to connect V# and IV#.[28] Since the period does not reach its harmonic goal until bar 26, it is clear that the return of the theme in the left hand, at bar 25, overlaps the concluding half cadence. The first bar of the theme, which in bar 1 would probably be taken to represent an arpeggiated tonic harmony, now arpeggiates the cadential $\frac{6}{4}$ – resolving, in bar 26, to the simple V harmony.[29]

This combination of phrase expansion and phrase overlap is complicated, particularly for a dance piece. That it is done within the framework of an apparently symmetrical structure, 3×12 bars – for the thematic reprise at bar 25 is complete and basically unaltered – is extraordinary. It is ironic that by recognising an expansion in the middle period we are positing an asymmetrical underlying structure, since the prototype for bars 13–26 will inevitably be shorter than twelve bars. Just what the prototype would be is rather difficult to say in this instance, although I think it would look something like Example 13.

Example 13.

I have simplified some of the melodic detail in this reconstruction, but – more important – I have assigned exactly one bar each to the bass tones D, D#, and E. This follows the harmonic rhythm of the rest of the prototype, and thus revokes Chopin's composed-out *ritardando* (which is itself a kind of expansion). I have separated the middle period cleanly from the reprise, revoking the

---

[28] Note that this harmonic skeleton is an enlargement of the harmonic motion in bars 10–11, although there the IV was minor. In both cases, the V–IV–V motion acts as a prolongation of the dominant.

[29] This time Chopin's slurring clarifies rather than obfuscates the phrase structure; so does the continuation of the dotted rhythm through bar 26.

overlap and thus giving the phrase juncture a more 'normal' appearance. Altogether, Example 13 makes a plausible prototype; note also that the $\hat{4}$–$\hat{3}$–$\hat{2}$ linear motion which Chopin divides between two voices (compare Example 12) is here contained entirely in the soprano.[30]

Chopin sometimes expresses the urge to unify the melody of a large section of a piece by writing a single, very long slur to cover the entire section. Such a slur appears, for example, in the middle section of the G minor Nocturne op. 37 no. 1 (1838). By itself, such a slur does not constitute endless melody, although it may perhaps be taken as an indication of Chopin's desire to overcome any obvious division of his melody into separate phrases. Such may not have been his intention in the chorale-like middle section of op. 37 no. 1 – if it was, the attempt would have to be deemed unsuccessful – but endless melody does appear to be a strong factor in the slightly later F♯ minor Nocturne op. 48 no. 2 (1841; the melody is given in Example 14). A single slur covers bars 3–25 (the repetition of this section, bars 31–53, is similarly slurred); unfortunately, these slurs are not reproduced in all editions of the nocturne.

It may seem paradoxical that a melody which contains so much repetition could be thought of as 'endless'. Melodic repetition – whether literal, varied, or sequential – has the effect of delineating and emphasising the melodic segments being repeated. Thus, in this nocturne, the slightly varied repetition of bars 3–4 (as bars 5–6) stresses the two-bar unit. The sequential repetition of bars 7–8 a third higher (as bars 9–10) strengthens the identification of the two-bar unit as a basic length for melodic segments in this piece. Then, as if the consistent repetition of two-bar units were not enough, an entire eight-bar segment is repeated sequentially: bars 11–18 are simply a repetition a fifth higher of bars 3–10. Only the beginning of the cadential process in bar 19 breaks the pattern of repetitions. (But once the section finally concludes in bar 28, the whole thing is repeated!) With so much attention drawn to the individual melodic segment – whether of two, four, or eight bars – how could it possibly be claimed that the boundaries of phrases and sub-phrases have been transcended, that being the essential precondition of endless melody?

This is indeed a paradox; but it is a paradox fundamental to this piece. We could even say that the contradiction between the small size and frequent repetition of melodic segments, on the one hand, and the attempt to overcome all segmentation within the large section, on the other, is the source of the peculiar tension which permeates this nocturne. The segments are *always* ending, but the larger thrust of the melody never allows them to end peacefully.

---

[30] The fact that this feature leads to an immediate repetition of c″–b′ ($\hat{3}$–$\hat{2}$) at the beginning of the thematic reprise may give a clue as to why Chopin employed a phrase overlap at this juncture.

Example 14.

Example 15 is a simple foreground reduction of the first section (bars 1–30), written almost entirely in actual note values. Only a rather small amount of melodic embellishment has been stripped away, and some of the polyphonic implications of the melody have been realised explicitly.[31] Double barlines are again used to delineate hypermeasures, which are mostly of four bars (subdivided into 2×2).

[31] A few notes from the left hand are shown an octave higher in Example 15 – for example, a and g♯ in bars 7–8, c♯' and b♯ in bars 9–10. This has been done to illustrate better the voice-leading connections between melody and accompaniment.

Example 15.

The two-bar introduction is critical to the phrase rhythm of the entire section. The opening gesture, a bare double octave on C♯ with its second and higher note syncopated, prepares the similar rising octave in the melody in bar 3, which returns many times in various guises. The recognition of these two gestures as related is vital to a proper understanding of the melody; for, without such recognition, one is liable to hear the first note of bar 3 simply as the end of the introductory cadence, rather than as end and beginning simultaneously. The parallel between bar 1 and bar 3 – supported by the hint contained in Chopin's long slur – propels f♯' (bar 3) to its higher octave, thus establishing a pattern to be followed two bars later and in all corresponding bars subsequently.

Another function of the introduction is to establish the importance of the tone a' ($\hat{3}$), which proves to be the primary melodic note of the piece. The descent $\hat{3}$–$\hat{2}$–$\hat{1}$ over the introductory cadence (a V–I auxiliary cadence)[32] immediately foreshadows the similar descent in bars 5–7 (see Example 15). The introductory descent has a visionary, unreal quality because its first tone is dissonant (an appoggiatura) against the V harmony. Further, $\hat{3}$ appears here on a relatively weak beat, compared to bar 5, and as the goal of a crescendo. Surely the most effective performance of these first two bars would include a slight acceleration up to a' (the $\hat{3}$) and a corresponding slackening of tempo for the descent itself. The pattern of accenting the third beat melodically, first adumbrated here, is continued in bar 3 and in every odd-numbered bar thereafter until bar 19.

The syncopation in bar 1 also suggests a slight hurrying of the second beat.[33] (One would then relax a moment before starting a new acceleration for the ascent to a'.) Having pressed forward here, one should do likewise – though probably more subtly – each time the octave leap or one of its derivatives is heard (see the square brackets in Example 15). This will help to achieve the required overlapping of melodic segments, and thus keep the endless melody going.

The first complete phrase extends from bar 3 to the downbeat of bar 7, and comprises the consonant establishment of $\hat{3}$ and its provisional descent to $\hat{1}$ (f♯'). The division of this phrase into two sub-phrases is made obvious by the two-bar repetition referred to above. But the double function of f♯' in bar 5 – it is simultaneously the end of the first sub-phrase and initiator of the octave leap connecting the two – covers over the division with an overlap (see the arrow at this point in the example). The end of the entire phrase, though marked by an

---

[32] On the concept of the auxiliary cadence, see Schenker, *Free Composition*, 88–9 and Figure 110.

[33] Schenker advised that, as a general rule, all accented weak beats should be slightly rushed or anticipated. See the present author's 'Heinrich Schenker as an Interpreter of Beethoven's Piano Sonatas', *19th-Century Music* viii (1984), 3–28.

emphatic descent in triplet rhythm (the first triplet to appear in the melody), is subverted by both rhythmic and voice-leading means. The voice-leading, as shown in Example 15, connects b′ in bar 6 to a′ in bar 7; this connection is confirmed by the left hand, which states the same notes an octave lower. Thus the descent to f#′ becomes merely a foreground event, superseded by the return of $\hat{3}$. Rhythmically, the use of the figure ♩ ♫ (bar 7) carries the motion forward in a manner reminiscent of bars 3 and 5, where the same figure was used in the second half of the bar. (A minim f#′ would have ended the phrase more conventionally and more conclusively.)

Even here, where the octave leaps of bars 1, 3, and 5 are absent, the pattern of motion toward an accented third beat helps to propel the melody beyond the cadence in bar 7. This pattern, which by now is well established, serves consistently to de-emphasise the downbeats of the odd-numbered bars. The accented third beats, on the other hand, are always dissonant; therefore the presence of a longer note there – these accents are mostly of the durational or 'agogic' type – cannot stop the forward motion, since the dissonances demand resolution. Thus, although it is certainly clear that each new sub-phrase (two bars long) ends with the downbeat of an odd-numbered bar, the following sub-phrase always begins with the same note, leading quickly to a new accent (and a dissonance) on the third beat.

The phrase motions up to bar 19 are readily apparent from Example 15. Bars 7–11 describe an ascending fifth from a′ to e″ and a harmonic motion from I to (minor) V. The goal tone, e″, however, is omitted from bar 11, and g#″ appears in its place; e″ is nevertheless implied by the previous ascending motion, by parallelism with c#″ in bar 9, and as the resolution of the seventh f#″ in bar 10. The presence of g#″ serves to differentiate melodically between bar 11 and bar 13 (compare bars 3 and 5); it also foreshadows the $\hat{2}$ (g#′) which is the melodic goal of the entire section.

The first important change in the pattern of repetitions is the bass passing note c# in bar 18 (compare bar 10). This note leads to a I⁶ harmony of G# minor, in preparation for a stronger approach to V of G# and a decisive cadence in that key. The renewed approach to V causes an expansion of the four-bar hypermeasure to five bars, an expansion that is significantly clarified by Chopin's dynamics (a crescendo through bars 18–19, to a *forte* at the arrival of the cadential six-four in bar 20).[34]

The cadence itself, beginning at bar 20, is sharply distinguished from all that has preceded it by the abruptly slower rhythm of its melody and by the two stentorian leaps of a fifth that announce its onset. The first of these fifths is an augmentation, an octave lower, of the falling fifth that was due in bar 19

---

[34] Note that there is no third-beat accent in bar 19. This break in the established rhythmic pattern also heralds the expansion.

(to correspond to bar 11); that fifth, D#–G#, is present in the quaver figuration of bar 19, but its unadorned statement is delayed until the following bar – thus further supporting our assumption of a one-bar expansion and a hypermetrical downbeat at bar 20.

The four cadential bars (20–3), considered apart from the motivic reprise in the last bar, form a hypermeasure (see the numbering in Example 15). But the motivic reprise transforms bar 23 from a metrically weak bar into a strong one; this is an example of *metrical reinterpretation*, a common device but one not very often found in Chopin's short character pieces. The thematic echoes over the G# pedal constitute an extension of the cadence (hence an expansion). The six-bar length of this cadential extension allows two bars (29–30) to be used for a return of the introduction, without further disturbing the four-bar hypermetre. Bars 29–30, like bars 1–2, thus quite literally constitute a two-bar-long upbeat.

The impression of endless melody in this opening section is only partly due to the unbroken legato articulation of its melodic line. That articulation is merely a symptom of 'endlessness', not its cause. The cause, in this case, is the consistent pattern of overlaps occurring every two bars from bar 3 to bar 19, and the extended cadential process thereafter. The overlaps, and thus the seamlessness of the melody, are in constant conflict with the urge of each two-bar segment to end undisturbed. Some of these endings – the one at bar 7, for example – are so definite that the continuation seems almost forced. In fact, if bars 1 and 3 had not established a pattern of first-beat beginnings to compete with the more obvious and simultaneous pattern of second-beat beginnings, it is doubtful whether the attempt at melodic seamlessness would have succeeded at all. As it is, the tension between repetition/regularity/division and overlap/ambiguity/continuity is unrelieved until bar 27.

I have devoted so much space to op. 48 no. 2 because it is such a good example of Chopin's endless melody, and yet it is relatively simple. It is, of course, not a very late work (earlier than the A minor Mazurka). The last two nocturnes, op. 62 (1846), are considerably more complex – especially the first one in B major, which is perhaps Chopin's most breathtaking venture into endless melody. A bare exposition of the opening period will have to suffice for this great nocturne (Example 16), along with a very tentative reconstruction of a possible eight-bar prototype (Example 17).

It would require too much additional space to explain fully the derivation of Example 17, but the reader can test this hypothesis against his own intuitions. I would only point out the equivocal nature of the strong beats in Chopin's 4/4 metre (the metrical shifts are reminiscent of eighteenth-century practice),[35]

---

[35] See Floyd K. Grave, 'Metrical Displacement and the Compound Measure in Eighteenth-Century Theory and Practice', *Theoria* i (1985), 25–60.

Example 16.

Example 17.

and also note that I interpret the cadence in bar 10 as a contraction or compression of a more leisurely close. The repeated melodic F♯s seem like obvious expansions, given the motivic pattern. And there is clearly a phrase overlap in bar 7. Beyond this lie several mysteries, including the precise co-ordination of melody and harmony in the prototype (the harmony is merely sketched in Example 17). But these mysteries lie very close to the heart of Chopin's late style, in which the rhythmic practices of a lifetime (however brief the lifetime!) reach a peak of complexity and refinement.

The conclusions we alluded to at the beginning should by now be clear. In his nocturnes and mazurkas, Chopin adopted the formal and rhythmic conventions of his time, and with them the Rhythm Problem. He seems to have conceived the latter as a problem of continuity above all, and he set about solving it by finding means (many of them traditional) to enhance melodic continuity. These became increasingly elaborate, although a marvellous suppleness of rhythm was present from the first. By 1845 the quantitative accumulation of rhythmic devices produced a qualitative change, a change which points forward to the dissolution of those same conventions that still form the foundation of Chopin's rhythmic technique.

The nocturnes and studies: selected problems of piano texture

ZOFIA CHECHLIŃSKA

The concept of texture is used ambiguously in musicological literature, and therefore the semantic scope of the word as employed in this article requires some explanation. For the most part it concurs with Berry's definition: 'Texture is conceived as that element of musical structure shaped. . .by the voice or number of voices and other components *projecting the musical materials in the sounding medium* [my italics] and (when there are two or more components) by the interrelations and interactions among them',[1] but naturally there are a few modifications. We are dealing here with the texture of a specific performance medium. The scope of the concept as used in this article will therefore cover only those interdependencies amongst the components of a musical structure which are connected with the piano – with its specific properties and capabilities. In other words, texture is understood here as the external layer of a musical structure, whose shape depends upon the performance medium. Texture is also influenced by all the shaping factors of a work, although it is not identical with them. Likewise, such specific devices of piano technique as octave sequences and trills are not in themselves texture. It is only when these devices are inserted into a musical fabric, or indeed when a specific musical fabric is woven from them, that they constitute texture.

In his monograph on Chopin, Arthur Hedley writes, 'Although the Studies were composed early in Chopin's career they thoroughly cover the ground which he was to explore at leisure in later years. Wherever a pianistic difficulty makes its appearance in his works, you may be sure that somewhere in the Studies a suitable preparation will be found.'[2] This view, widespread in the

[1] Wallace Berry, *Structural Functions in Music* (New Jersey, 1976), 191.
[2] Arthur Hedley, *Chopin* (London, 1947), 141–2.

143

literature on Chopin,[3] applies primarily to pianistic devices and difficult technical performance problems. It could, however, be extended to Chopin's piano texture, treating the studies as a compendium not of texture in its entirety, but of texture of primarily one type, i.e. where the main component is figuration in its many different varieties. This type does not account for every single kind of texture encountered in the studies but it is definitely predominant. It also occupies an important position in Chopin's oeuvre as a whole, occuring in the preludes and in sections of the larger pieces (e.g. the impromptus, scherzos, ballades, sonatas, and the Fantasy op. 49). Textures based on figuration may of course take many different forms. By no means every figurative texture used by Chopin has its exact counterpart in the studies. And even amongst the studies it would be difficult to point to two pieces whose texture is identical. Moreover, Chopin does not duplicate the texture of the studies in his other compositions but modifies, alters and develops it. It is rather as though the studies present us with a collection of patterns – models of a particular kind of texture, models which each time are realised in a different way.

Another texture typical of Chopin is that which characterises the nocturnes, comprising – in simple terms – the combination of a cantilena melodic line with an harmonic accompaniment. Fragments of this kind of texture are scattered throughout the composer's work (the preludes, middle sections of the impromptus, particularly op. 29 and op. 66, middle sections of the scherzos, the second subjects of the Sonatas op. 35 and op. 58 etc.). Both these broadly-defined types of texture are characteristic in general of the piano music of the first half of nineteenth century. In Chopin, however, they acquire a special significance as the principal form-building materials for much of his music. It is for this reason, too, that the nocturnes and studies have been selected as case-studies in Chopin's piano texture.

Naturally, this does not mean that all the innovations and ideas in the domain of texture saw the light of day in the music of the studies and nocturnes and were subsequently carried over into the other genres. Perhaps this is true to a certain extent of the studies, which were written in a relatively short period of time at an early stage of Chopin's career. But it certainly does not apply in the case of the nocturnes, which Chopin composed throughout his life and in which he was able to develop ideas derived from other works. Nor does it mean that all Chopin's ideas about texture have their counterparts in the genres of study and nocturne. It is, however, true that the shape of the individual layers of notes and the manner of co-ordination and interdependence amongst them, which characterises the studies and nocturnes, permeates nearly all Chopin's oeuvre.

[3] As in Gerald Abraham, *Chopin's Musical Style* (London, 1939), 37.

From his predecessors Chopin took on the pianistic devices and instrumental figures (*Spielfiguren*)[4] that were in general circulation. He transformed and developed them, through *inter alia* a significant increase in the span of the individual figures; the use of a wide-spread textural layout; an increase in the distances between the components of the figures and, by contrast, their reduction through the figuration's saturation with changing, passing and leading notes.[5] The way the existing figures were developed is already evidence of Chopin's characteristic tendency towards fullness and at the same time elasticity and flexibility of tone in his piano texture. Of course not all the existing pianistic devices were employed by Chopin to the same extent. In fact some he almost completely eliminated, at least in the form in which they were current. Robert Collet[6] wonders whether Chopin's elimination from the studies of certain pianistic devices in general use among his predecessors might have been occasioned by his own limitations as a pianist. Collet numbers amongst these devices difficult trills, tremolo patterns, broken octaves and cross-hand playing. He also stresses Chopin's very restricted use of octave technique. It seems highly unlikely that this could have been the reason. Everything suggests rather that purely musical considerations were the decisive factor. Of the devices mentioned by Collet only rapid successions of either octaves or chords played by alternate hands cannot be found in Chopin. This essentially percussive device was used by Beethoven in an attempt to expand the tone of the piano by imitating the orchestra,[7] and by other composers primarily for virtuosic effect. Chopin did not employ virtuosity for its own sake, nor did he ever attempt to imitate the sound of another instrument. Moreover the non-legato of these alternating figures ran contrary to his desire for fluidity in musical movement. The transformation of existing technical devices and the adoption of other specific figures were dictated above all by Chopin's search for new colours. He took over only those devices which would harmonise with his overall conception of a pianistic sound-world. Tremolos, trills and rapid octave motion, particularly in the low register, instantly increase the density of sound, producing a rather heavy tone. Chopin avoided such sonorities as we can easily

---

[4] I take this concept from H. Besseler, 'Spielfiguren in der Instrumentalmusik', *Deutsche Jahrbuch der Musikwissenschaft für 1956* (Leipzig, 1957).

[5] The question of Chopin's instrumental figures and their genesis is discussed by Józef Chomiński, 'Z zagadnień faktury fortepianowej Chopina' in Zofia Lissa, ed., *F.F. Chopin* (Warsaw, 1960), and by Jim Samson, *The Music of Chopin* (London, 1985), who points out the transformations to which these figures were subjected and emphasises the different artistic result which Chopin obtained through their use.

[6] Robert Collet, 'Studies, Preludes and Impromptus' in Alan Walker, ed., *Frederic Chopin. Profiles of the Man and the Musician* (New York, 1967), 120.

[7] This question is discussed further in Irena Poniatowska, *Faktura fortepianowa Beethovena* (Warsaw, 1972), 118ff.

see by examining his use of the low register.[8] Such devices also tend to produce schematic figures, which Chopin also shunned. This is almost certainly the main reason for the rare appearance in his music of tremolos and broken octaves in the form in which they were common at the time. They do appear, however, in modified form through the use of additional or 'inessential' notes, or through octave transposition – as in the Study in A♭ major op. 10 no. 10. In Chopin's later compositions figures of this kind were further expanded, and from the performance viewpoint were considerably more complex than their prototypes (Example 1). Depending upon the register, these figures may per-

Example 1.

(A) Study in A♭ major op. 10 no. 10, bar 43

(B) Ballade in A♭ major op. 47

---

[8] Regarding the problem of Chopin's use of particular piano registers cf. Zofia Chechlińska, 'Zakres materiału dźwiękowego i jego dyspozycja w utworach Chopina', *Muzyka* i (1969).

form either a dynamic or a colouristic, function. In the high register it will be colouristic, for the sound is poor in harmonics, producing a 'murmuring' effect in rapid movement, so that melodic meaning is relegated to the background. This results in a light texture, whose quality is as a rule underlined by the composer's indications 'leggierissimo' or 'legatissimo' (Example 2).

Example 2. Study in Ab major op. 10 no. 10, bars 49–51

Although the Study in B minor op. 25 no. 10 is devoted to octave technique, passages consisting of octaves in both hands together are rather rare in Chopin. They are normally only used when he wants to produce a special display of energy and strength of tone, as for example in the Nocturne in C minor op. 48 and the Scherzo in C# minor op. 39. More frequently octaves occur in one hand alone (e.g. the polonaises and ballades) and here again as a dynamic device. Their combination with other technical devices produces a quite different sort of texture – more elastic and less massive. Great intensification of dynamic levels is not typical of Chopin's compositions, as it is, for example, of Beethoven's and Liszt's – and this is also a reason for Chopin's severe restriction of octave technique. Once again this is seen in the total subordination of the texture and its constituent pianistic devices to the demands of expression. This is true even in the treatment of seemingly minor, non-essential details in a piece, as for example the replacement of the octave by a single note at the phrase end in the middle section of the Study in B minor op. 25, where by weakening the sound Chopin gives special emphasis to the conclusion of the phrase (Example 3).

Example 3. Study in B minor op. 25 no. 10, bars 33–4

By treating existing pianistic devices in new ways, and permitting unusual interactions with other elements in a work, Chopin ensured that these devices take on a new significance.[9] This involves, *inter alia*, novel relationships between the two hands, or – in other words – between the melodic line and the accompaniment. This problem presents itself differently in individual genres, and even in individual pieces. In the studies both parts are frequently marked by such significant melodic activity that concepts of melodic line and accompaniment become completely inadequate.[10] It is true that Beethoven had already given considerable independence to each hand, but Chopin goes much further. Some scholars even draw an analogy with Bach's preludes and define the structure of the studies as contrapuntal.[11] Clearly, one is not dealing with strictly contrapuntal voices in the Bachian sense, but with thematically independent layers composed either of one voice or of several simultaneously sounding components. At least one of these layers, irrespective of its degree of independence, always fulfils an harmonic role, confirming that the starting-point of Chopin's thought was homophony.

An example of a two-layer texture is the Study in C major op. 10 no. 1 whose harmonic figuration, encompassing practically the whole range of the piano of the day, defines the piece's dynamic character, while the melodic line simultaneously functions as its harmonic basis. A similar type of relationship occurs in the Study in C minor op. 25 no. 12, but with the difference that the figuration is now located in both hands and is fused into a single layer, while the bottom notes bring out the melodic line. The dynamic properties of the figuration are determined by the tonal space employed, by the rapidity of motion and by the density, which is intensified by the dissonances between the figurative lines. Successive repetitions of the figurative curves accumulate to produce a powerful sound whose apogee is reached at the end of the piece.[12] This amounts to a transformation of harmonic figuration into an effect of dynamic power and energy. This is not an entirely new phenomenon. It had already appeared in Beethoven.[13] But never before Chopin had this kind of figuration covered such an extended time-span, nor displayed such artistry of construction.

Despite the repetition of its components, the structure of this figuration exhibits an internal differentiation entirely characteristic of Chopin. We see

---

[9] Jim Samson addresses this issue in *The Music of Chopin*, 71.

[10] The problem is further discussed in Zofia Chechlińska, 'Faktura fortepianowa Chopina' (Diss., Instytut Sztuki Polskiej Akademii Nauk, 1966).

[11] Robert Collet, 'Studies, Preludes and Impromptus', 116ff. The author warns that this is not counterpoint in the strict sense of the word; the question of the links between Chopin's studies and the Baroque tradition is further discussed by Jim Samson, *The Music of Chopin*, 60ff.

[12] In an editorial copy of this study (Krystyna Kobylańska, *Rękopisy Utworów Chopina, Katalog*, 2 vols. (Cracow, 1977), i, 342) the only *fff* marking comes in the last two bars of the piece.

[13] Irena Poniatowska, 'Faktura fortepianowa Beethovena', 176ff.

Example 4. Study in C minor op. 25 no. 12, bars 19–20

here the intersection, as it were, of three-note groups, distinguished by their direction of motion, with four-note rhythmic figures, so that each time the repeated notes fall at a different place in the figure and at a different place in the bar. As a result of this, and of the rapid tempo of the study, the figurative curves do not disintegrate into their component elements but create a fluid line which in this instance causes the dynamics to come to the fore. Moreover the non-congruence of the figures with the metric groups eliminates any possible schematicism and is yet another characteristic sign of the diversification and purposeful ambivalence in Chopin's music, evident not only in the harmony and the macrostructure, but also in the details of his works (Example 4).

Another characteristic feature of Chopin's texture is the balance between separate layers, frequently coinciding with the parts of the two hands. The division into right-hand and left-hand parts may appear an insignificant technical-performance detail, yet in reality it is an important component of the texture. The space covered by one part, and above all the compass of the figures, is limited by anatomical considerations (the span of the hand), whereas this restriction does not exist *between* the hands. The two hands may be placed closely together, so that their parts may be either fused or separated. They may be maintained in equilibrium, or one of them may predominate, not only in the way that it functions (melody, accompaniment) but also in the character of its sound. In Chopin both parts as a rule act as sonoristic counterweights. Changes in one part entail corresponding changes in the other. For example in the Study in C# minor op. 10 no. 4 (bars 1–4) the enlargement of the area covered by the individual figures of the line produces an increased number of notes in the accompanying chords, and subsequently an augmentation of the area covered by these chords. In the Study in C major op. 10 no. 1 the role of counterweight to the powerfully dynamic figuration is taken by the held octaves in the low register, which are in themselves a dynamic device. The powerful convergence and recession of the layers while notes are sustained in the pedal means that in actual fact the instrument's entire tonal space is sounding. The registral relations are therefore basically constant throughout the whole piece, while at the same time each part has its own clearly defined area.

A texture composed of two parallel unfolding layers rarely remains constant throughout a work. In the Study in C op. 10 no. 1 melodic motives emerge from the notes of the figuration (e.g., bar 26) over short sections creating a third quasi-layer. At times these layers merge into one. A maximally homogeneous layer, which in Berry's terminology would be defined as 'texture of one real factor',[14] is represented by monophonic sections, but ones which – as for example the Study in A minor op. 25 no. 11 – very quickly separate into two different lines, often in distant registers. The rapid passage from the narrow

Example 5. Study in A minor op. 25 no. 11, bars 65–9

space occupied by the monophonic motives to a command of the full range of the instrument elicits a powerful crescendo. Here the texture is the fundamental means of shaping the music, despite the obvious importance of underlying harmonic functions (Example 5).

Sometimes, however, the emancipation of texture eliminates the functional connections between chords. Often in Chopin we find chromatic or scalar movement in a homorhythmic series of definite instrumental figures (e.g., op. 10 no. 4 bars 27–32; no. 8 bars 41–6); in sixths and tritones (e.g., op. 10 no. 3 bars 38–42); in thirds (op. 25 no. 6 bars 31–4); or in sixth, minor third and seventh chords (e.g., Study in Db major from the *Méthode des Méthodes*, bars 61–3). In such cases only the beginning and end of the sequence are functionally unambiguous.

Lissa[15] even detected embryonic atonality in this phenomenon and at any

[14] Wallace Berry, *Structural Functions in Music*, 186.
[15] Zofia Lissa 'Harmonika Chopina z perspektywy techniki dźwiękowej XX wieku', *Annales Chopin*, iv (Warsaw, 1959), 16–24.

rate perceived a considerable impairment in the workings of the functional system. There is no doubt that these non-functional interpolations were innovatory in the harmony of the time, but purely pianistic devices were at their source.[16]

On the whole, however, texture enriches Chopin's harmony while functional relations are retained. In the Study in F minor op. 25 no. 2, also two-layer, the 'accompaniment' built upon chord notes is functionally unambiguous. Superimposed upon it is a figurative line saturated with passing, leading and changing notes, leaving the harmonic function spiced with many dissonances. The area of figuration is restricted to the middle register of the piano, scalar motion predominates, the tempo is very quick and there is a strict legato and *piano* which exploits the instrument's characteristic nuances of tone. As a result the notes fuse together in combination and the melodic values of the figuration recede into the background, exposing primarily movement and colour. A single-note, thinned-out 'accompaniment' layer close to the area of figuration constitutes a sort of parallel figurative line, creating along with the main line an exceptionally homogeneous texture.

Chopin also obtains colouristic effects through an appropriate fashioning of figuration based on chord notes alone. In the Study in Ab major op. 25 no. 1 the static arpeggio figuration in the right-hand and left-hand parts, the small distance between them and the contradirectional motion fuse both figurative lines into a single layer – a static arabesque from whose top notes a cantilena melody emerges. The texture pulsates incessantly. On the one hand, the tonal space is basically constant resulting from the rapid movement and the holding of the figuration notes in the pedal; on the other hand, changes in the pedal plus the circular motion of the figures cause nuances of fluctuation in the density, producing as it were a continual vibration of colour. And in places the notes of the figuration create motives that counterpoint the main melody. A similar texture, but realized by a completely different pianistic device, is to be found in the Study in Eb major op. 10 no. 11. Arpeggiated chords correspond to the chordal figuration of the Ab study, while their top notes form a melodic line. Both studies encompass an area of similar size, although the Eb major is written in a slightly higher register. The hands remain very close together resulting in the maximum uniformity of sound. However, the homodirectional chordal motion as opposed to the Ab study's circular figuration means that the density does not vacillate but through each grows phrase so, despite the similarity the character of the sound is somewhat different. The lightness of texture is assured primarily by the spread of the chords and their wide layout.

---

[16] This kind of series of displaced chords or figures can be found throughout the whole of Chopin's oeuvre; e.g., the scherzo from the Sonata op. 35 (bar 37ff.) the first movement of the Sonata in B minor op. 58 (bar 20ff.), the Polonaise in Ab major op. 53 (the opening).

This study is an excellent illustration of Chopin's characteristic tendency to thin out the pianistic sonority.[17] It also displays another typical Chopinesque feature, which Wójcik-Keuprulian[18] has labelled 'polyphonisation', or 'polyphonic illusion'; this is based upon a shifting of the melodic motive from one line to another, while the homophonic structure of the whole is preserved intact (Example 6).

Example 6. Study in E♭ major op. 10 no. 11, bars 25–7

In the Study in C♯ minor op. 25 no. 7 there is already evidence of imitation, but this is combined with an harmonic accompaniment which fills in the space between the imitative outer voices. The introduction of the harmonically motivated pitches has a bearing upon the shape of the melodic lines and also restricts the imitation to the initial motive. The bottom line develops completely unhampered in broad curves and is ornamented in a manner characteristic of Chopin's nocturnes. The top line – for reasons of performance – is composed exclusively of phrases enclosed within a narrow tonal space. The harmonic pitches also reduce the distance between the two lines thereby increasing the density of the musical structure and contributing to the equilibrium between the lowest voice and the right-hand part. The harmonic pitches are obviously particularly important in places where the hands are wide apart. Above all, however, the extra pitches attest to Chopin's essentially harmonic thought, where voice-leading is always firmly rooted in and subordinate to an harmonic foundation.

A similar kind of texture occurs in the middle section of the Nocturne in E major op. 62 no. 2, but here the lowest voice has less independence and its initial relation to the rest of the structure varies. The lowest voice imitates the melody of the top voice over short sections, then turns into an independent counterpoint which in places combines with the harmonic pitches of the middle layer to create a subtle and effective accompaniment pattern. Through-

[17] Józef Chomiński, 'Z zagadnień faktury fortepianowej Chopina', 152–3 and Jim Samson, *The Music of Chopin*, 69–71 compare this study with Moscheles's Study in G major op. 70 no. 2 indicating *inter alia* the thinning out of the sound which takes place in Chopin.

[18] Bronisława Wójcik-Keuprulian 'O polifonii Chopina' in *Studia, krytyki, szkice* (Warsaw, 1933), 30.

Example 7. Nocturne in E major op. 62 no. 2, bars 42–6

out, the top voice predominates, as we would expect of the nocturne texture. Unlike the study, the thickness of the harmonic layer also changes. As a result the relations between the layers, and their respective functions, are continually changing. Chopin does not introduce any innovatory pianistic devices here, but the way in which the individual layers are fashioned, their changing relations and the compressed sound resulting from the limited tonal space all give the texture a novel quality. These features underline the *agitato* character of this section in marked contrast to the texture of the nocturne's outer sections (Example 7).

The prototype of this texture in Chopin can be seen in the Study in E major op. 10 no. 3, where, however, the lowest voice functions exclusively as a bass foundation. It is built upon the same rhythmic formula as the nocturne.

The Study in E♭ minor op. 10 no. 6 is even more dense in texture; here the tonal space is one of the most limited in the whole of Chopin's oeuvre.[19] Jim Samson refers to an 'intricate counterpoint. . . . perfectly suited to the

---

[19] Zofia Chechlińska *Zakres materiału dźwiękowego. . .*

piano, with its capacity to shade and differentiate voices' and distinguishes a melody, a countermelody, a bass line and a semiquaver accompaniment,[20] rightly insisting that the term 'accompaniment' is an inadequate description of the figurative voice. The 'voices' are not present continually throughout the piece. The countermelody appears mainly in the outer sections, this being splendidly reflected in Chopin's notation. The bass line, only sporadically more independent,[21] is doubled at the octave in the central section. And so both the number of lines and their thickness changes, in a manner typical of Chopin's texture. Texture in this piece plays an important role from the viewpoint of harmony. The sequential repetition of the chromaticised semiquaver figure, the semitone shifts and the sustained notes all lead to successions of very distant harmonic functions and an exceptionally saturated chromaticism.[22] Conglomerations of seconds and the dissonances between the individual 'voices' further increase the density.

In the Study in E minor op. 25 no. 5 texture also influences harmony, but in a completely different way. Appoggiatura figures are here superimposed on to chords with basically simple harmonic functions, and – because of the quick tempo – this creates dissonances which stand out from the overall body of sound, causing its stratification. As a result simple harmonic functions take on a quite different role. The texture is modified here in a very subtle way. In the

Example 8. Study in E minor op. 25 no. 5

(a) bar 1   (b) bar 9   (c) bar 17

(d) bar 21   (e) bar 29   (f) bar 37

---

[20] Jim Samson, *The Music of Chopin*, 67.

[21] E.g., bars 21–3, where there is imitation contradirectional to the principal melody.

[22] Attention is drawn to this by Robert Collet, 'Studies, Preludes and Impromptus', 132, who detects Wagnerian traits and the anticipation of Debussy. Jim Samson discusses this problem further in *The Music of Chopin*, 66–7.

first three sections (a, b, c) the melodic layer remains constant while the accompaniment is transformed, resulting in a displacement of accents. In the fourth section (d) the appoggiatura figure is homorhythmic, so that it no longer produces such an incisive colouristic impact. At this point, however, Chopin introduces appoggiaturas in the accompaniment, though they appear less frequently and so have a different effect. In the following section (e) the appoggiaturas resume their initial role, but now with the top part sustained. And finally in the last section (f) the appoggiaturas are not isolated and the musical sonority has a uniform character. The texture here acts as a preparation for the middle section with its highly distinctive character. As a result, given the same succession of functions, pitches and intervals, the transformation of the instrumental figures produces subtle nuances of colour (Example 8). Because of the slower tempo, similar appoggiatura figures in the Study in F major op. 25 no. 3 do not stratify the sound, even though they enrich the harmony. The texture of this study is similar – but not identical – to that of the Prelude in C major op. 28 no. 1 and the middle section of the Nocturne in F♯ major op. 15 no. 2. On the basis of the notation some commentators have detected a direct parallel with Bach, and even with four-part chorale texture.[23] We can indeed distinguish several voices in this study: the melodic line anticipated an octave lower, the countermelody repeating it at the fifth, and the bass part, whose lower line represents the tonic function and whose upper line adds the complementary simultaneous pitches (Example 9).

Example 9.
(a) Study in F major op. 25 no. 3, bars 1–4

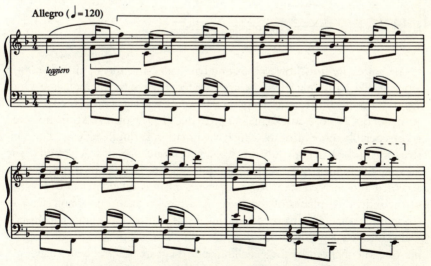

[23] Bronisława Wójcik-Keuprulian, 'O polifonii Chopina', 30ff.

Example 9. (*cont.*)

(b) Prelude in C major op. 28 no. 1, bars 1–4

(c) Nocturne in F♯ major op. 15 no. 2, bars 25–8

The voices are not, however, distinctly separate but merge into a uniform arpeggio-like harmonic layer whose top notes produce the melodic line. Once again – from the functional viewpoint – there are two layers, as in the Studies in A♭ major op. 25 no. 1 and E♭ major op. 10 no. 11. The piano texture, however, is considerably more intricate, which the notation faithfully reflects. The construction of the F major study is based largely on nuances of articulation of the melodic line which, preceded by an appoggiatura motive, or a trill, is then accented and marked staccato and *sforzato*. All this differentiates the colour of the individual phases of the piece. Articulation is an important factor in Chopin's texture. Legato predominates in his compositions and is painstakingly indicated (e.g., the Study in F minor op. 25 no. 2 or the E♭ minor op. 10 no. 6) and enhanced by the pedalling. But there are also frequent changes in articulation, contrasts and varying shades of legato and staccato. Articulation also plays a structural role. In the Study in G♭ major op. 25 no. 9 the basic figure hinges upon the opposition of legato and staccato which, combined with the staccato chords in the accompaniment, is the main reason for the lightness and delicacy of this piece. In the Study in F minor op. 10 no. 9 the contrast in articulation emphasises the differentiation between the melodic line and the 'nocturnal' accompaniment though it is only one of several elements of contrast between the two layers. It points up contrasts in the construction of phrases and sentences as in bars 17–20, and it highlights points of climax, as with the change of the melodic line's articulation to legato at bars 27–8 and 53–7. In the Study in E major op. 10 no. 3 the figures of the middle section also differ in their articulation from the broad legato curves of the outer sections. In the D♭ major study from the *Méthode des Méthodes*, articulation is again a means of stratifying the sound. The melodic line and its counterpoint are built from small intervals grouped closely together, so that given homorhythmic movement they would fuse into a single melodic layer. However, the staccato of the lower line gives it special prominence, so that the texture is perceived as three distinct lines. Another effect of stratification results from the repetition of the lowest notes of the figuration in the Study in C major op. 10 no. 7,[24] though here the quick tempo of the work simultaneously takes on an integrating role. Chopin also frequently uses staccato chords as a sonoristic counterpart to a light figuration, as in op. 10 nos. 2, 4 and 5.

Example 10. Study in A♭ major op. 10 no. 10

---

[24] Robert Collet, 'Studies, Preludes and Impromptus', 133, draws attention to this atypical device in Chopin.

Example 10. (*cont.*)

Articulation may in some cases take on the major form-building role in a piece. In the Study in A♭ major op. 10 no. 10, for example, it is the chief means of diversification while pitch and interval structures remain relatively constant. Syncopated figures composed of successions of two quavers (a) are successively transformed into three-note groups (b), and into two-note groups with a reversed arrangement of the components (c) until as the result of uniform articulation they combine in a continual staccato (d) and legato line (e). Differences of articulation bring with them changes of colour, and also mean that different pitches create the melodic line emerging from the figuration. As a result the melodic line's pitch changes ((a) and (c)), and variants arise through the repetition of the constituent notes (d) and their octave displacement (b). The shift of accents also modifies the metrical relations between the right- and left-hand part (Example 10).

Similarly in the Study in A minor op. 25 no. 4 articulation is a means of shaping the form. But here it leads to the division of an originally uniform texture into layers. In the second phase of the piece (bars 9 onwards) the melody-notes are played legato. The sound is stratified into a staccato accompaniment and legato melody. Later (bar 31ff.) as a result of different rhythmic values and different articulation the part played by each hand creates a distinctly separate layer. The uniform and the stratified sections with different inter-relations of layers alternate and produce the contrast upon which the piece's form rests.

In the nocturnes texture serves to emphasise the genre's characteristic lyrical properties by means of a cantabile style, where the melodic line is presented in the top voice, to which the accompaniment in the lower voice is subordinate. The starting-points for the accompaniments in Chopin's nocturnes were figures drawn from the arsenal of current pianistic devices, comprising various configurations of bass note with complementary chords, or – more frequently – notes of a chord presented successively, sometimes with additional pitches. By comparison with Field's nocturnes and other lyrical piano pieces of the period, Chopin diversified and developed both the layout of the harmonic accompaniment[25] and the shape of the melodic layer. For one thing he significantly enlarged the area covered by the accompaniments, sometimes to over three octaves, as in the nocturne in Eb major op. 55 no. 2. In earlier composers' works figures covering such a vast area rarely appeared. They seldom extended beyond a tenth, and were more frequently confined within the octave. In Chopin, extended, widely-ranging figures became the norm, as did the wide-spread arrangement of notes within a figure: this increased distance between components resulted in a general thinning-out of sonority in the nocturnes. The detailed formulation of accompaniment figures is on the whole different in successive nocturnes. Only in the early nocturnes (op. 72 no. 1; op. 9, nos. 1 and 3) is an identical formula repeated. By doubling or eliminating notes, changing their order and enriching them with 'inessential' notes, Chopin created different, yet highly characteristic, types of accompaniment. Also, particularly in the later period, accompaniment figures may be gradually differentiated within sections of a single nocturne. Besides their harmonic function they have another very important role. The cantabile style demands fluidity in the musical movement. To exhibit this quality on the piano, which by its very nature is a non-legato instrument – or at any rate considerably less legato than the human voice or a stringed instrument – demands a specific shaping of the musical sound-world. One aspect of this must be a rhythmically homogeneous accompaniment adjacent to, or even interlocking with, the melodic line. The accompaniment increases the fluidity of the music and at the same time takes on an integrating role. In Chopin, accompaniments of this type occur not only in lyrical compositions or lyrical parts of compositions[26] but also in the studies (op. 10 nos. 9 and 10) and in figurative fragments of other works, and this across his entire oeuvre.[27]

---

[25] Cf. n. 5, and also Józef Chomiński, 'Harmonika a faktura fortepianowa Chopina', *Muzyka* iv (1959).

[26] E.g., the Prelude op. 28 no. 13; the second subject of the Sonata in B minor op. 58; the central section of the Impromptu in C♯ minor op. 66.

[27] E.g. Scherzo in Bb minor op. 31; Impromptu op. 66; Ballade in G minor op. 23; Fantasy in F minor op. 49; finale of the Sonata in B minor op. 58.

The youthful Nocturne in E minor op. 72 no. 1 is unusually interesting in relation to the development of texture in the nocturnes as a whole. It is rather like an encyclopaedia of textures, which, when subsequently perfected, were to become the basis of later individual nocturnes, or at any rate of their outer, more lyrical sections. Considerable heterogeneity is already evident in the accompaniment figures, ranging from heterodirectional spread chords through chords with different orders and numbers of notes to figures containing 'inessential' notes outlining broad curves. Similarly the melodic line is presented in ornaments; in octaves, thirds and chords; with an attendant countermelody, and with trills.

The lack of rhythmic congruence between the melodic line and the accompaniment, so characteristic of Chopin, already appears in this piece. The distance between melody and accompaniment also ranges from several octaves in the ornamental sections right down to an overlapping of the two parts; this nocturne therefore displays the many different degrees of textural density employed in the genre as a whole, and the many different kinds of note distribution. All the devices mentioned here are only hinted at, occurring in an embryonic, incompletely developed form. While this may be a shortcoming from the artistic viewpoint, it does indicate how the germs of Chopin's later texture lay dormant in his youthful compositions; it also shows the selection which Chopin made from the existing resources of lyrical pianism.

The nocturnes mainly revolve around the middle register of the piano, excluding the lowest register and restricting the highest. An increased use of the higher register occurs in broadly expansive ornamental writing, thanks to which the sonority is even further diluted. In such instances the melodic line distances itself significantly from the accompaniment, the sound-structure fragments and the colouristic properties of the upper register are displayed in light, lace-like sound (e.g., Nocturne in Db major op. 27 no. 2). The ornaments which unfurl the melodic line of the nocturnes are at the same time an important factor in their texture. In the Eb major and B major Nocturnes from op. 9 and the F# major from op. 15 the basic melodic phrase appears in a succession of ever more elaborated ornaments. The irregular tightening and slackening of the motion, its continual changes of direction, bring about minute fluctuations of dynamics, similar to those which occur naturally in singing. The melodic line is constructed such that it exploits the piano's ability to produce nuances of sound, using the subtlest shades, and thus heightening the impression of its fluidity. At the same time the ornaments affect the relationship between the melody and the harmonic layer. Irregular rhythmic groups arise, each time with a different number of notes, and these are superimposed upon the homorhythmic regular accompaniment pattern, undermining the rhythmic homogeneity.

In the later nocturnes, the extended ornamental fioriture are more rhythmically even. In the Nocturne in Ab major op. 32 no. 2 the ornamentation of the theme near the end of the piece gives rise to a melodic line of homorhythmic motion (bars 71–2), while in the Nocturne in B major op. 62 the cantilena melody, when embellished, is transformed into a figurative line with wide curves. The texture here approaches that of a study and is in marked contrast to that of the cantilena section.

In the early nocturnes the texture is primarily diversified by means of ornaments. In the later nocturnes there are other, more subtle, changes. In the Nocturne in F♯ minor op. 48 no. 2 a constant piano dynamic is maintained, but the melodic line, either alone or together with the harmonic layer, is transposed at the fifth, the eleventh, and the octave, with the different registral placings resulting in marked differences in colour. In the Nocturne in C♯ minor op. 27 no. 1 the single melodic line acquires a countermelody on repetition, and this displays considerable melodic activity, imitating motives from the main melody from bar 19 onwards. Typically this part writing rests upon a clearly-defined harmonic accompaniment. Apart from the melodic animation at this repetition there is, of course, a slight increase in the thickness of the texture. Chopin's melody is often doubled in thirds, sixths[28] and octaves creating – in opposition to the single line – a double line, occasionally splitting into two layers in dialogue with one another (Nocturne in Db major op. 27 no. 2, bars 69–74), but more often creating a uniform layer. In the Nocturne in G major op. 37 no. 2 the melodic line unwinds a ribbon of thirds and sixths, acting as a counterweight to the wide curves of the accompaniment. The minute changes of texture also apply to the bass part. Chopin modifies the shape of the accompaniment figures in this nocturne, widening the distances between their successive components to an octave and, most importantly, introducing 'inessential' notes which saturate the harmony with chromaticism. All this creates a texture which is in sharp contrast to the 'sostenuto' section. In the Nocturne in B major op. 32 no. 1 the accompaniment is even more diversified, with heterodirectional movement of the figures, and with 'additional' notes placed variously within them.

The two-voice melodic layer is maintained over longer sections in the late Nocturnes in Eb major op. 55 no. 2 and B major op. 62 no. 1. The countermelody thickens and compresses the texture and – for obvious practical reasons – confines the curves of both lines of the melodic layer, narrowing the tonal space occupied by that layer and keeping the two voices in close proximity. In the Eb major nocturne the density of texture is intensified by the accompani-

[28] In the thirds and sixths doublings Jim Samson (*The Music of Chopin*, 84) sees a tendency to sweeten the melody. In his opinion this texture is analogous to that of the vocal duet, being yet another Italian trait in Chopin's melody.

ment, whose area overlaps with that of the melodic layer. The countermelody complements the main melody and starts a dialogue which, thanks to the differences of pitch and articulation, becomes the source of a play of colours in the melodic layer. Novel colouristic effects are also produced by the use of the

Example 11. Nocturne in E♭ major op. 55 no. 2, bars 35–7

trill as a countermelody (op. 55 no. 2) or as an ornament of the theme (op. 62 no. 1).[29] As a rule where there is a countermelody the texture does not remain constant. Even in these, the two most contrapuntal nocturnes, this voice emerges only from time to time. At some points the additional pitches in the melodic layer are really just an harmonic support for the main melody, and they usually recede quickly from the texture, allowing the melodic layer to return once more to a single line. The variable number and function of simultaneously employed layers is a characteristic feature of Chopin's piano texture (Example 11).

Texture is a means of contrast in the nocturnes. In the middle sections, with their often quite different expressive characters, it is first and foremost texture, as the external layer of the work, that expresses this dissimilarity.

In the *sotto voce* passage of the Nocturne in B♭ minor op. 9 no. 1, the entire musical process is shifted down to a lower register. The shape of the accompaniment figures and their layout become more concentrated and the ornamented single melodic line is replaced by a melody in octaves. This latter change results in a subtle change of articulation, since octave legato can never be as fluent as

---

[29] Jim Samson, *The Music of Chopin*, 93 sees a foretaste of Scriabin's music.

single-note legato. In the Nocturne in B major op. 9 no. 3 the *agitato* part also falls within a lower register, and more importantly in a narrower range, more restricted at the top than was the first part of the nocturne. This narrow-range melodic line is sharply contrasted with the wider curves of the ornamental melody of the first part. Moreover, the area of the bass figures is also restricted. The two-layer texture is replaced by a three-layer texture, in which the harmonic function is taken over by supplementary pitches which fill out the space between the outer voices. Some of the other compositions described above also have a three-layer texture with a central harmonic layer. But in this nocturne the texture is rather different. The bass line here does not imitate the top voice, nor does it serve exclusively as an harmonic basis, but rather constitutes an independent line which conveys the motoric element of the music. There is a compression of movement, while the semitone steps increase the tension within the individual harmonies (Example 12).

Example 12. Nocturne in B major op. 9 no. 3, bars 90–1

In the middle section of the Nocturne in C♯ minor op. 27 no. 1 the bass line is also a motoric factor, imparting dynamism to the musical flow. The oscillation in the low register, because of its recurrence, does not increase the tension within successive chords, however, but rather colours them in a specific way. Unlike the central section of the B major Nocturne, the texture here changes and is subordinated to the formal (two-phase) organisation of the section. After successive transformations it finally merges with the melodic layer into a uniform chordal texture. The diversification of texture in this section is in marked contrast to the consistent, uniform texture of the outer sections.

Just as in the Nocturne in C♯ minor op. 27 no. 1, texture in the Nocturne in F minor op. 55 is a means of energising the middle section. Here the effect is achieved through a contrast of monophonic and chordal sections, with the contrast sharpened by means of register. The opposition of chordal and monophonic motives is also the basis of the middle section of the Nocturne in F♯ minor op. 48, no. 2, but the considerably sparser, thinner texture here means that the expressive effect is completely different. The texture in the

Nocturne in C minor op. 48 no. 1, on the other hand, performs an exceptionally dynamic function.[30] Here texture creates the main expressive character of
the piece, generating contrasts on several different planes, between the central
section and the outer sections, and within the central section itself. It is also
the means by which the main theme of the nocturne is transformed into its
expressive opposite. The consistent octave doubling of the bass in the main
section – a device not previously encountered in the nocturnes – gives it a fuller
sound. In the Poco piu lento section Chopin introduces thick chords, of a kind
which had been in use since Beethoven's day to emphasise the strength of tone.
In a manner untypical for his era Chopin combines these chords with a piano
dynamic, inverting the proportions of density and volume, as composers of
the second half of the nineteenth century were later to do. Thus, despite
limited dynamics the fullness of sound is again ensured. The return of the main
theme is really a continuation of the second section. While the melody and
harmonic progressions are retained the chordal accompaniment of the first
section is replaced by the rapid motion of thick chords. The more compact
texture at this quick tempo alters the theme's character.

This type of texture composed of repeated chords was of course popular
among piano composers of the day. But by making it more dynamic and
condensed Chopin invested it with a quite new meaning.

A similar type of texture, but thinner and lighter, occurs in the Prelude in Ab
major op. 28 no. 17 and in the middle section of the Nocturne in Ab major
op. 32 no. 2. Here the melodic line emerges from the top notes of the repeated chords. Chopin painstakingly chisels this kind of texture, extracting
melodic motives from the subsidiary voices and introducing subtle articulative
differentiations.

In the late nocturnes (op. 62) the central sections are more closely related
to the outer sections, in textural as in other respects. In the first part of the
B major Nocturne (bars 20–6) the melodic line and countermelody give way
to a single ornamented line, while the harmonic figuration of the accompaniment gives way to repeated notes and chords which foreshadow the accompaniment in the middle section. An analogous section expanded into a virtuosic coda integrates the piece as a whole. Likewise the thinning-out of the
texture in bars 20–6 anticipates the middle section. The latter – in contrast
to the dense, polyphonic texture of the first section – is sparser and more
homophonic in conception. The texture is enriched by the rhythmic non-
congruence of the accompaniment and the melodic line, caused by the continual syncopations in the accompaniment.

The E major Nocturne, by referring explicitly to the vocal, three-layer texture

[30] For a detailed discussion of the role of texture in this nocturne see Józef Chomiński 'Mis-
trzostwo kompozytorskie Chopina' in *Rocznik Chopinowski*, (Warsaw, 1956).

of the *agitato* section, provides 'codetta'-like extensions to the outer sections. In these study-like passages the bass line, strikingly independent, moves in semiquaver motion, and thus in the motion which prevails in the middle section. In places the melodic line is doubled, but the central layer, clearly isolated in the *agitato* section, is here only sporadically prominent. This texture is the indirect link between the texture of the outer sections and that of the middle section.

Chopin's texture is highly differentiated. It would be difficult to find two pieces in which it is identical. Even where there are obvious similarities there is always some difference, if only of detail. Despite the fact that harmony and melody play leading structural roles in Chopin's music, texture is an important contributing factor. It determines the piece's integration and its internal differentiation; it influences its character and the way in which its individual coefficients interact. It also influences the harmony, facilitating the succession of distant harmonic functions, and giving additional meaning to functional connections between chords. But above all it defines the character of the sound. Subtle changes in the texture's density, thickness, registers, articulation, and relations between individual layers all contribute to the richness of Chopin's music, and in particular to its characteristic colouristic nuances.

Twenty-four Preludes op. 28: genre, structure, significance

JEAN-JACQUES EIGELDINGER

Nearly a century and a half after they were first published the Twenty-four Preludes[1] still give off a sparkle and exercise a fascination unique in the literature of the piano. This volume gazes at us like a sphinx proposing a riddle, and one that has remained more or less unsolved. In the words of André Gide 'Some of Chopin's shortest works have the pure, necessary beauty of the solution to a problem. In art, solving a problem is a matter of formulating it correctly.'[2] I shall attempt in this chapter to formulate the problem of the Preludes correctly and then uncover the lines of force of the solution through its architecture. With this in mind, I shall first examine Chopin's op. 28 with reference to the traditions of the prelude; the significance of the work in Chopin's own output will be considered subsequently.

Thanks to the Majorca episode the Preludes have given rise to a spate of literature, much of it anecdotal in character. Even so there are few important Chopin works about whose genesis and purpose we know so little. Let us remind ourselves that they were published in June 1839 by the Parisian publisher Catelin who, for purely commercial reasons, split them into two volumes: nos. 1–12 and 13–24. The French rights in the edition were given to Camille Pleyel, who was also the dedicatee; the German edition, published the same year by Kistner in Leipzig, was offered to J.C. Kessler in gratitude for the dedication of his own Twenty-four Preludes op. 31. Chopin sent his manuscript to Fontana for copying on 22 January 1839, which therefore marks

---

[1] This chapter refers to the edition of the Preludes by Thomas Higgins, Norton critical scores (New York and London, 1973) which copies the musical text edited by E. Zimmermann/ H. Keller for Henle Verlag (Munich-Duisburg, 1956, rev. 1969).

[2] André Gide, *Notes sur Chopin* (Paris, 1948), 111.

the final date for his revisions. This is not the place to go into the controversy about how many and which pieces were composed or completed in Majorca[3] – it is in any case almost insoluble for lack of sound evidence. Whatever may have been its origins and chronological development, I shall consider it syn-

[3] On this question see Ludwik Bronarski, *Études sur Chopin* (Lausanne, 1944), 40–2; M.J.E. Brown, 'The Chronology of Chopin's Preludes', *The Musical Times* xcviii (August, 1957), 423–4; G. Belotti, 'Il problema delle date dei preludi di Chopin', *Rivista Italiana di Musicologia* v (1970), 159–215.

The only thing we can be certain of is that op. 28 nos. 2 and 4 were composed on Majorca, as the autograph sketch for them (coll. Mrs Daniel Drachman, Baltimore, USA) is to be found on the recto-verso sheet which contains the sketch of the Mazurka op. 41 no. 1, dated *Palma*. 28 *9bre* [November] (see figures 1a+1b). It is possible to deduce this – as Bronarski had already done – from a study of Chopin's graphological habits; and I am grateful to Jeffrey Kallberg for his detailed information on this point and for having checked my transcription. Brown inferred that op. 28 nos. 10 and 21 were written on Majorca from the fact that the sketch mentioned above also contains six bars marked *Cis moll* [C♯ minor] and four others which he interprets as being in B♭ major (Examples 1 and 2 are transcriptions). In order to read the second in B♭ one has

Example 1.

(a) Cis moll

(b)

to change the orthography of the left-hand chord on the fifth quaver of bar 2 to C♯–G instead of C–G♭ in the original, which does admittedly omit several accidentals in the course of its modulations. If one retains the original C–G♭, then the sketch must be in F minor (see Example 2).

Example 2.

Whatever the truth of the matter, there can be no doubt that these two sketches are of abandoned preludes, since they include the motivic cell which I discuss later (in the left hand for *Cis moll*, in the right for the other). In support of Brown's hypothesis over op. 28 no. 10, we may note that the harmonic substance of this piece is one of the least rich in the volume, relying on

Figures 1a, 1b: Sketch autograph of the Mazurka op. 41 no. 1, the Prelude op. 28 no. 4 (recto), and the Prelude op. 28 no. 2, with two other rejected fragments for op. 28 (verso). (Photograph courtesy of TiFC, Warsaw)

chronously and as a whole,[4] basing my study on its final realisation at the midpoint of Chopin's composing career.

The keyboard prelude (and by extension that for lute and other similar instruments) can trace its history back to the German organ tablatures of the fifteenth century. From then until the numerous piano collections of the years 1810–30, and despite a sometimes loose use of terminology, it was linked to elements of *improvisation* and was defined above all by its *functions*. These have, at various times, included: testing the instrument and checking its tuning; establishing silence before a performance and putting the audience in the mood for the piece or pieces that are to follow; giving practice in the modes or keys to be used; and, if necessary, providing an opportunity for virtuosity. It has inspired a number of varied and distinct types both of texture and of composition, depending on the period, the geographical location and the affiliations of the composer in question: for example, the unmeasured preludes of the seventeenth-century French lute and harpsichord composers, the alternations of *stile fantastico* and *osservato* in the various sections of Baroque toccatas of the Italian school, or the pairing of prelude and fugue in German music of the High and Late Baroque. The dimensions of the prelude can extend from a barely developed cadential formula to several elaborate and stirring pages. Although it has always been an open form *par excellence*, it came to take on a monothematic aspect at the turn of the seventeenth and eighteenth centuries. After J.S. Bach had, for clearly defined pedagogical reasons, explored the fifteen most commonly used major and minor tonalities in his Inventions and Sinfonias,[5] he gave his *Wohltemperirtes Clavier* (1722)[6] a defini-

two consecutive ideas (bars 1–2, 3–4 etc.) which rather curiously echo the beginning of Schubert's *Impromptu* op. 90 no. 4: perhaps not wholly coincidental, if Chopin was in a hurry to complete the collection?

I have indicated elsewhere that the 'Raindrop' Prelude is certainly op. 28 no. 15 and that it must therefore have been composed at Valldemosa, if one interprets George Sand's description correctly: 'Le prélude "de la goutte d'eau" de Chopin: état de la question et essai d'interprétation', *Revue de musicologie* lxi (1975), 70–90.

[4] The fact that Chopin never played the complete op. 28 in public is irrelevant to my argument. At most he performed four preludes on the platform (26 April 1841), which was not uncharacteristic of him or of the customs of the period. On the other hand the tonal relationships between eight preludes destined for a pupil's studies reveal a concern for organisation. On the back of a copy of the Nocturnes op. 9 presented to Jane Stirling, he prescribed two groups of four preludes: the first based on two pairs with identical tonics, a fifth apart (nos. 9, 4; 6, 11), and a second in which relationships of a fifth predominate (nos. 15, 21, 13 (marked Gb major!) and 17). See F. Chopin, *Oeuvres pour piano: fac-similé de l'exemplaire de Jane W. Stirling*, ed. Jean-Jacques Eigeldinger and Jean-Michel Nectoux (Paris, 1982), xxviii and [25] (facsimile).

[5] They are entitled *Praeambula* and *Fantasien* in their first version in the *Clavier-Büchlein vor Wilhelm Friedemann* (1720).

[6] An early version of Preludes 1–6 and 8–12 also appears in the *Clavier-Büchlein vor Wilhelm Friedemann*. In both versions they can be regarded essentially as textural variations on the harmonic basis of the first Prelude in C major (bars 1–11 in particular), which is the cornerstone of the volume. As we shall see, op. 28 no. 1 could, up to a point, play an analogous role in Chopin's collection.

tive form, building on the groundwork laid most notably by J.K.F. Fischer. A didactic, even polemical work, it sets out to show the excellence of a temperament which, for the first time in the history of keyboard music, explores the cycle of twenty-four keys arranged in ascending chromatic order. It was a great step forward but it marked not so much a break with the past as a summing up from every point of view. For our purpose, the immense impact of the *Wohltemperirtes Clavier* works in two main directions, aided by the spread of equal temperament and similar solutions after 1800. For one thing it led to Reicha's bold thirty-six Fugues op. 36 (*c*. 1805), as well as to the neo-Baroque counterpoint of Clementi's *Gradus ad Parnassum* (1817–26, see the pieces in the 'severe manner') and Klengel's (48) *Canons et Fugues dans tous les tons majeurs et mineurs* (1855), the composer's own performance of which attracted Chopin's attention in 1829. But chiefly it led to a wide proliferation of preludes and studies in the twenty-four keys from the first years of the nineteenth century.[7] These were closely linked with the rise in the piano's popularity and acquired a status of their own in the post-Classical, Romantic era. The two genres[8] offer some points of contact (an educational purpose and a monothematic principle) and at times in the course of their evolution have tended to be confused with one another. The prelude, for instance, can lose its improvisatory character and its introductory function, and the study its didactic intention, veering towards the concert study (Chopin, Liszt) or towards the so-called, stylistic, salon or 'characteristic' studies (Moscheles,[9] Henselt, Alkan, Liszt): here it comes closest to the prelude in its restricted dimensions. Lenz, a one-time pupil of Chopin, proposed the following relationship: 'The (24) Preludes op. 28 are on a small scale what the Etudes are on a large one, less developed but no less interesting or full of ideas. They are suitable for use as advanced keyboard exercises.'[10] I shall return to this comment in due course.

---

[7] Any number of the textural formulae in the *Wohltemperirtes Clavier* serve as the basis for technical studies by Clementi, Czerny, Moscheles (op. 70) and especially Cramer.

[8] The modulating prelude belongs to a different tradition again. It goes back at least to Attaingnant (*Prélude sur chacun ton*, 1531), passing through J.S. Bach (*Kleines harmonisches Labyrinth* BWV 591 – of doubtful authenticity), Reicha (*Étude de transitions et 2 fantaisies* op. 31), Beethoven (*Zwei Praeludien durch alle Dur-Tonarten* op. 39), Clementi (*Étude journalière des Gammes dans tous les tons majeurs et mineurs*) and Field (*Exercice modulé dans tous les tons majeurs et mineurs*). In my opinion, Chopin's Prelude op. 45 constitutes his essay in the genre, a personal stylisation of an improvisatory manner. I shall return to this point in a later article.

[9] This tendency is confirmed by the title of Moscheles's op. 70: *Études ou Leçons de Perfectionnement* destinées aux Elèves avancés, contenant une suite de 24 Morceaux caractéristiques *dans les différents Tons Majeurs et Mineurs* [*c*. 1828]. Apart from no. 23, none of this collection bears a programmatic title, as was to be the case in the same composer's *Characteristiche Studien* op. 95 [1837].

[10] W. von Lenz, 'Uebersichtliche Beurtheilung der Pianoforte-Kompositionen von Chopin . . .', *Neue Berliner Musikzeitung* xxvi (1872), 298.

Our next task is to look at Chopin's immediate predecessors in the field of the piano prelude and see how they organised their collections and what their influence on Chopin might have been. The volumes which Chopin certainly, or in all probability, knew are the following:

Clementi, (25) *Preludes and Exercises in all major and minor keys* (1811, rev. 2/ *c.* 1821)

Hummel, *Vorspiele vor Anfänge eines Stükes* [sic] *aus allen 24 Dur und mol Tonarten* op. 67 (*c.* 1814)

Cramer, *Twenty six Preludes or Short Introductions in the principal Major and Minor Keys* (1818)

Szymanowska, *Vingt Exercices et Préludes* (1819)

Würfel, *Zbiór exercycyi w kształcie preludyów ze wszystkich tonów maior i minor* (1821)[11]

Kalkbrenner, *Vingt-quatre Préludes dans tous les Tons majeurs et mineurs, pouvant servir d'exemple pour apprendre à préluder* op. 88 (1827)

Moscheles, *50 Préludes ou Introductions dans tous les tons Majeurs & Mineurs* (. . .) op. 73 (1828). N.B. Cet ouvrage est destiné a servir d'Exercices préparatifs aux Etudes (op. 70) du même Auteur.[12]

Led by Clementi and Hummel, these composers represent the main schools of pianism in the aftermath of the Classical era. These volumes, though diverse in character, have in common their stated utilitarian and pedagogical purpose, tied as they are to the *functions* that I listed above – Szymanowska, in mixing the genres of prelude and study leans towards the latter. None of them offers any internal unity, beyond what is guaranteed by inclusion of all twenty-four keys, which they handle differently[13] (Clementi, Hummel, Würfel, Kalkbrenner). Hummel is the only one to adopt the cycle of major keys moving in fifths followed by their relative minors, ascending through the sharp side and descending through the flat one with an enharmonic link between F♯ major and E♭ minor. The absence of tonal architecture in Cramer's and Moscheles's collections means that they are no more than a motley assortment. The preludes are isolated entities in every case except that of Clementi, and there only partially.[14] Their length remains fairly constant within each volume, going from a minimum of one or two systems to an exceptional maximum of three pages in the case of Szymanowska. This collection apart, most of them

[11] I have been unable to trace this volume either in Switzerland, Paris, or Warsaw. Wilhelm Würfel (1790–1832) was a professor at the Warsaw Conservatory and is supposed to have given the adolescent Chopin basic organ lessons.

[12] This editorial notice is no more than a disguised advertisement.

[13] In his *Exercices* only, Clementi adopts the succession of major and minor descending and ascending alternatively in a cycle of fifths and their relative minors (C major–A minor; F major–D minor; G major–E minor; B♭ major–G minor etc.). Kalkbrenner follows the ascending chromatic pattern of the *Wohltemperirtes Clavier.*

[14] The work underwent some revision. In its final form it presents one or more preludes going only as far as C♯ minor. On the other hand, three keys are given more than one prelude: C major (5), F major (2) and G major (3) – hence the total of twenty-five.

are based on ready-made pianistic formulae – *topoi* inherited from post-Classicism – and less often on rudimentary counterpoint, while the conventional characters of keys are generally respected. Their form is open[15] and they remain within the prelude's traditionally accepted confines, that is to say the cadenza or instrumental recitativo, without impinging on other genres except on occasion the cognate one of the exercise or study based on motivic repetition (these last comments do not apply to Szymanowska).

Altogether these points show that Chopin was in only the slightest degree dependent on his predecessors. If some of his preludes give the impression of being improvised, it is by means that have nothing to do with anything that had gone before. The only real similarity is in the pattern of key arrangement borrowed from Hummel. As for the varied length of the pieces in op. 28,[16] this seems to be a necessary concomitant of their musical substance and of their place in the overall musical sequence; certainly this variation is a unique feature of Chopin's collection. His monothematic writing here looks back not so much to previous preludes as to certain studies. Finally, such passing reminiscences as there are in this collection are confined to a single analogy with Szymanowska[17] and, if one looks very hard, a single phrase in Hummel.[18] The sum of influences is, then, meagre and not very persuasive, though it is as well to mention them.

André Gide's questioning attitude therefore seems justified: 'I admit that I do not wholly understand the title that Chopin chose to give these short pieces: *Preludes*. Preludes to what? Each of Bach's preludes is followed by its fugue; it is an integral part of it. But I can no more imagine one of these Chopin preludes followed by some other piece in the same key, even if by the same composer, than I can hearing all these Chopin preludes played immediately one after the other.'[19] That last comment aside, Gide asks an important question even though it is obscured by the pairing of prelude and fugue. The name Bach is the nub of the matter. Bach's influence on the Preludes, as on Chopin's music in general, is infinitely more powerful and subtle than that of any of the post-classical composers; but as this has been the subject of attention elsewhere I do not intend to deal with it here.[20]

---

[15] The stylised improvisation is emphasised by, among other things, the absence of barlines in Cramer and partially in Moscheles.

[16] According to Alfred Cortot (*Edition de Travail des Oeuvres de Chopin, 24 Préludes op. 28* (Paris, 1926)) the durations range from some 30–5 seconds to 4 minutes, 20–5 seconds.

[17] See op. 28 no. 23 and *Vingt Exercices. . .* no. 1, both in F major.

[18] See op. 28 no. 10 (bar 1) and *Vorspiele* op. 67 no. 10 (bar 1).

[19] André Gide, *Notes sur Chopin*, 32.

[20] See Walter Wiora, 'Chopins Preludes und Etudes und Bachs Wohltemperiertes Klavier', *The Book of the First International Musicological Congress Devoted to the Works of Frederick Chopin*, ed. Zofia Lissa (Warsaw, 1963), 73–81; K. Hławiczka, 'Chopin a Jan Sebastian Bach', *Chopin a muzyka europejska*, ed. K. Musioł (Katowice, 1977), 3–17; Jean-Jacques Eigeldinger, *Chopin:*

Chopin was called by Liszt 'an enthusiastic student of Bach'[21] and he took the *Wohltemperirtes Clavier* for his gospel, whether as composer, pianist or teacher. Certainly it was no coincidence that he took it with him to Majorca[22] at the time when he was putting the finishing touches to his own Preludes. His decision to compose them in the twenty-four keys appears not so much as a concession to a genre inherited from his predecessors as a mark of his grounding in the work of Bach. If Chopin does not follow his chromatically ascending pattern (as Kalkbrenner does), that is because he is not engaged in a polemic about temperament. The cycle of fifths and relative minors, beyond its appearance also in Hummel, has a structural purpose, as I shall show later. Walter Wiora (see n. 20) has demonstrated the influence of the *Wohltemperirtes Clavier* both on the Preludes op. 28 and on the Studies opp. 10 and 25. He makes persuasive claims for the succession of keys inside opp. 10 and 25 (though the latter is less amenable to his efforts) and presents a hypothesis of an initial project of studies in all twenty-four keys which would have been abandoned in the course of composition and resumed in a different form with op. 28. But this hypothesis is invalidated by the separate publication of opp. 10 and 25 four years apart, in 1833 and 1837 respectively, the second book being in no sense complementary to the first in the matter of keys as well as being invested with a profounder poetic content. In any case, the question of what relationship there might be between the Twenty-four Preludes and the two books of Twelve Studies can be answered only by means of a further hypothesis, which must itself be immediately called into question: the idea of a corpus of twenty-four preludes and studies (by analogy with Bach, Clementi and Klengel). This conjecture, too, is invalidated by the date of publication for op. 28, after the two books of Studies. These judgements are clearly made a posteriori. On the other hand, this does nothing to reduce the force of Wiora's analogies between the first prelude of the *Wohltemperirtes Clavier* I[23] and the opening pieces of

Pianist and Teacher, 3rd, English edn., (Cambridge, 1986), 135 n. 137, and *passim*. G.P. Minardi, 'L'élève enthousiaste de Bach', *Chopin: Opera omnia*, ed. C. de Incontrera (Monfalcone, 1985), 43–50.

[21] Frederick Niecks, *Frederick Chopin as a Man and Musician*, 3rd edn., 2 vols. (London, 1902), i, 30.

[22] See *Korespondencja Fryderyka Chopina*, ed. Bronisław Edward Sydow, 2 vols. (Warsaw, 1955), i, 332, letter to Fontana (Palma, 28 December 1838) which mentions the name of Bach without being more specific. A piece of contemporary evidence, hitherto unknown to Chopin experts, confirms that the work in question is the *Wohltemperirtes Clavier*: 'Le Clavecin bien tempéré has been the *vade mecum* of all the great pianists; it was the only music Chopin took with him on his journey to Majorca . . .', wrote J.-J.-B. Laurens, 'Lettre d'un touriste peintre-musicien, à son ami Castil-Blaze, sur quelques artistes et sur l'art en Allemagne', *La France musicale* vi (1843), 145. On his return from Majorca, Chopin mentioned that he had been indulging in some textual criticism by the light of instinct – a unique instance of his involvement in such an activity; this was at the time he was finishing his Sonata op. 35, and the subject was Bach: see *Korespondencja . . .*, i, 353–4, letter to Fontana [Nohant, 8 August 1839].

[23] Bach's model was obviously Kuhnau, *Neue Clavier Übung* (1689), 'Partie v', Praeludium, both for the textures and for the substance of the harmony.

opp. 10 and 28. All three are in the paradigmatic key of C major, are based on a single motive and are essentially chordal. They begin by announcing the major triad and develop a continuous pattern of arpeggios derived from the opening bar (both in the Bach and in op. 10 no. 1 the third is at the top). The differences in texture and range are, of course, explained by the respective instruments, styles, genres and intentions. I would add two things to Wiora's analysis with respect to op. 28 no. 1. Through a succession of what strikes the listener as waves of sound, Chopin's complex notation, with the help of the sustaining pedal, may be taken as an instinctive, stylised development of the 'brisé' lute writing of which Bach's piece is an obvious example. This detail is enough on its own to substantiate Chopin's debt to Bach; but Chopin is at the same time an innovator in the way he draws from his arpeggios a melodic line which proves a determining element in the structural unity of the volume.

The transfigured imprint of Bach in the Twenty-four Preludes is to be seen most clearly in their texture; powerful and new as this is, the harmony is often clearly the result of superimposed lines.[24] Many of the pieces are built from a polymelodic texture of the most inventive kind, and a very long way from the neo-Baroque counterpoint practised at this same period by Mendelssohn or Schumann.

We may take as an example the Prelude no. 2, the boldest in texture and the more so by its placing in the volume (we are uncertain at this point of the tonal pattern since it reaches A minor only in the final bars). Interesting information can be gleaned from the sketch and from the manuscript fair copy used as the basis for the French edition. The sketch begins by notating the start of the left hand figuration (Example 3), followed at once by a revised version for the two opening bars and bar 8 (Example 4). In the fair copy the disposition from bar 3 onwards is simplified, for ease of writing and engraving (Example 5).

Example 3.   Example 4.   Example 5.

The current Urtext editions are the only ones to follow the revised version (not retained in the first French edition), which shows the development of a horizontal conception (Example 6). We have here a piece entirely made up of four 'voices' and the tensions derive from the movement of the parts, especially

[24] See especially Bronisława Wójcik-Keuprulian, *Melodyka Chopina* (Lvov, 1930); the same author's 'O polifonii Chopina', *Kwartalnik muzyczny* i (1929), 251–9; J. Chomiński, 'La maîtrise de Chopin compositeur', *Annales Chopin* ii (1958), 179–237; J.-J. Eigeldinger, 'Autour des Préludes de Chopin', *Revue musicale de Suisse romande* xxv/1–2 (1972), 3–7 and 3–5; C. Burkhart, 'The Polyphonic Melodic Line of Chopin's B-minor Prelude', in Thomas Higgins, ed., *Preludes op. 28*, 80–8.

Example 6.

the clashes between the upper part and the embroideries of the 'baritone' – variations on a *Dies Irae* archetype, perhaps. Heard like this, the piece is very close to the Study op. 10 no. 6 which is notated in four real parts. If, at the other end of the volume, we look at Prelude no. 21 and seek out its polyphonic basis, we obtain a result (see Example 7) in which the contrary movement of

Example 7.

the inner parts foreshadows the importance they are going to have at the 'reprise' (bars 33–45), over a dominant pedal that is at first explicit and then implicit. In op. 28 no. 3 the left hand presents a gyratory formula from which the leaping motive in the right hand, appearing in short sections and enriched with doublings at the third and sixth, is derived by free augmentation. Although the texture is utterly pianistic, it is nonetheless a reworking of a two-part 'Invention' or 'Prelude'. In op. 28 no. 4 the layout of the left hand, with its chords in close position, cloaks the descending, chromatic movement of three independent lines; superimposed lines which represent Chopin's response to the harmonic polyphony of the 'Crucifixus' from the B minor Mass.

In writing this elegy in E minor, Chopin had recourse to the key traditionally associated with lamentation in the Baroque catalogue of affects.[25] Similarly we find in op. 28 no. 20 a chromatic line descending through a perfect fourth (bars 5–6, 9–10) which was a symbol of affliction for Bach as for his contemporaries and predecessors. The texture of op. 28 no. 18 recreates

---

[25] See also *Wohltemperirtes Clavier* I no. 10, the prelude in arioso style (bars 1–22).

after a fashion a recitativo section from a Baroque toccata or fantasy, and there are several instances of *moto perpetuo* in the Preludes, turning the frequent formula of so many of the preludes from the *Wohltemperirtes Clavier* to other esthetic purposes. There is no question but that Bach determines many of the elements of texture and layout in these Preludes in advance of the influence he was to have on Chopin's final period of creativity, as Gerald Abraham has shown.[26]

Rooted as they are in Bach, the Preludes represent the precise moment at which Chopin broke away from the tradition he had inherited from post-Classicism. Clearly the collection no longer fulfils any of the functions to which its title had laid claim hitherto. To take out some of the Preludes and couple them with other Chopin pieces in the same key might be an interesting experiment at best, but could hardly be termed necessary. At this point in the discussion the elements which so far justify the title *Preludes* are: the cycle of twenty-four keys; the impression given by some of the pieces of being stylised improvisations,[27] their brevity; and a basic monothematic principle. Even if these characteristics could, singly, be attributed to the genre of the *Study*, the volume of Preludes taken as a whole reveals no pedagogical intention so that Lenz's conclusion, quoted earlier, is clearly reductive and inadequate.[28]

The break marked by these Preludes did not escape the attention of either Schumann or Liszt, both of whom expressed their feelings in a highly revealing manner in their well-known reviews:

The Preludes are strange pieces. I confess I imagined them differently, and designed in the grandest style, like his Etudes. But almost the opposite is true: they are sketches, beginnings of Etudes, or, so to speak, ruins, eagle wings, a wild motley of pieces. But each piece, written in a fine, pearly hand, shows: 'Frederick Chopin wrote it.' One recognises him in the pauses by the passionate breathing. He is and remains the boldest and proudest poetic mind of the time. The collection also contains the morbid, the feverish, the repellent. May each search what suits him; may only the philistine stay away![29]

Chopin's Preludes are compositions of an order entirely apart: they are not merely, as the title would indicate, introductions to other *morceaux* – they are preludes instinct with poesy, analogous to those of another great contemporary poet, who cradles the

---

[26] Gerald Abraham, *Chopin's Musical Style* (London, 1939), xi–xii and 96–111.

[27] The improvisatory element is more noticeable in the Prelude op. 45, in certain sections of the Fantasy op. 49 (bars 43–67, 180–98), and at the start of the Polonaise-fantasy op. 61 (the alternation of *stile fantastico* and *osservato*).

[28] Lenz's judgement is most nearly applicable to the *Trois Nouvelles Études* for Moscheles's and Fétis's *Méthode des Méthodes* [1840]. They stand halfway between the Studies and the Preludes by their substance (more musical than technical), form and dimensions.

[29] *Neue Zeitschrift für Musik* xli (19 November 1839), 163. Trans. Edward Lowinsky in Higgins, *Preludes op. 28*, 91.

soul in golden dreams, and elevates it to the regions of the ideal. Admirable for their variety, the labour and learning with which they abound are appreciable only by the aid of a scrupulous examination; everything seems fresh, elastic, created at the impulse of the moment, abounding with that freedom of expression which is characteristic of works of genius.[30]

Liszt, with his quick understanding, saw straight away the work's unique identity and the window it opened on to the future. Besides George Sand, from another point of view, nobody else has written with such acumen: 'What melancholy, what finesse, what wisdom, above all what *art* there is in the masterpieces of La Fontaine, the subjects of which are so mundane and the titles so modest! It is the same with the Studies and Preludes; but the Chopin pieces which bear these titles will remain nonetheless as types of perfection, in a genre which he has created and which, like all his works, partakes of the inspiration of his poetic genius.'[31] By contrast we find in Schumann's ambiguous tone, for the first time in his Chopin criticisms, a nuance of reserve and puzzlement. The volume's bold and enigmatic style disconcerted him to the degree that he himself tended to shelter under the protective banner of Mendelssohn. In particular, it ran counter to his own aspirations – his problem, in fact, as a composer – towards writing in ever more extended forms. Beyond its diversity, the unity of the collection escaped him; he saw only extracts, incompleteness and ruins. This opinion of the Preludes was predominant for the next century. Certainly the volume contains the shortest pieces, in time and in number of bars,[32] that Chopin ever published. But brevity does not predicate a sketch, nor extreme concision incompleteness. Together with the view of the Preludes as unconnected pieces, this confusion between size and content has been at the root of a prolonged misunderstanding, reducing the volume to a collection of isolated miniatures, lyrical pieces or *Charakterstücke*. The Preludes do not in any sense belong to the esthetic of the fragment which dominates Schumann's *Bunte Blätter* op. 99 or, to a still greater extent, his

---

[30] *Revue et gazette musicale de Paris* viii (2 May 1842), 246. Trans. in *Preludes op. 28*, 91–2.

[31] Franz Liszt, *F. Chopin* (Leipzig, 1882), 3rd edn., 15.

[32] Op. 28 no. 9 is the shortest in bars (twelve) but also the most compact – the most artfully condensed. But op. 28 no. 20, which is thirteen bars long in the published version, has only nine bars in the original manuscript (two phrases: a–a'). For bars 5–8 the autograph has the signs a–b–c–d, indicating their repetition for bars 9–12 at a different dynamic level, with these words: '*note* pour l'éditeur (*de la rue de Rochechouard* [sic]) *petite concession faite à Mr xxx qui a souvent raison*. Chopin obviously deferred here to the advice of Pleyel who must have felt that the piece was outrageously short, too much so to be published. When Chopin wrote the piece into the Szeriemietiev's family album (20 May 1845) he followed the complete, published text; but in A. de Beauchesne's album (30 January 1840) he wrote only the original nine-bar version. Clearly he had not renounced it, as there is no question here of a lack of space or a lack of energy (a double bar would have sufficed). In my opinion, one is justified in adopting the earlier version which, in the economical climate of the volume as a whole, comes over all the more strongly – and at the same time prevents pianists being embarrassed by having to repeat something.

Albumblätter op. 124 – and, *a fortiori*, so many minor works by his imitators. In a manner quite foreign to Chopin's own artistic habits[33] and by means of labels which belittle what they are attached to, the Preludes have become the object of literary interpretation: titles, epigraphs, programmatic commentaries – merely so many verbal compensations for a musical perception that is demeaning and normative.[34]

This so-called tradition goes back to George Sand, if we are to believe her daughter's reminiscences: 'George Sand gave a title to each of Chopin's wonderful Preludes. They have been preserved on a copy he gave her.'[35] This volume has not so far been discovered and the six preludes copied by Mme Sand into her album[36] (nos. 2, 4, 6, 7, 9, 20) are not accompanied by any literary allusions. On the other hand Solange's jottings on the subject of Chopin at the piano come near to being twenty-four in number and several of them can be collated with Mme Sand's famous description of the Preludes in Majorca.[37] There is then a chance that Solange's words might reflect, even if they do not exactly reproduce, the titles imagined by her mother.

On 3 November 1849, Ferdinand Hiller organised in Düsseldorf a soirée in honour of Chopin, who had just died. On this occasion the performance of each piece was preceded by the recital of some poetry; in the case of op. 28 no. 4 a five-line stanza.[38]

Liszt, who was a proponent of programme music, quotes in his book *Frédéric Chopin* (pp. 238–9, n. 1) some perceptive remarks on the Preludes by Count Załuski, including two quatrains inspired by no. 8.

Individual titles and passionate, detailed scenarios for each piece were published by Laura Rappoldi-Kahrer[39] as being reminiscences, supposedly handed down by Bülow and 'authenticated' by their similarity to reminiscences from Lenz and Mrs Mouchanoff-Kalergis – both Chopin pupils.

Around the turn of the century, R. Koczalski used to add verbal commentary to his

---

[33] On Chopin's aversion to the French titles thought up for his compositions by the English publisher Wessel, see *Korespondencja* . . ., ii, 37, 42 and 396, the last of which reads: '. . .my latest pieces won't any longer make people think of *warblers twittering*, or even of *broken porcelain*'; there is an implied pun here between Wessel and 'vaisselle'. This is not to deny the images Chopin sometimes had recourse to when teaching to make his intentions understood: see Eigeldinger, *Chopin: Pianist and Teacher*, 12, 69, 75–6, 81, 85, 87.

[34] Even Hugo Leichtentritt (*Analyse der Chopin'schen Klavierwerke*, 2 vols. (Berlin, 1921–2), i, 125–76) does not avoid it, despite his positivist approach.

[35] J.-J. Eigeldinger, 'Frédéric Chopin: Souvenirs inédits par Solange Clésinger', *Revue musicale de Suisse romande* xxxi (1978), 226–7.

[36] Krystyna Kobylańska, *Rękopisy utworów Chopina. Katalog*, 2 vols. (Cracow, 1977), i, items 381, 392, 401, 408, 416, 461; ii, 45, 46, 50 (facsimiles). Other facsimiles in Kobylańska, *Korespondencja Fryderyka Chopina z George Sand i jej dziećmi*, 2 vols. (Warsaw, 1981), i, ill. 27–9.

[37] George Sand, *Histoire de ma vie* in G. Lubin, ed., *Oeuvres autobiographiques*, 2 vols. (Paris, 1970–1), ii, 420–2.

[38] Ferdinand Hiller, *Aus dem Tonleben unserer Zeit*, 2 vols. (Leipzig, 1868), ii, 264–9.

[39] Julius Kapp, 'Chopin's Préludes (op. 28): Aufzeichnungen von Laura Rappoldi-Kahrer nach Angaben von Liszt, W. von Lenz und Frau von Mouckhanoff', *Die Musik* xxxiv (1909/10), 227–33.

Chopin recitals and in their published version they include a literary gloss for each prelude, followed by advice on technique and style.[40]

This tradition was continued beyond 1945 by Alfred Cortot, in his students' edition of the Preludes (see n. 16), programme notes for his concerts, lectures and in his master-classes.[41]

If op. 28 is not a miniature rejoinder to opp. 10 and 25, nor a collection of heterogeneous *feuillets d'album*, how should we describe it? Debussy wrote of Chopin's work in general: 'If his formal freedom has deceived his critics. . . we must none the less recognise the degree to which everything is in its place and carefully organised.'[42]

If the Preludes are an organic whole, they must be put together according to certain structural principles: it remains to discover what they are and how the volume's unity is achieved over and above its diversity.

It is certainly true that op. 28 exploits the principle of alternation: between the cycle of fifths ascending through the sharp side and that descending through the flat side;[43] between major and minor; between diatonic and chromatic; between opposing tempi and characters, sizes and lengths, rhythms and metres; between two oscillating harmonies; between ascending and descending melodic lines; between high and low, left hand and right hand, continuity and discontinuity in the passage from one piece to another;[44] between single and dual thematic bases. *Not* that these oscillations are systematic: in taking these parameters singly or in groups one discovers no more than *partial* structures. This is so with complementary pairs of preludes (nos. 1–6, 7–10, 13–18,

---

[40] Raoul Koczalski, *Frédéric Chopin: Quatre Conférences analytiques* (Paris, 1910), 173–95.

[41] Alfred Cortot, 'Frédéric Chopin: Les Préludes', *Conferencia* xxviii (1933/4), 252–61; B. Gavoty, *Alfred Cortot* (Paris, 1977), 277–81.

[42] Chopin, *Oeuvres complètes pour le piano*, révision par C. Debussy, *Valses*, Préface (Paris, 1915), ii.

[43] In the axial symmetry of the cycle of fifths, the bipolarity between four sharps and four flats plays an important role in Chopin. Preludes 9 and 17, which occupy symmetrical positions in op. 28, modulate respectively from E to Ab with a return to E (no. 9, bars 7–9) and from Ab to E (no. 17, bars 23–4, 43–6), both at dramatic high points. The two pieces seem to provide a syntactical clue to this bipolarity which, with changes in key signature, is a predominant feature in opp. 11(ii) and 54 (modulation from E to Ab) and in opp. 10 no. 10, 17 no. 3, 53, 61 and 64 no. 3 (modulation from Ab to E). To a lesser degree, it occurs in the relationship C♯ minor–Ab major/F minor (opp. 10 no. 4, 27 no. 1). It is possible that the structure of the tempered keyboard is what determines this axis, with Chopin, for pianistic reasons, preferring keys rich in sharps or flats (statistically, Ab major is by far his favourite key).

[44] The coherence between the odd-even pairs (major–relative minor) is signalled by the presence of one or more notes at the same pitch or in different registers: especially noticeable is the transference from high/medium to low in the transition between nos. 1–2 (e'–E') and nos. 15–16 (f'–F''). In the final pair, nos. 23–4, there is furthermore the tension of the seventh Eb'' (penultimate bar) which 'resolves' on to the first D of no. 24. The close link between nos. 3–4 is the result of a correction: the sketch for no. 4 shows clearly that the ascent b–b' (the third of G major becoming the fifth of E minor) was added as an afterthought. As for the links between the even- and odd-numbered Preludes, they consist mainly of a diatonic movement, whether conjunct or not.

21–4) or with the way the collection is punctuated by monothematic pieces in the nature of studies (nos. 8, 12, 16, 19, 24) or by bithematic ones that are close to being nocturnes (nos. 13, 15, 17, 21) – that is to say, coming in the second half of the volume! Considerations along these lines have led Chomiński to see in op. 28 sonata structures fitted into an ensemble of 'minia-tures'.[45] Such an interpretation cannot be other than purely speculative: Chopin, after all, was to give his current answer to the sonata problem in his op. 35, finished a few months after the Preludes. Taken all in all, the parameters outlined above are a stumbling block to any serious attempt at an internal grouping of these pieces. The unifying principle must therefore be looked for in another direction. Chomiński comes close to it when he proposes a *Sub-stanzgemeinschaft* common to twelve (even fourteen) of the twenty-four pieces, in the form of progressions of seconds. But any explanation must take ac-count of the volume as a whole.

In tackling his project of a collection of short pieces passing through all twenty-four keys, Chopin of necessity exercised maximum economy in the means he employed. Each piece in fact exploits a textural continuum based on a rhythmical ostinato, whether melodic or harmonic (nos. 6 and 15 take the process to its ultimate limits in the unrelenting repetition of a single note). Above all, the Twenty-four Preludes are a cycle by virtue of an omnipresent *motivic cell* which assures its unity through a variety of textures. Melodically, the cell is characterised by an ascending sixth which falls back on to the fifth. It appears first in the very opening phrase of Prelude no. 1 (Example 8). The

Example 8.

---

[45] Józef M. Chomiński, *Preludia Chopina* (Cracow, 1950), 300–33. A resumé of the author's views appears in his *Fryderyk Chopin*, trans. B. Schweinitz (Leipzig, 1980), 108–12.

A in bars 1–3, first a decoration and then a development of G, is balanced by the E appoggiatura to the D at the crest of the melodic wave in bars 5–7. The relationship is present again in a condensed form in the final cadence where we see the structural intervals (Example 9) in the implicative shape X (bars 25–6)

Example 9.

and then in the closed shape Y (bars 27–8). Either X or Y, and sometimes both, appear in each prelude at strategic points (see Example 10, pp. 186–93): at the beginning (and, in the case of bithematic pieces, at the beginnings of sections), at the final cadence and in the codas; more rarely at the piece's centre of gravity, where the various threads of the musical discourse are brought together (nos. 4, 9, 12).

Nor is this all. The shape of this melodic cell is generated by the dictates of the *temperament* of Chopin's piano; the rising sequence of fifths together with their thirds indicates step by step the way in which his instrument was tuned.[46] In the first bar of Prelude no. 1 the major triad is laid out according to its natural resonance, the fundamental being doubled at two octaves' distance, the fifth throughout three octaves and the third at the octave. The relationship C–G is thus highlighted. In bars 5–7 the second fifth G–D is introduced with an insistent E appoggiatura – following the practice of the tuner who plays the perfect triad with a six-four appoggiatura. The tuning therefore begins with the superimposition of the two fifths C–G, G–D, with their respective thirds E and B; this is where the motivic cell derives from and explains why in Preludes nos. 1, 2 and 3 it appears on identical notes (in no. 3 the E appoggiatura to the D is particularly striking in the left-hand pattern of bar 1, as well as in the right hand's augmented version in bars 3–4), going on to be transposed from Prelude no. 4 onwards. The piano's temperament is therefore arrived

---

[46] The discussion that follows is the fruit of a collaboration with my colleague Pierre Studer, professor at the Geneva Conservatory of Music. I shall deal elsewhere in more detail with the temperament of Chopin's piano and its possible relationship with the tuning of the *Wohltemperirtes Clavier.* Here I shall content myself with some general principles relevant to my argument.

at through the following process which mirrors the succession of Preludes nos. 1–13 (Example 11). The first turning-point comes in no. 5 where X is heard successively in D and A major and then in E and B minor. In nos. 8 and 9 the enharmonic synonyms on the flat side are tested, first of all successively

Example 11.

(no. 8, bars 7–18), then simultaneously (no. 9, bars 7–8). No. 12 regulates the enharmonic equivalences according to which sharps and double sharps become naturals (bars 9–12) and travels through a successive cycle of fifths, F♯–B–E–A–D–G–C♮ (bars 13–29), dividing the octave into two tritones. X now rings out in C major in the middle of the piece (bars 29–30) and the denouement is in sight. With the regulation of the thirds F♯–A♯ (=B♭) and C♯–E♯ (=F♮) in Prelude no. 13, the temperament is successfully achieved and the cycle of fifths now descends through the flat side to no. 24. This is the key point in the volume. The enharmonic switch from D♯ to E♭ is made between the beginning of the middle section of no. 13 and no. 14 – and here Chopin cleverly covers his tracks with a panchromatic unison texture.

With the temperament duly established in the first half of op. 28, the second half is given over to profiting from it with a symbolic 'counter-tuning'. As a result, the pieces are more elaborately constructed with particular use of enharmonic devices in the bithematic works (nos. 15, 17), which establish links with some of the sharp keys already heard in the first part. G♭ major, which appeared briefly in nos. 14 and 19, is given a paragraph of its own in the middle of no. 21, for example. With the move to the flat side, the motivic cell begins to take on modifications: chordal contraction (nos. 13, 21), inversions (no. 13, bars 16–18, 21–2, 23–4; no. 16, bar 2; no. 22, bars 40–1), 'apophonies' (no. 17, bars 19–21, 21–3, 23–4), permutations etc. The tension set up by the flattened seventh at the end of Prelude no. 23 (see n. 44) is released through a double presentation of the cell in no. 24, the first X (bars 4–5), the second X–Y (bars 8–9) being stated in the tonic D minor. As a final act of elegance on Chopin's part, the left-hand ostinato of no. 24 highlights the fifth D–A, the traditional test of equal temperament tuning!

In the final analysis, what governs op. 28 and makes it a *cycle*[47] is the logic of its temperament, which gives pride of place to the thirds. From this point of view the Twenty-four Preludes constitute a confirming response to the *Wohltemperirtes Clavier*. Where Chopin differed from Bach, who was moved by didactic considerations to arrange his preludes and fugues in isolated pairs, was in grasping straight away the tonal space opened up by his 'tempered piano'. Not that he wrote his Preludes with an eye to tuning his own instrument (something he must have had to do even in Valldemosa!) but the impact of op. 28 is made all the greater by the euphony of the temperament – giving us some idea of Chopin's views in the matter.[48] Any comparison with Hummel now becomes irrelevant.[49]

At the same time, the Preludes offer a clue as to the associations keys held for Chopin. If they are a *microcosm* in this respect, they are too for several of his

[47] Lawrence Kramer, *Music and Poetry: The Nineteenth Century and After* (Berkeley, 1984), 91–117, has shed light on a structural principle in op. 28, a sort of Schenkerian *Urlinie*. The unity of the cycle is assured by the harmonic rhythm I–vi–V (C major–A minor–G major), V becoming I in its turn (G major–E minor–D major) and so on to the final Prelude. This succession is carried over into the structure of several of the pieces themselves, inspiring either an initial harmonic formula, a final cadence or a coda, or even (as in no. 21) determining the form. Through his fascinating conception of 'Transit of Identity', the author comes to some of the same conclusions as myself. But it is the musical fact of temperament which in fact gives rise to the succession I–vi–V; this is therefore not a cause but a result.

[48] The importance Chopin attached to the temperament of his piano is documented in a poignant letter to Fontana (18 August 1848) in which he laments the death of his Paris tuner, who worked for Pleyel: 'All those with whom I was in most intimate harmony have died and left me. Even Ennike our best tuner has gone and drowned himself; and so I have not in the whole world a piano tuned to suit me'. *Selected Correspondence of Fryderyk Chopin*, trans. and ed. A. Hedley (London, 1962), 330.

[49] At the end of Hummel's *Méthode Complète Théorique et Pratique pour le Piano-Forte* (Paris, [1828]/R 1981), 466–7, a work Chopin admired, the author describes a system of tuning starting from A which is in no way illustrated by the succession of keys in his own *Vorspiele . . .* op. 67. His tuning, which relies on the superimposition of 'narrow fifths', does not lay emphasis on thirds from the start and so is very different from what we can deduce on the evidence of op. 28.

pianistic textures and compositional types. Apart from pieces of the study or nocturne variety, the volume contains brief passages in the style of mazurkas (no. 7; no. 10, bars 3–4 etc.), impromptus (no. 11), two *alla Marcia* types (nos. 9, 20), one *moto perpetuo all'unisono* (no. 14), one recitativo in fantasy style (no. 18), two elegies (nos. 4, 6), two arabesques (nos. 10, 23) and at least one prelude (no. 1), which quite possibly was the last to be written.

The volume is a kind of ordered catharsis. Chopin's volatile genius is perfectly captured in this succession of 'ideas' (as George Sand called them), snapshots like a concentric mirror of the man and the artist; aphorisms stretched at times to the limits of exaggeration, but never descending into rhetoric; a cycle of 'moments musicaux' or 'visions fugitives' without the titles. George Sand wrote of Chopin: 'It is a strange anomaly – he is the most original and individual genius who ever lived. But he does not like you to tell him so.'[50] Ignoring the legacy of his immediate predecessors, deaf to the contemporary world, the Chopin of the Preludes anchored himself in Bach so as to see himself more clearly – and, despite himself, into the future. This work is a two-faced Janus, not only within his own output, but in the development of keyboard music from Bach to the present day. Alfredo Casella emphasised the work's modern aspect: 'In these preludes we find a Chopin entirely exempt from even the most distant remembrance of society, who works heroically and in solitude, with his steady glance fixed upon the mists of the impressionistic future before him. . .'[51] A study of the influence of the Preludes on the nineteenth and twentieth centuries (beyond Debussy)[52] could lead to an a posteriori evaluation of their uniqueness. But that is another story.

[50] George Sand, *Impressions et souvenirs* (Paris, 1896), 81 – taken from chapter 5, dated January 1841.

[51] F. Chopin, *Preludi*, revisione critico-tecnica di A. Casella (Milan, 1967), 'Note on the Preludes', n.p.

[52] Such a study would have to take account of the principal collections of Preludes after op. 28 from the point of view of whether their arrangement was by keys or not, whether they were homogeneous or not, the way one followed another, their thematic material etc. It would be possible to distinguish a number of different groups:

  (a) collections using the twenty-four keys: Alkan, op. 31 [1847]; Heller, op. 81 [1853]; Busoni, op. 37 [c. 1882]; Scriabin, op. 11 (1897); Rachmaninov, op. 3 no. 2 (1892), op. 23 (1903), op. 32 (1910); Shostakovich, op. 34 (1932–3);

  (b) collections of Preludes that enlarged the concept of tonality, such as those of Debussy (1910, 1913) or that were uninvolved with tonality, such as those of Ohana (1974);

  (c) sets of Preludes made up of various numbers of pieces below twelve, from the numerous collections of Lyadov and Scriabin; Szymanowski, op. 1 (1906); Fauré, op. 103 (1910–11), to those of Frank Martin (1949).

  (d) One could then establish links in many directions with cycles of short pieces such as Schönberg's *Sechs kleine Klavierstücke* op. 19 (1911) and his *Fünf Klavierstücke* op. 23 (1923), Prokofiev's *Visions fugitives* (1922) etc.

  (e) Another section of the study might examine Liszt's organ arrangement of op. 28 nos. 4 and 9 (Raabe 404; Searle 662), as well as variations on the Chopin Preludes, no. 20 of which was

Example 10.

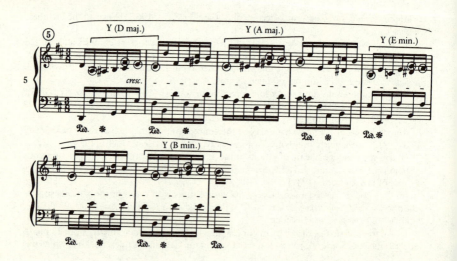

Example 10. (*cont.*)

taken as a theme by Busoni for his op. 22 (1885; 2nd edn. 1922) and by Rachmaninov for his op. 22 (1904).

It would also be a simple matter to show the influence of op. 28 no. 8 on Liszt's harmony in 'Au bord d'une source' and even in 'Les cloches de Genève' (bars 140ff.). Op. 28 no. 2 exercised a direct influence not only on Liszt's *Via crucis* (Stations ii, v, x), but also on Rachmaninov's Prelude op. 23 no. 1, Bartók's *Ten Easy Piano Pieces*, no. 2 (1908), Kodály's *10 Pièces pour le piano*, op. 3, no. 1 (1909) – as I. Kecskeméti demonstrated in these two cases – and Frank Martin's Prelude 3. Finally, Ohana openly proclaims his allegiance to Chopin in his Twenty-four Preludes and, like his model, finishes the final piece of the set on a low D.

Example 10. (*cont.*)

Example 10. (*cont.*)

Example 10. (*cont.*)

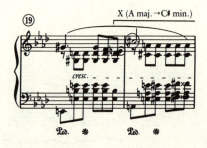

Example 10. (*cont.*)

Example 10. (*cont.*)

Example 10. (*cont.*)

The *Barcarolle*:
Auskomponierung and apotheosis

JOHN RINK

Chopin's *Barcarolle* has inspired the enthusiastic admiration of musicians and writers ever since its publication in 1846.[1] A work unlike any other by Chopin, neither in the 'epic' vein nor among his more reflective compositions, the *Barcarolle* can be called a masterpiece of Romantic piano music not only for its profoundly expressive musical language and unique form, but further-more for the remarkable structural synthesis that Chopin achieves in it.

Chopin ensures compositional unity in the *Barcarolle* at two levels by his commitment to what Heinrich Schenker, with reference to Bach, later called the 'principle of variety' (*Prinzip der Mannigfaltigkeit*).[2] Only rarely will Chopin express an idea more than once in the same manner: whether subtle (for instance, an added grace note) or more substantial (a new harmonic context), variation acts as the music's lifeblood. Taken to its full potential,

---

[1] Although virtually no analytical literature exists for the *Barcarolle*, numerous authors discuss the work, admittedly in rather general terms. See for instance Jarosław Iwaszkiewicz, '"Bar-carolla" Chopina', *Wiadomości Literackie* x/55 (526) (24 December 1933): 25; Karol Stromenger, 'Mesjaniczna "Barkarola" Chopina', *Wiadomości Literackie* xi/9 (536) (4 March 1934): 6; and Maurice Ravel, 'Les Polonaises, les Nocturnes, les Impromptus, la Barcarolle – Impressions', *Le Courrier Musical* (1 January 1910), 31–2 (although Arbie Orenstein questions the authenticity of Ravel's article in *Ravel Man and Musician* (New York, 1975), 124n.). See also Karl Tausig's programmatic description of the *Barcarolle* in Wilhelm von Lenz, *Die grossen Pianoforte-Virtuosen unserer Zeit aus persönlicher Bekanntschaft* (Berlin, 1872), 64–5.

The only substantial analytical discussion in the literature on the *Barcarolle* can be found in Hugo Leichtentritt, *Frédéric Chopin* (Berlin, 1905), 117, and *Analyse der Chopin'schen Klavier-werke*, 2 vols. (Berlin, 1922), ii, 274–9. See also Louis Ehlert, 'Frederic Chopin', *Aus der Tonwelt* (Berlin, 1877), 305, for criticism of the 'harmonic congestion' Ehlert perceived in the work.

[2] Heinrich Schenker, ed., *J.S. Bach Chromatische Phantasie und Fuge* (Vienna, 1910), 20. English translation from *J.S. Bach's Chromatic Fantasy and Fugue*, trans. Hedi Siegel (New York, 1984), 25.

195

the 'principle of variety' initiates a comprehensive process of intensification or 'apotheosis', where recapitulation '. . .reveals unexpected harmonic richness and textural excitement in a theme previously presented with a deliberately restricted harmonization and a relatively drab accompaniment'.[3]

'Apotheosis' in the *Barcarolle* engages virtually every element of the music, so that seemingly independent sections work together to create powerful climaxes. Rhythm, dynamics, phrasing, and even sonority increase the musical momentum that erupts in those climaxes, as do recurrent cadential patterns, motivic references, registral connections, and, on a larger scale, the return of thematic groups in the composer's unique interpretation of the 'sonata principle'.[4]

Although no one analytical approach can fully capture the work or address all of its parameters, graphic analysis elucidates the particularly strong tonal foundations on which Chopin builds the *Barcarolle*. The *Auskomponierung* or composing-out of a fundamental structure acts in conjunction with other agents of synthesis to define the 'essence' of the work: *Auskomponierung* enhances unity through the elaboration of an all-embracing harmonic plan and thus effectively overcomes the sense of thematic concatenation implicit in the *Barcarolle's* form.

The analysis that follows shows first how composing-out draws together apparently disjunct thematic and harmonic areas in the work (as seen in Example 1). Graphic analysis leads in turn to a discussion of other compositional features and their contribution to synthesis.[5]

---

[3] Edward Cone, *Musical Form and Musical Performance* (New York, 1968), 84.

[4] 'Chopin's early works display either a fundamental lack of comprehension of the sonata principle or a deliberate flouting of it; but of all the composers of the period he ultimately achieves the most personal and in some ways the most successful transformation of the form for his own purposes. I refer not only to the Fantasy and the last two Ballades, all openly based on modified sonata patterns, but to the Polonaise-Fantasy and the Barcarolle as well, which apply the sonata principle to forms derived elsewhere.' Cone, 83.

[5] A few words about the manuscripts of op. 60 should precede the analysis. In August 1846 Chopin forwarded the autograph manuscript of the *Barcarolle* and a copy he had made to the cellist Auguste Franchomme, who then passed on the first manuscript to Brandus for publication in Paris, and the copy to Maho, the Paris agent of Breitkopf and Härtel. At the same time, Chopin sent a further copy of the work to Auguste Léo for dispatch to Wessel in London.

The first manuscript has been classified as KK 808 in Krystyna Kobylańska, *Rękopisy utworów Chopina Katalog*, 2 vols. (Cracow, 1977), i, 324. (Hereafter this manuscript will be referred to as Ab, as in the German translation of the *Katalog: Frédéric Chopin Thematisch-bibliographisches Werkverzeichnis*, trans. Helmut Stolze (Munich, 1979), 130.) The Breitkopf *Stichvorlage* hereafter Ac) has the number KK 809 in the *Katalog*; the Wessel copy has been lost. A short sketch of the work (KK 807, or Aa) survives.

The Towarzystwo im. Fryderyka Chopina in Warsaw currently holds Aa. Manuscript Ab, reproduced in vol. iv of the series *Faksymilowane Wydanie Autografów F. Chopina* (Cracow, 1953), is in the Biblioteka Jagiellońska, and in 1986 Ac was acquired by the British Museum in London.

Example 1. Formal synopsis of the *Barcarolle*

Bars	Formal Division	Main harmonic area
1–3	Introduction	V (C♯)
4–16	Theme A	I (F♯)
17–23	'Development'	
24–34	Theme A′	
35–9	Transition	i → ♭III (f♯ → A)
40–50	Theme B(1)	♭III (A)
51–61	Theme B(1)′	
62–71	Theme B(2)	
72–7	Transition	V (C♯)
78–83	'Dolce sfogato'	
84–92	Theme A′	I (F♯)
93–102	Theme B(2)′	
103–10	Coda (B(1)″)	
111–16	Coda	

The background

The background structure of the *Barcarolle* shown in Example 2 incorporates the main harmonic areas outlined in the formal synopsis above: the dominant in the introduction leads into a large-scale progression from I through ♭III to V and back to I. The note in common to these harmonies, c♯″, acts as the primary melodic tone (*Kopfton*) of the fundamental line.[6] Only after the return of the tonic in bar 84 does the fundamental line complete its descent from $\hat{5}$ to $\hat{1}$, supported by another V–I cadence. As the I–♭III–V–I progression embellishes the tonic harmony, a simpler fundamental structure should be considered as the genesis of the background and thus of the entire work.

Example 2. Background

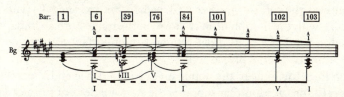

[6] The insistent focus throughout the *Barcarolle* on c♯″, and more generally on pitch class c♯, justifies its designation as primary melodic tone, although pitch class a♯ plays an important role as well. (Chopin occasionally highlights the tension between c♯ and a♯, as in the coda.)

The first middleground level

The composing-out of the background structure at the first middleground level (Mg_1) gives rise to an extensive elaboration of the primary melodic tone, c♯″, as shown in Example 3. The structural $\hat{5}$ generates several linear descents. The first two, c♯″–b′–a♯′ and c♯″–b′–a♯′–g♯′–f♯′, imitate the fundamental line and form the basis of Themes A and A′. The third, a stepwise descent from c♯″ to c♯′, comprises the transition to A major, Theme B(1) and the initial statement of B(2).

The first middleground level points to the process of intensification or 'apotheosis' important at more immediate structural levels. Initially Theme B(2) descends from e′–d′–c♯′ (($\hat{5}$–$\hat{4}$–$\hat{3}$) in the context of A major), failing to reach the local ($\hat{1}$) and thus emphasising c♯′, the link to the tonic F♯ major. When the theme returns in bars 93–103, however, it completes the descent from $\hat{5}$ to $\hat{1}$ and thereby resolves the tension latent in the music for thirty-two bars. In the piece itself, Chopin embellishes the $\hat{5}$ to $\hat{1}$ descent and the long-range resolution of tension it effects with intensely exciting harmony in a foretaste of the first eight bars of the coda (although at this stage the coda appears merely as a reminiscence of the fundamental line, harmonised like the other ($\hat{5}$–$\hat{1}$) elaborations by an authentic cadence).

The second middleground level

The second middleground level (Mg_2) reveals important features of the *Barcarolle* such as the prevalence of cadences based on ii–V–I progressions and the tonicisation of new harmonic areas through secondary dominants. The prolongation of background and first middleground structures generally manifests itself in third-based harmonic juxtapositions, linearly filled-in thirds, and the heightened tension between major and minor sonorities. (In the following graphs of Mg_2, the bass lies an octave higher than in the piece.)

Bars 1–39 – Although referred to as 'dominant ninth' in the literature,[7] in fact the dissonant sonority in the introduction acts as appoggiatura to the dominant seventh in the form of ii$^{6}_{5}$ over a C♯ pedal. (See Example 4.) The tonic then follows, with the motion from c♯″ to a♯′ in the treble both an imitation of the filled-in third c♯″–b′–a♯′ from Mg_1 and an important feature not only of Theme A but of Theme B(2) as well.

The resolution from the tonic to the dominant in bar 15 (via vi and V of V) leads to a V–IV–III♯³ progression that supports the stepwise descent from c♯″

---

[7] See for instance Paul Badura-Skoda, 'Chopin's Influence', in Alan Walker, ed., *Frédéric Chopin: Profiles of the Man and the Musician* (London, 1966), 271.

Example 3. Middleground₁

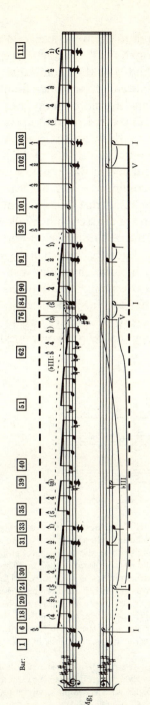

Example 4. Middleground₂, bars 1–39

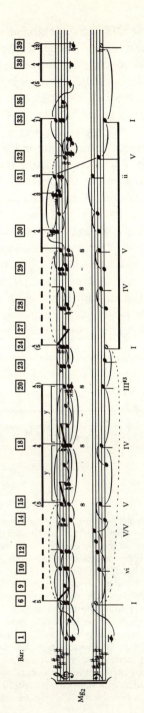

to b′ to a♯′. III♯³ acts as chromatic appoggiatura to the tonic in bar 24 and effects the return of Theme A′, where the motion from c♯″ to a♯′ appears (as in Theme A), followed by the tonicisation of IV and V via their dominants.

The cadence on the dominant in bar 29 (reminiscent of the motion from I to V in bars 6 to 15, although here at a more rapid harmonic pace) gives rise to an elaboration of the local (4̂), (3̂), and (2̂) centred on the supertonic harmony. The progression from V⁷ (bar 30) to ii (31) by way of ii♭₄ and V⁷ of ii culminates in a dissonance in bar 32 similar to that at the start of the piece both in its role as appoggiatura to the dominant and in the combination of supertonic harmony and pedal on c♯. Once the dominant resolves to the tonic, the motion from a♯′ to a♮′ cancels F♯ major; the resultant F♯ minor harmony assumes the role of vi in A major, the tonal centre of the section that follows.[8]

As Example 4 shows, the octave descent in the bass from bar 6 to bar 24 comprises an F♯ major scale without the seventh degree. Each pitch in the scale (marked with stems in the graph) supports a tonicised harmony with the exception of the penultimate, G♯, which serves as a passing note between the roots of the mediant and tonic harmonies. The bass thus articulates a concealed but nonetheless remarkable motivic reference to bar 115, where the same scale features prominently after a fleeting appearance in the previous bar.[9]

Example 5. Middleground₂, bars 39–51

[8] In the autograph manuscripts of the *Barcarolle*, Chopin carefully ensures the clarity of the voice-leading from bars 35–9. In Ab he adds quaver flags underneath the c♯s on beats three and four of bar 36 (having crossed out the beams connecting them to the three-quaver group), further highlighting the c♯s by adding fingering: they would thus be played by the second finger of the left hand, whereas the right hand would play the other pitches on beats three and four. Although Ac has neither the quaver flags nor the fingering (either a deliberate omission or an oversight – Chopin left out many details in copying Ac), both Ab and Ac emphasise the second pitch in the descent from c♯′ to b to a by two crotchet stems added to the b and B on the last beat of bar 38. (Unlike most editions of the *Barcarolle*, the Henle *Urtext* edition accurately reproduces the stems.) Chopin further suggests the importance of the bs by adding an accent in Ab (not present in Ac, however).

[9] Although the motivic reference might appear tenuous, it seems remarkable that Chopin should have changed the sketch of the coda (which has very different figuration) to this final version. Admittedly other factors might have led to the change, such as Chopin's wish simply to highlight the motive f♯″–d♯″–c♯″ important throughout the *Barcarolle*.

Bars 39–51 – Just as the passage from bar 15 to bar 20 features a chain of triads at the second middleground level, Theme B(1) similarly harmonises the linear descent from a′ to e′ with a succession of parallel triads. (See Example 5.) The tonicisation of each step in the perfect fourth comprises a progression based on a ii–V–I pattern. The A major triad in bar 40 assumes the role of ♭II of G♯ major, resolving first to the dominant and then to the tonic of G♯ major. In the next few bars, G♯ minor (with lowered third, b♮′) becomes ii in a ii–V⁷–I resolution in F♯ major. The change from a♯′ to a♮′, reminiscent of bar 35, gives rise to a descent from f♯′ to c♯′ (anticipating the descent to c♯″ later articulated by Theme B(2)), ultimately achieving a C♯ major triad in bar 50 which acts both as V of F♯ major/minor and as III♯³ of the local tonic, A major.

Theme B(1) in part derives its essential character and forward impetus from the tension between F♯ major and A major, each of which lays claim to the role of tonic. The rapidity with which B(1) abandons the newly established A major (so soon after leaving the tonic in bar 35) and enters into an harmonic excursion through G♯ major and then F♯ major seriously undermines A major as tonic. Unstable harmonic foundations lend to B(1) an episodic character (particularly in comparison with other themes in the work). Chopin exploits the tensions from conflicting harmonic implications by delaying until bar 50 (in fact until the last beat of the bar) both the local dominant, necessary to re-establish A major as the tonic, and the arrival of e″, the final pitch in the linear descent that started with a′.

Further tensions arise from a second line in bars 41–9 – a chromatic descent from c♯″ to a′ – which challenges the stepwise motion from a′ to e′ as the most important linear connection. At the foreground level and in the piece itself, the two-octave arpeggiations (as at bars 43 and 47) reinforce g♯′ and f♯′ in the structurally more significant linear descent from a′.

Bars 62–84 – Just as the delay of e″ until bar 50 creates middleground (and foreground) tensions, not until the arrival of the local tonic A major and Theme B(2) in bar 62 can the linear descent from a″ (bar 51) reach its goal, e″, with B(2) formed by the continuation of the linear motion to c♯″. (See Example 6.) The linearly filled-in sixth from a″ that follows imitates the descent from a″ to c♯″ initiated by B(1)′ in bar 51, followed by two more statements of the line e″–d″–c♯″ and then another at a higher registral level. Unlike Theme A, where the initial (5̂–4̂–3̂) is answered and completed by a (5̂–4̂–3̂–2̂–1̂) descent, here the line from e‴ to c♯‴ stops abruptly at the local (3̂) (an interruption caused by the e′ in bar 71), leaving unfinished the descent from 5̂ to 1̂ that only later B(2)′ completes.

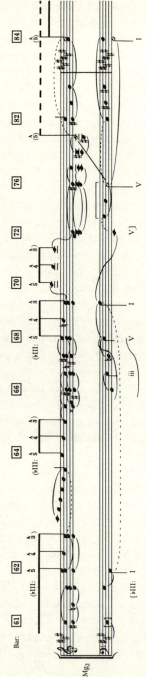

Example 6. Middleground₂, bars 61–84

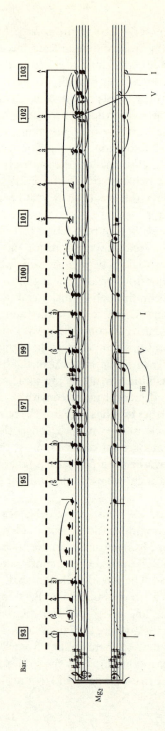

Example 7. Middleground₂, bars 93–103

Whereas harmonic instability pervades B(1) at the second middleground level, Theme B(2) rests on secure tonal foundations with only a brief excursion to the local mediant and dominant. A chain of secondary dominants effects the third-based progression from I through iii to V, whereupon the ($\hat{5}$–$\hat{4}$–$\hat{3}$) descent characteristic of B(2) returns, harmonised by a V–I cadence.

The re-establishment of the F♯ major tonic has as its first stage a motivically imitative descent from e to d to c♯ in the bass. The c♯ supports a tonicisation of C♯ major (its role as dominant to F♯ major also implied), in the context of which the ascent in tenths leads to the return of the tonic and Theme A'.

Bars 93–103 – After the reprise of A' (virtually identical to the graph of A' in Example 4) Theme B(2) returns, its second statement characterised by more complex harmonic activity, registral expansion, and the completion of the fundamental line, $\hat{5}$ to $\hat{1}$, at a new registral position, c♯''' to f♯''. (See Example 7.) The initial pitch in the treble, c♯''' (bar 93), appears only implicitly, due to the overlap of Themes A' and B(2)'; unlike its counterpart in the parallel bar (62), the c♯''' lacks a linear connection to the preceding thematic statement.

B(2)' once again focuses insistently on the motion from ($\hat{5}$–$\hat{4}$–$\hat{3}$) (now c♯'''–b''–a♯'') , although within a more elaborate harmonic context than in its first statement. First of all, a V–I cadence decorates the descent in bar 95 (as opposed to the unembellished A major harmony in the parallel bar), followed by a secondary dominant (V of V of iii) not present in the earlier passage. The heightened activity in bars 99–100 leads to a more expansive harmonisation of the final linear descent from $\hat{5}$ (shown in greater detail at the foreground level in Example 15). The cadence from II$_{♯3}^{7}$ through V^7 to I in bar 102 now supports the structural $\hat{2}$ and $\hat{1}$ in what amounts to the most compelling moment of closure in the work.

Bars 103–11 – Whereas at the first middleground level the coda offers a last reminiscence of the fundamental line, harmonised by a simple V–I cadence, its representation at the second middleground level indicates the tremendous harmonic complexity of the music after the completion of the fundamental line. (See Example 8.) The fermata at the end signifies the unfolding of the

Example 8. Middleground$_2$, bars 103–11

tonic harmony that takes place at the foreground level in a larger two-part division of the coda. Although no significant harmonic change occurs in the coda from bars 111–16 (hence the representation as I in Mg_2), Chopin invests the passage with particular beauty as well as an important structural function, as the discussion of the foreground level will point out.

The foreground

The prolongation of middleground structures in the foreground creates highly contrapuntal textures, where inner lines complement melodic and bass lines established at more remote structural levels. Thirds and sixths now accompany the melody, and enhanced enharmonic implications highlight the play between harmonic colour and harmonic function, as expressed for instance in the prevalent augmented sixth and dominant seventh harmonies. Throughout the foreground, various harmonies (among them augmented sixths) chromatically embellish the cadences – particularly the ii–V–I cadences – from the middleground.

Bars 1–16 – The introduction at the foreground level arises through the articulation of the ii$^6_3$ appoggiatura an octave higher. (See Example 9.) This generates a stepwise descent of first-inversion triads decorated by 'échappées', creating an alternation of harmonic colours as the chords descend. The bass, now expanded to the lower octave, supports an arpeggiation in the middle register from c#′ to c# to C#. In the piece itself, Chopin effectively conceals the structural skeleton of the introduction with slight variations and rhythmic subtleties.

The minor third from c#″ to a#′ in bar 6 imitates the same interval extended from bar 6 to bar 9 at the second middleground level. With the inflection to IV$^6_4$ in bar 8, the melodic third is restated at a higher register. After the return to the tonic, an inner line ascends chromatically (in contrary motion to the bass) and precipitates the arrival of vi, decorated by a linearly filled-in third in the treble. A second inner figure (motive y, shown in Example 4 and again in Example 19) then leads through the secondary dominant to V. In bar 12 another imitation of y follows, preceding a stepwise ascent to g#″ and then a leap to c#‴, the registral peak of the passage. The ensuing descent in sixths resolves to the tonicised dominant in bar 15, followed by a cadential extension incorporating the retrograde of motive y (labelled y′ here and in Example 19) framed by two outer lines.

Bars 20–4 – The decoration of III$^{#3}$ by its minor subdominant in bar 20

Example 9. Foreground, bars 1–16

Bar:

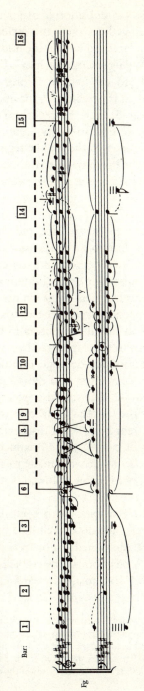

Example 10. Foreground, bars 20–4

Bar:

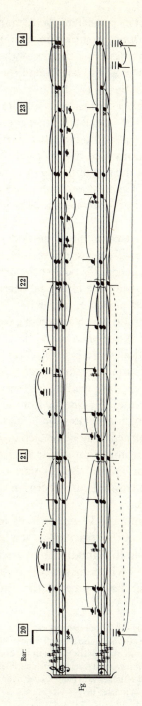

culminates in its parallel minor, A♯ minor, in another opposition of major and minor sonorities (as shown in Example 10). Inner lines carry the melodic weight, with a descent (imitative of the $\hat{5}$ to $\hat{1}$ fundamental line) in the middle register from bar 20 to bar 21 and then 21 to 22 (answered in each case by a third-progression in the treble from e♯″ to d♯″ to c×″ which restores A♯ major). Registral expansion establishes a new peak in the treble, f♯‴, the upper neighbour to e♯‴ (itself an anticipation of the local ($\hat{5}$) in the descent from e♯″ to c×″). In bar 22 the cadential extension figure returns in a new harmonic context, accompanied by two parallel descending lines in the middle register (the upper of the two imitating in augmentation the bottom line of the extension figure). The final assertion of A♯ major in bar 23 acts as appoggiatura to the tonic, as in the second middleground level.

Bars 28–39 – Contrapuntal motion predominates in this passage and thus creates a 'layered' foreground texture, as shown in Example 11. The cadences on IV and V in bars 28 and 29 now appear with added inner parts and descents in the treble from the fifth scale degrees of the subdominant and dominant harmonies (f♯″ and g♯″), prepared by appoggiaturas (respectively g♯″ in bar 28 and a♯″ in bar 29) which ascend in a registral connection over three bars to the local ($\hat{4}$), b″. No sooner has b″ been reached than the linear motion in the treble turns downward in a reflection of the ascent to ($\hat{4}$), supported by chromatic and diatonic passing notes. Other linear motions decorate the local ($\hat{2}$) (g♯‴) as the bass climbs to c♯, with C♯ the foundation of a remarkable embellishment of the cadence from ii⁷ to V in bar 32. The stepwise ascent in the treble which decorates the ii⁷ harmony over the C♯/c♯ pedal reaches d♯‴ only to be turned away before achieving its apparent goal, f♯‴ (thus creating a sense of incompletion whose later resolution in bars 92 and 93 launches the reprise of Theme (B(2)). After the cadence from the dominant to the tonic, the extension figure returns in the context of F♯ major, followed by the parallel minor.

The resolution to F♯ minor leads into a prolonged focus on c♯′ (another reminiscence of the structural $\hat{5}$, at a lower register), initially embellished by a filled-in fifth from f♯ and then by a descent from f♯′ (decorated first by its upper neighbour g♯′) which answers the bass motion. A neighbour-note embellishment of c♯′ in bar 38 prepares the descent from c♯′ to b to a, now reinforced by octaves.[10]

---

[10] Although bars 40–77 are not represented at the foreground level, certain features warrant attention. The canonic figure characteristic of B(1) first appears in the foreground (see Example 16 for the later statement of the canon in the coda). In the treble, important registral connections occur at the foreground level, first from g♯‴ in bar 43 to f♯‴ in bar 47, then from g♯‴ in 54 to f♯‴ in 58 and ultimately, in bar 60, to a‴ (the registral peak thus far, articulated again at the end of Theme B(2) in bar 70).

Example 11. Foreground, bars 28–39

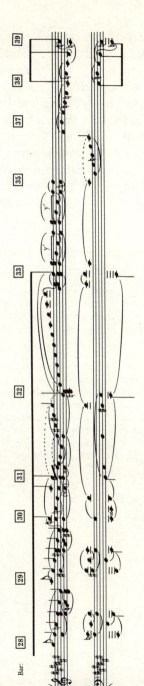

Example 12. Foreground, bars 78–84

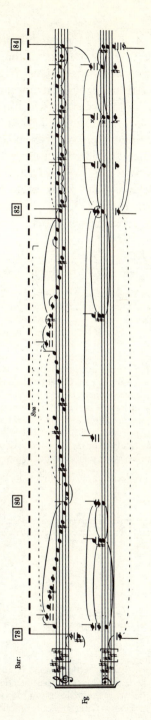

Bars 78–84 – The 'enraptured improvisation'[11] that ultimately leads into the reprise of Theme A transforms the simple C♯ major harmony of the middleground into a passage of great beauty. Marked 'sfogato' (freely given out), graceful fioriture highlight triadic pitches, first in a descent from e♯‴ to g♯′ and then in a two-octave ascent which culminates in a leap to e♯″″, the new registral peak (as shown in Example 12). Although it articulates a C♯ major scale virtually in entirety, the descent from e♯″″ skips from a♯″″ to f♯‴ and from a♯‴ to f♯″, delicately shaping the otherwise smooth linear motion. Middle lines from g♯′ to f♯′ to e♯′ ((5̂–4̂–3̂) in C♯ major) support the improvisatory fioriture in the treble. Above the chromatically embellished motion in the bass and middle registers in bars 82–3, an ornamental figure decorates c♯″, a figure whose motivic significance will be seen later.

Bars 93–103[12] – Chopin 'symphonically' elaborates the middleground structure of Theme B(2)′ in the foreground, where three linear strands weave a

The prolongation of the dominant of A major in bars 71–5 comprises three separate embellishments, each slightly different from the others (in keeping with Chopin's commitment to the 'principle of variety'). The two-bar tonicisation of C♯ major that follows exploits the adjacency of whole tones and semitones in a manner that suggests the passage had its genesis at the keyboard.

11 My translation. Leichtentritt, *Frédéric Chopin*, 117.
12 At the foreground level, the return of Theme A′ in bars 84–92 closely resembles its first appearance (shown in part in Example 11), and in the piece itself the two passages are also quite similar. But the second statement of A′ differs from the first in at least one important respect, if only in one of the two extant autograph manuscripts (Ac) and the editions prepared from it (Breitkopf and Härtel, 1846 and 1879, and Henle, 1978), as well as the first English edition (and thus presumably the Wessel *Stichvorlage*). Bar 92 appears in manuscript Ac with the ascending scale articulated by the upper notes of the right-hand chords doubled an octave below by the left hand, at every point except the first two chords of the third beat. (See Example 13a.)

Example 13. Left-hand chords, bar 92, after Ab and Ac

(a) After Ac   *cres.* _ _ _ _ _ _ _ _ _ _ _ _ _ _ _ _ _ _ _

(b) After Ab   *cres.* _ _ _ _ _ _ _ _ _ _ _ _ _ _ _ _ _ _ _

As for the first of these, Chopin intended the 'melodic' g♯′ to be played by the right-hand thumb. But what about the missing a♯′ on the second quaver of the third beat, whose omission seems curious if not musically unsound?

thickly textured contrapuntal fabric as a backdrop to the complex harmonic motion in the passage. Chromatic passing notes decorate both the bass and the melody (now harmonised in thirds), while triads in the middle register not only offer harmonic support to the melody but also create a third contrapuntal strand, articulated by their uppermost pitches.[13]

The answer lies in manuscript Ab. When he prepared Ac and/or the Wessel *Stichvorlage* from Ab (the order of the two copies is uncertain, although it appears that Chopin completed the Wessel manuscript before Ac), Chopin inaccurately copied the original version of bar 92, where compressed ledger lines above the second left-hand chord from beat three make the a♯′ appear at precisely the same level as the f♯′ of the previous chord. (See Example 13b.) In Ab Chopin omits not a♯′ but f♯′ in the second chord of the third beat (with the f♯′ as well, the chord would have been awkward to play in tempo) so that with the exception of the g♯′ played by the right hand, the left hand doubles the entire ascending scale.

Why Chopin did not later notice his copying error is unclear. Another similar mistake in bar 95 (discussed in n. 13) suggests that he failed to spot errors, even ones of musical import, if they stayed within the prevailing harmonic context.

[13] The second left-hand chord on the third beat of bar 95 differs in manuscripts Ab and Ac, almost certainly the result of another copying error. In Ab the chord comprises a♯–c♯′–f♯′, whereas it appears in Ac as c♯–f♯–a♯, as shown in Example 14.

Example 14. Left hand, bar 95, after Ab and Ac

(a) After Ab

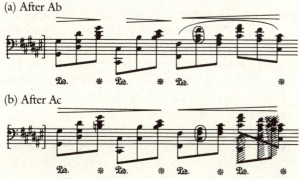

(b) After Ac

In preparing Ac from Ab or from the Wessel *Stichvorlage*, Chopin inadvertently copied the third and fourth beats of bar 94 twice, first in bar 94 itself and then (incorrectly) a second time, as the third and fourth beats of bar 95. The fourth beat of bar 95 in Ac reveals his error: Chopin crossed out a first version of the fourth beat which on close inspection proves to be identical to the fourth beat of bar 94. The resultant harmonic clash on the fourth beat alerted him to his mistake, so he obliterated the first version of beat four and changed it to conform to Ab. But as the *third* beat sounded consonant, he failed to notice the incorrectly copied chordal configuration (as well as the pedalling from bar 94), an oversight which has haunted editions of the *Barcarolle* to this day, even the Henle *Urtext* edition.

Several other factors suggest that the difference stems from a copying error made in the preparation of Ac. The first English edition 'correctly' prints the passage, that is, as in Ab. Furthermore the voice-leading of the middle line requires an f♯′ on the third beat of bar 95 to complete the motion from g♯′ to e♯′ at the ends of the first and second beats of bar 95 (and in general Chopin paid careful attention to resolutions of this kind). Finally, in the original, 'correct' version in Ab, the third and fourth beats of bar 95 match in configuration the last two beats of bar 93 but at a higher registral level, thus contributing to the apotheotic excitement of the passage.

Harmonic density reaches its peak in the elaboration of the fundamental line in bars 100–3, where each pitch in the line appears in the context of a consonant although not necessarily diatonic harmony. (See Example 15.)

Example 15. Foreground, bars 100–3

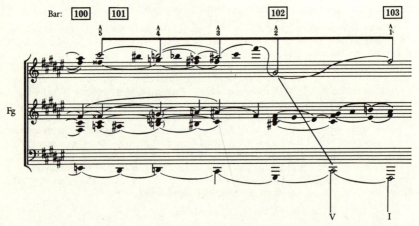

An augmented sixth chord in bar 100 supports the structural $\hat{5}$, c♯‴, resolving chromatically to V⁷ of II in bar 101. Harmonised by ♭II⁶₄, the $\hat{4}$ appears in a chromatic descent from c♯‴ that ends with the arrival of the structural $\hat{3}$, a♯″, and the I⁶₄ harmony (preceded by another augmented sixth chord). The prolonged decoration of $\hat{2}$ that follows elaborates the harmonic foundation laid in the middleground and dramatically completes the descent of the fundamental line with the resolution to $\hat{1}$ in bar 103.

Bars 103–11 – Chopin reserves the most dramatic musical gesture in the *Barcarolle* for the coda, where he fleshes out the middleground structure with complex counterpoint and sonorities of extraordinary dissonance in relation to the pedal on F♯′. Furthermore he counters the registral contraction prevalent in the passage by a four-octave arpeggiation of the augmented sixth harmony in bar 110. (See Example 16.) The canonic figure characteristic of Theme B(1) appears in the treble, set against two contrapuntal lines in the bass (the lower of the two highlighted in the score by crotchet stems).

Whereas in the piece itself Chopin plays upon subtle enharmonic implications, the foreground graph represents harmonic colours in functional terms, with reference to the underlying progression generated in the middleground. For instance the harmony on the first beat of bar 109 appears in the foreground not as A♯ major (let alone B♭ major, as Badura-Skoda would have it)[14] but as a diminished-seventh chord with appoggiatura, a♯′.

---

[14] Badura-Skoda, 266.

Example 16. Foreground, bars 103–11

Bars 111–16 – The resolution to the tonic in bar 111 (initially with the third only implicitly stated) leads into a six-bar prolongation of F♯ major that forms the second part of the coda. The cadential extension figure appears again and resolves a sense of imbalance latent since bar 93, where it had been elided by the overlap of Themes A′ and B(2)′. A linear descent in the middle register from c♯′ to a♯ accompanies the extension motive (bars 111–13), with the goal of the descent, a♯, the first note of the new theme that follows in the left hand. Both the new theme and the fioriture in the treble highlight pitch classes f♯, a♯, and c♯ in an arpeggiation of the tonic triad that first establishes the *Barcarolle*'s registral peak, f♯′′′′ (related by semitone to the previous registral high point, the e♯′′′′ in bar 80), and then plummets six octaves from the peak to F♯′, the bass foundation of the coda. Although essentially an accompaniment to the middle-register theme, the fioriture articulate several motives with connections elsewhere in the piece (in particular x and x′, to be discussed later, as well as the f♯–b–a♯ figure heard earlier in bar 7) in a final motivic summing-up. At the end, the motion in octaves from pitch classes c♯ to f♯ concludes the three-bar arpeggiation of the tonic triad.

Beyond the foreground

Chopin fully reveals his compositional mastery in the elaboration from the foreground level to the *Barcarolle* itself, where rhythm, phrase rhythm, dynamics, sonority and timbre breathe life into the tonal foundation of the work. The remarkable ingenuity with which Chopin employs these 'energising' forces not only enhances the overall compositional synthesis: Chopin furthermore ensures that the *Barcarolle* stands apart from other works in the genre, many of which have a predictable or even trite character.[15]

Although various rhythmic features in the work clearly derive from the genre, the *Barcarolle* lacks the sense of rhythmic monotony virtually inherent in other pieces reliant on those same features through Chopin's commitment to the 'principle of variety'. The 'rocking barcarolle rhythm' (to borrow Leichtentritt's phrase)[16] takes three forms, as shown in Example 17. The first

---

[15] Carl Dahlhaus makes a related point regarding the demise of genres in the nineteenth century. Until about 1800, he writes, 'A work formed not so much an isolated, closed whole, an individuality enduring in itself, as, rather, it exemplified a type, feeding on the historical substance of this type, which had developed in the course of decades or even centuries, and requiring listeners to connect the work with the type in order to understand it. Thus, if a piece of music bore the title "Barcarole," it was at least as important, as Ernst Bloch has noticed, that the piece conspicuously represent the type, barcarole, as that it be an individual work with its definite, unrepeatable characteristics.

  'But since the late eighteenth century all genres have rapidly lost substance. In Chopin's Barcarole (although even this piece invokes a picture of Venice) the peculiar, unrepeatable features are more essential than any general qualities that it shares with other pieces of the same name.' *Esthetics of Music* [*Musikästhetik*], trans. William W. Austin (Cambridge, 1982), 15.

[16] My translation. Leichtentritt, *Frédéric Chopin*, 117.

Example 17. Rhythmic cells

of these enters after the three-bar introduction and establishes the rhythmic foundation of Theme A, lasting until the end of bar 11 where steady quavers make their way into the accompaniment. As the piece progresses, the first rhythm appears again only in the context of Theme A′. Its registral disposition changes, however, when the rhythm passes from the right hand to the left hand in bars 28 and 29 and later in the parallel passage.

After the remarkable rhythmic unfolding in bar 1, the six-quaver rhythm propels the harmonic descent through the rest of the introduction. The six-quaver figure features prominently thereafter, primarily in Theme A, the accompaniment of B(2), the reprise of B(2) in bars 93–102, and finally the first part of the coda, where it imbues the music with particular energy. The rhythm furthermore participates in the process of thematic intensification. In its first appearance in bars 40–50, Theme B(1) derives momentum in part from the middle voice (in steady quavers) and in part from the rocking rhythm in the bass (the third rhythmic group in Example 17, the most characteristic barcarolle rhythm). At bar 50, however, the bass yields entirely to the six-quaver rhythm and channels the impetus it generates towards the first expansion of B(1) in bars 51–61, an expansion which sets the stage for the later 'apotheosis' of B(1) in the coda.

Chopin establishes the characteristic crotchet–quaver rhythmic pattern as a salient feature only in bar 12, with subtle hints of the rhythm in bar 2 (highlighting the f♯″ and d♯″ of later motivic importance as well as ensuring rhythmic variety in the introduction) and then in bars 9 and 11. The cadential extension figure in bar 15 combines the pattern with a three-quaver group in preparation for the more emphatic statement of the crotchet–quaver rhythm in the left hand in bars 20–3. In the transition from bar 35 to bar 39, the crotchet–quaver pattern insinuates itself into the steady flow of quavers so that bar 39 grows directly out of the transitional passage. Later the characteristic rhythm appears prominently in B(2) and B(2)′, in the transition from V of ♭III to V in bars 72–7, and finally in the middle-register theme in bars 113 and 114 and the octaves in bar 116.

Although the three rhythmic groups shown in Example 17 predominate, Chopin constructs the *Barcarolle* from other rhythmic materials as well. The dotted figure first heard in bar 11 acts motivically throughout the piece: further appearances in bars 13 and 30 and the variation of the rhythm in bars 17, 19, and 21 prepare the most important manifestation of the figure, the canon in B(1) and B(1)' (bars 42, 46, 53, and 57) and in the coda (bars 103, 104, 107, and 108). The dotted rhythm also colours both the first appearance of Theme B(2) (bar 70) and its 'apotheosis' (bars 95 and 101).

Semiquavers appear gradually, first in the accompaniment of Theme A; then in the trill figures at the ends of bars 11, 12, and 13; and finally in the descent in sixths in bar 14 and the extension figure that grows from it. Throughout the work semiquavers act in an ornamental capacity, as in Theme B(1)'s arpeggiations, the fioritura in bars 80 and 81, and the two-bar transition that follows, with even more rapid rhythms to come in bars 110 and 113–15.

Occasionally rhythmic activity ceases altogether, usually at moments of structural importance: the end of the introduction (bar 3); the interruption of the fundamental line in Theme B(2) (bars 70–1); and, at the end of B(2)', the arrival of the structural $\hat{2}$ and the imminent completion of the fundamental line (bar 102).

Unlike certain rhythmic features, the phrase structure of the *Barcarolle* appears to have little or no relation to the genre, nor for that matter is it characteristic of Chopin's music more generally. When one considers that Chopin '. . .absorbed, digested, assimilated, and nourished himself on the four-measure concept. . .',[17] the phrase structure of the *Barcarolle* seems particularly remarkable in its asymmetry.

Short phrases often only one or two bars in length appear throughout the work as the result of the many cadences articulated at the foreground level. The short phrase units form nine-, ten-, and eleven-bar periods, as opposed to the four-bar period typical of the barcarolle genre. (Regular four-bar periods occur only in the coda in bars 103–6, 107–10, and finally 113–16.)

Chopin ensures the coherence of the phrase structure by the large-scale repetition of periods, as in the two statements of B(1) in bars 40–50 and bars 51–61. A and A' have the same phrase structure (a remarkable feature, as otherwise the two passages substantially differ), similarly B(2) and B(2)' (although they differ in important respects as well). On a smaller scale, Chopin enhances the connection of short phrases by extending slurs over barlines and by subtleties in dynamics: crescendos and decrescendos often link phrases and overcome the sense of fragmentation potential in the series of one- and two-bar units.

Throughout the *Barcarolle*, dynamics articulate a clearly defined structure of their own. Chopin carefully distinguishes between words such as 'crescendo',

---

[17] Cone, 80.

'*forte*', and '*sotto voce*' (usually abbreviated in the standard way) with which he establishes a dynamic background for a certain passage or theme, and symbols such as hairpins which create shadings within that general dynamic background.[18] Various dynamic shadings colour Theme A, for instance, with the *p* in bar 4 a point of reference for those shadings until bar 12, when the word 'cresc.' signals a departure from *p* to the *f* in bar 14. Chopin makes the distinction between word and symbol particularly clear in Theme B(1), where in bar 43 he reminds the performer of the dynamic background of the theme (*sotto voce*, from bar 40) by the words 'sempre *p*' but in the same bar specifies a hairpin crescendo. Of the various thematic statements, only B(2) fails to establish a dynamic context at the outset (although *p* appears later in bar 68); otherwise Chopin clearly specifies the dynamic background of each theme.[19]

The dynamic structure of the *Barcarolle* enhances the overall momentum towards 'apotheosis' in part through the contrast of dynamic backgrounds. Theme A appears first in the context of *p* but in later statements (bars 24–34 and 84–92) with *f* as its dynamic background. Similarly B(1) initially establishes a context of *sotto voce* (bars 40–50), later to become *f* (bars 51–61). The two statements of B(2) have remarkably different dynamic backgrounds: the expansion of B(2)'s initial *piano* or *mezzo piano* to the *fortissimo* of Theme B(2)' heightens the sense of 'apotheosis' in bars 93–103.

Chopin creates a particularly beautiful effect in the dynamic contrast of bars 32 and 92. The first chordal ascent fades away in a striking diminuendo ('dim.', with a hairpin decrescendo as well) as opposed to the crescendo in bar 92, which lends such energy to the second ascent that it attains its registral goal ($f\sharp''''$) and thereby initiates the return of B(2) in expanded form. The striking 'impressionistic'[20] pedal effect that colours the two passages makes the chordal ascents all the more breathtaking.

Perhaps more than any other work by Chopin (with the possible exception of the Polonaise-fantasy op. 61), the *Barcarolle* reveals the composer's great sensitivity to pedalling and its importance in the creation of piano sonority and

---

[18] Schenker comments in several of his essays on the 'layered' nature of a piece's dynamics, with apparent interest in developing a theory relating dynamic structure to pitch levels. See for instance 'Joh. S. Bach: Sechs Sonaten für Violine. Sonata III, Largo', *Das Meisterwerk in der Musik*, (Munich, 1925), i, 71, as well as *J.S. Bach Chromatische Phantasie und Fuge*, 42–5. Charles Burkhart discusses the notion, later abandoned by Schenker, in 'Schenker's Theory of Levels and Musical Performance', *Aspects of Schenkerian Theory*, ed. David Beach (New Haven, 1983), 95–112.

[19] In his dissertation, Jeffrey Kallberg points out the not unrelated way in which Chopin attaches structural importance to the term 'ritenuto'. ('The Chopin Sources: Variants and Versions in Later Manuscripts and Printed Editions' (Diss., U. of Chicago, 1982), 303ff.) In the *Barcarolle*, 'ritenuto' appears in three places, all of structural importance: bar 61, just before B(2) enters; bar 83, before the reprise of A'; and bar 102, at the cadence completing the fundamental line, after which the coda begins.

[20] My translation. Leichtentritt, *Analyse der Chopin'schen Klavierwerke*, ii, 276.

resonance. Although the two autograph manuscripts vary somewhat, Chopin painstakingly notates pedal markings in the *Barcarolle* not only to attain maximum resonance and to create 'impressionistic' effects (as in bars 32 and 92, as well as in bar 14), but to imply harmonic rhythm and to highlight individual pitches (for instance the left-hand a♯ in bar 4 *et seq.*). The sensitively notated pedalling furthermore ensures that thickly scored 'symphonic' textures never sound unclear.

Various compositional features indicate that the *Barcarolle* had its genesis at the keyboard,[21] not least among them the pedalling. The improvisatory *dolce sfogato* passage, the fioriture in bar 110, and the six-octave cascade at the end point to the work's 'instrumentally idiomatic' conception,[22] as well as the disposition of the left-hand chords (similar to other passages in Chopin's music, such as the Ballade op. 47, bars 213ff. and the Polonaise-fantasy op. 61, bars 32ff. and 249ff.) in the reprise of B(2). The composer's considerations of 'pianistic comfort' extend to the F♯ major tonality itself, as Eigeldinger suggests with regard to Chopin's more general predilection for keys with many sharps or flats.[23]

Chopin builds his themes with great sensitivity to the way they lie on the keyboard, often with powerful pianistic effect: the performer feels all the more keenly the contrast between B(2)'s first appearance in A major and its reprise in F♯ major by virtue of the two different keyboard layouts. As in the G♭ major Study op. 10 no. 5, certain motivic shapes stem directly from the disposition of black and white keys, for instance motive x and its inversion x' (shown in Example 18), played only on the black keys.

Example 18. Motives x and x'

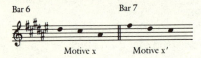

Bar 6   Bar 7

Motive x   Motive x'

Their appearance throughout the *Barcarolle* means that motives x and x' help to enhance compositional synthesis, as if through a process of improvisation[24] (where, as traditionally practised, motivic and thematic connections played an important role in ensuring unity). The two shapes appear in various con-

[21] Numerous contemporary sources indicate that Chopin completed the most essential work on a composition while at the piano. See Kallberg, 154–7.

[22] Cone, 84; furthermore see his comments on the '. . .unique key-preferences of Romantic themes. . .' (84 and 86).

[23] Jean-Jacques Eigeldinger, *Chopin: Pianist and Teacher*, 3rd, English edn. (Cambridge, 1986), 100, n. 30.

[24] Schenker often characterises the act of composition in terms of improvisation (with reference to the historical improvisation tradition), claiming for instance that '. . .only what is composed

texts: first in Theme A (bars 6, 7, 8, 9, and 11) and A' (24 and 25; later, 84, 85, and 86); then in the transition from F♯ major to A major (bars 35 and 36, and bar 38 in retrograde); and finally in B(1) (in the middle voice, in retrograde, and more profoundly in the canon in 42, 46, 53, and 57). Later appearances in the coda (bars 103, 104, 107, and 108) lead to the last elaboration of the motives in bars 113–15.

Other motivic and thematic connections similarly enhance synthesis in the *Barcarolle*. Motive y and its retrograde y' (shown in Example 19) appear often,

Example 19. Motives y and y'

Bars 11–12   Bar 15

Motive y   Motive y'

particularly at moments of cadential significance such as the tonicisation of the dominant in bar 11 (imitated in the next bar) and in bars 17 and 19 in the harmonic descent from V through IV to III[13]. The middle voice in the extension figure articulates y' in bars 15, 18, 33, 111, and 112. Elsewhere in the piece recurrent cadential progressions subtly draw together various passages, as in bars 92 and 102 and, later, bars 105 and 109.

Melodic contour acts as an equally subtle agent of synthesis. As a pattern for various cadential and ornamental figures in the work, the melodic contour of bar 6 reappears first as the trill figure in bar 11 (transposed down a fourth) and later at the cadence in bar 50 (with chromatic alterations). In the parallel bar 61, interpolations extend the basic pattern over the barline to form the first few notes of Theme B(2) in bar 62 (just as B(2) completes the linear descent from the previous passage in the middleground and foreground). Later appearances include the trill figure[25] in bar 71 (culminating in bar 72) and, more profoundly, bars 82–4, where the contour appears four times in preparation for its return in the original context of Theme A.

Bass contours similarly enhance synthesis, although perhaps less explicitly than the melodic pattern. The keyboard genesis of the *Barcarolle* suggests itself

with the sweep of improvisation [*aus dem Stegreif*] guarantees unity in a composition'. ('Organic Structure in Sonata Form', trans. Orin Grossman, in Maury Yeston, ed., *Readings in Schenker Analysis and Other Approaches* (New Haven, 1977), 39.). See also Schenker's 'Die Kunst der Improvisation', *Das Meisterwerk*, i, 9–40. My paper '"Improvisation" in Schenkerian Theory and its Relation to Musical Structure', delivered at the Cambridge University Music Analysis Conference (Cambridge, 26–9 September 1986), focused on this aspect of Schenker's theoretical work.

[25] Perhaps Chopin's wish to ensure the clarity of the connection explains why the trill figure appears in the sketch, which otherwise features only the coda.

again in the linear nature of the bass: Chopin builds the work largely on the foundation of ascending and descending lines, some of which connect several bars in a single bass gesture. Pedal points (a general feature of Chopin's late style) occur throughout the work, not only in the introduction and coda but in Theme A (on F♯), the 'development' in bars 20–3 (on A♯ and A♯′), Theme A′ (on F♯ and F♯′ in bars 24–8 and on F♯′ in bars 84–8), and Theme B(2) (on A). Finally a C♯ pedal supports the *dolce sfogato* passage.

Both bass and treble articulate registral connections that extend over many bars. As we have seen, Chopin links the resolution from the e♯′′′′ in bar 80 to the registral peak of the composition, f♯′′′′, in the penultimate bar. A similar registral connection occurs in the bass descent from A′ (51) to G♯′ (53) to F♯′ (57) to E′, the goal of the descent attained not in bar 61 (where E, not E′, appears as the foundation of the local dominant chord) but in bar 72, after a ten-bar delay.

Throughout the *Barcarolle*, F♯′ and C♯′ act as the cornerstones of the bass foundation, with particularly frequent reference made to F♯′ after it enters in bar 24. The opening octave on C♯′ establishes a lower registral boundary touched upon only one other time (at the registrally and dynamically enhanced chordal ascent in bar 92) in a gesture that spans over ninety bars.

Apart from this registral connection, it is not immediately clear what relation the three-bar introduction has to the rest of the work. Such introductions tend to remain structurally independent in Chopin's music, as Gerald Abraham points out: whereas Chopin's codas '. . .not infrequently have a structural function. . .his introductions are seldom important structurally; they serve only to attract attention, or in his later works, more subtly, to place a harmonic curtain before the tonic key and so heighten the effect of its first appearance'.[26]

In the *Barcarolle*, however, Chopin invests the introduction with particular importance by laying the foundation for subtle connections throughout the work: the registral boundary on C♯′; the elaboration of the supertonic over a dominant pedal; and motives such as y (in the inner voice) and the third from f♯′′ to d♯′′ important not only in x but, with the two notes that precede it, as a hint of the melodic figure in bars 47–8 and 58–9. Of even greater importance, the introduction states from the outset Chopin's commitment to the 'principle of variety' in the way he fleshes out its structural skeleton with subtle variations in contour, rhythm, and harmonic colour.

That commitment more generally enables Chopin to transcend a sense of the derivative in the *Barcarolle*, even though the melodic thirds and sixths, grace notes, rhythm, and lyrical character show that he borrowed from the genre. Although a more detailed study of the work's relation to the genre

[26] Gerald Abraham, *Chopin's Musical Style* (London, 1939), 47.

might shed light on Chopin's conception of the piece, here it suffices to note the extreme subtlety and beauty with which he fills in the tonal framework of the music through the 'principle of variety', and by continually building towards 'apotheosis'. In the masterful integration of its expressive effect and structural foundations, Chopin has secured for the work a place among the most powerful and compelling compositions of the nineteenth century.

Chopin's Fantasy, op. 49: the two-key scheme

CARL SCHACHTER

Introduction

'If a well-written composition can be compared with a noble architectural edifice in which symmetry must predominate, then a fantasy well done is akin to a beautiful English garden, seemingly irregular, but full of surprising variety, and executed rationally, meaningfully, and according to plan.'[1] Carl Czerny, who wrote this passage around 1836, was using the word 'fantasy' to mean an improvised, as distinct from a composed, piece. His remarks, however, apply equally well to the written-out fantasies of J.S. and C.P.E. Bach, Mozart, and Beethoven, for as the name suggests, these are pieces designed to sound like improvisations, abounding in evaded cadences, abrupt modulations, and unexpected juxtapositions, and tending strongly to emphasise flux and surprise at the expense of stability and order.

Few genres of tonal composition offer the musical analyst so many difficulties as does the fantasy; most of these difficulties relate to issues of unity and continuity, for the disruptions at the surface can make it hard to discern any guiding idea or underlying plan. Such is the case with the piece that forms the subject of this chapter, Chopin's great Fantasy op. 49. Written some five years after Czerny's words, it represents one of the last manifestations of a remarkable musical tradition; probably the decline in public improvisation spelled the end of the composed fantasy as a viable genre, except in debased and popularised forms like the medley of national airs and the operatic pot-pourri.

---

[1] Carl Czerny, *A Systematic Introduction to Improvisation on the Pianoforte* op. 200, trans. and ed. A. Mitchell (New York, 1983), 2.

This Fantasy has a complex and highly original tonal structure, one feature of which it shares with a fair number of Chopin's larger works. Like the Second Ballade, the Second Scherzo, and the Bolero, to name some of the others, our Fantasy begins and ends in different keys. Such a departure from the norms of tonal composition always poses certain questions for anyone trying to understand a piece in which it occurs. These are: (1) Is the piece tonally unified? Can one understand it in relation to a single governing tonal centre, or does it flesh out a progression from an initial centre to a closing one of equal status? (2) If there is a single primary tonic, which one is it? (3) How does the composer establish its primacy? and (4) What is the artistic purpose of the two-key scheme; how does it influence the piece's larger shape, its details, and its expressive character?[2]

With respect to the Fantasy, I have always felt that the answers to the first two questions were clear: there is a governing tonal centre, and it is Ab major, the closing key, rather than F minor, the opening one. The fact that the piece is almost universally known as the 'Fantasy in F Minor' is, I think, beside the point. Pieces that change their main (or seemingly main) tonic are usually known by the first 'key'; this is for easy identification and does not represent an analytical judgement. Many musicians (among them Czerny) refer to Beethoven's op. 77 as the 'Fantasy in G minor', although the initial G minor lasts for about three bars.[3] It is my impression, by the way, that most musicians who have thought about the Chopin Fantasy's tonal scheme agree with me in hearing Ab as the primary centre.[4]

In this paper I shall try to support my judgement about the Fantasy's tonal structure by pointing out the strategies that tend to establish Ab as main tonic (the third of the questions listed above). I shall also attempt to examine the compositional implications of the two-key scheme (the last of my four questions). In doing so, I shall make use of the analytical approach of Heinrich Schenker, who regarded Chopin as one of the greatest composers, and whose work has done so much to illuminate his genius.

The form: an overview

In one important way Chopin's op. 49 differs from the description by Czerny quoted at the beginning of the chapter, and interestingly enough it differs in the direction of regularity, for symmetry, created by the transposed repetition of

---

[2] See Felix Salzer, 'Tonality in Medieval Polyphony' in *The Music Forum* (New York, 1967), i, 65-7. See also Harald Krebs, 'Alternatives to Monotonality', *Journal of Music Theory* xxv/1 (1981), 1-16.
[3] Czerny, *A Systematic Introduction*, 177.
[4] See, for example, Harald Krebs, 'Third Relation and Dominant in Late 18th- and Early 19th-Century Music', (Diss., Yale University, 1980), 138-42.

large sections, predominates far more than in any of the great eighteenth-century fantasies that I know. Example 1, a chart of the form, shows the extent of this repetition. After an introductory slow march in two strains comes a passage in the arpeggiated texture that might well begin a keyboard fantasy (compare Mozart's Fantasy in D minor). Here, however, it forms a transition from the march to a chain of linked phrases; most of the phrases are eight bars long, and most of them change the previous texture, rhythm, melody, or harmonic focus in some noticeable way. I call this chain a 'cycle', for it recurs twice, the first time broken off, and the second time complete. Consulting Example 1 together with the score will show that bars 155–79 (the incomplete cycle) contain the same material as 68–92 and that 235–315 are a slightly varied transposition of 68–148; this is more large-scale repetition than would be usual in a sonata-form movement, let alone a fantasy. That it is artistically possible here is due, first of all, to the richly varied thematic design, whose many elements are indicated in a rather simple-minded way by lower-case letters above the horizontal line in Example 1. And more importantly, the three cycles are phases of one continuous process; each return – even in exact transposition – brings with it a new function and a new meaning.

The tonal structure: an overview

The uncharacteristically symmetrical form relates closely to the Fantasy's tonal structure, about which I can now begin to make some preliminary observations. (The following brief discussion is based upon Example 1, which should be consulted together with the score.) The opening march clearly centres on F. The mode, basically minor, changes to major for the second of its two strains; the codetta hints at the return to minor that coincides with the beginning of the arpeggiated transitional passage.

At the beginning of the first cycle, we still hear F as tonic, but the ensuing tonal instability weakens its pull without at first establishing a new centre of comparable strength. Gradually, however, E♭ major emerges as just such a centre, and before the cycle ends, we are solidly in E♭. Of course the transposition of this process that occurs during the third cycle leads us to A♭, our closing centre. The A♭ receives the additional emphasis of the extended cadence and coda, which provide the structural resolution of a melodic $\hat{3}$–$\hat{2}$–$\hat{1}$ over I–V–I. And owing to the repetitive, cyclical design, the ear can easily connect the final A♭ with the previous E♭ and infer a large-scale progression of dominant to tonic.

The second, incomplete, cycle and the Lento sostenuto section that follows it remain, I believe, in the domain of the E♭ harmony. I hope to substantiate this belief when I discuss these sections in detail; here I shall simply point to

Example 1. Chart of form

Form:

Large	March					
Small	1st strain	2nd strain	Codetta	Transition — 1st phrase	2nd phrase	descending run
Groups of bars:	4+6 ⌒ 4+6,	8, 8,	6	11	10	4+downbeat
	①1	㉑21	㊲37	㊸43	㊵54	㉔64

(⌒ = phrase link; | = phrase separation)

1st cycle

	a	b	c	d	e	f	g	Transition — h (from bars 43–68)
	1+8	8	8	8	8	8+10	8 8	12+downbeat
	68	77	85	93	101	109	127	143

2nd cycle (incomplete) — Lento sostenuto (3-part form)

	a	b	c	h	j	k	j	Transition — h
	1+8	8	8	4+4+11	8,	8	8	12+downbeat
	155	164	172	180	199	207	215	223

3rd cycle — Extended cadence and coda

	a	b	c	d	e	f	g	h	adagio j	coda h
	1+8	8	8	8	8	8+10	8 8	10	2	11
	235	244	252	260	268	276	294	310	320 322	332

the emphasised tonal areas – E♭ major and minor, G♭ major, and B major (=C♭) – and suggest that their combined presence is certainly compatible with the assumption of an underlying E♭ centre that mixes major and minor modes.

Now the succession F minor, E♭ major, A♭ major makes a logical progression toward A♭ as a goal; it makes no such progression in F minor. Therefore the possibility that F represents the governing tonic of the Fantasy can, I think, be ruled out. And the march's closure occurs much too soon and is much too weak to bear comparison with the powerful final cadence, which forms the resolution not just of one section but of the whole Fantasy. This makes most unlikely the notion that F and A♭ enjoy equal status.

Of course only a comprehensive view of the Fantasy – one that relates detail to the large structure – can provide a fuller answer to the question of tonal unity. I hope to provide such a view in a section-by-section discussion. And since one needs some feeling for the whole in order to make any sense of the parts, I should like to present first a picture of the Fantasy's large-scale tonal structure, encompassing the background and the earlier levels of the middle-ground (Example 2). The reader can regard this picture, in its several stages, as a hypothetical construct to be tested against the discussion of detail that follows.

Example 2a shows the Fantasy's background structure together with what I would regard as the first level of middleground. (In its harmonic aspect and in the contour of the bass line, the example corresponds to none of Schenker's models of the first middleground level – a fact that points to the uniqueness of the Fantasy's tonal plan.) The bass line divides into two phases, indicated in the graph by ascending and descending stems. The first phase consists of what Schenker calls an 'auxiliary cadence' – a progression that leads via V to I, but that lacks a structural I at the beginning. Here, of course, the F minor chord replaces the missing opening tonic; from the perspective of the whole piece, the F minor represents VI of A♭ (or, expressed in contrapuntal terms, the V's upper neighbour). At the beginning, however, and for a long time thereafter, the F minor seems to function as the Fantasy's tonic, as is indicated in the graph.

Auxiliary cadences often shape individual thematic elements in tonal compositions – the opening idea in the first movement of Beethoven's Piano Sonata op. 31 no. 3, for example. Very occasionally, as Schenker has pointed out, the harmonic framework of a whole piece (Brahms's Intermezzo op. 118 no. 1 is an instance) will consist of an auxiliary cadence.[5] The Fantasy represents an intermediate case: most of the piece is taken up with the auxiliary cadence, but the structural closure at the end includes a complete background progression: $\hat{3}$–$\hat{2}$–$\hat{1}$ over I–V–I.

[5] Heinrich Schenker, *Free Composition*, trans. and ed. Ernst Oster (New York, 1979), 88–9.

Example 2. Tonal plan

The upper voice of Example 2a is much less unusual than the bass. $\hat{3}$, the first note of the Fundamental Line, is already present over the F minor triad; a registral coupling, c''–c''', shifts the $\hat{3}$ from its original position into the Fantasy's normative register (*obligate Lage*), in which the resolution to $\hat{1}$ takes place. The coupling is achieved by means of two upward register transfers, indicated in the graph by diagonal lines.

In any graph as distant from the foreground of the piece as this one, bar numbers can serve only as a rough guide, for notes that occur together in the graph will often shift away from each other at later levels. The F at the beginning of the bass line, for instance, occurs in bar 1, but the c'' of the upper voice enters only in bar 3. Using the bar numbers as an approximate guide, we can see that the auxiliary cadence spans almost the whole piece. The F minor chord governs the march and the transition; the E♭ chord appears in the course of the first cycle (see bar 109) and continues in force through the second cycle and the Lento sostenuto episode; A♭, the true tonic, arrives definitively in bar 276. The structural V coincides with the *adagio, sostenuto* of bar 320; the I follows in 322, but a♭'', the goal of the Fundamental Line ($\hat{1}$) is delayed until the very last bar.

The most striking aspect of the next level (Example 2b) is the filling out of the bass: two smaller auxiliary cadences replicate the main one and serve as prefixes to the V and I. The subordinate cadences shape the harmonic direction of the first and third cycles; of particular importance is the shift to minor within the prolonged C-chord of the first cycle (bar 93). This change is one of the most decisive tonal events in the Fantasy, for it marks the turn away from F minor and toward A♭.

The augmented sixth chord that precedes the beginning of the third cycle relates to the preceding E♭ chord through the technique of *chromaticised voice exchange*; the crossed diagonal lines express the chromatic relationships that connect notes belonging to different parts.

Example 2c adds enough detail to show the essential tonal contents of each of the Fantasy's developmental phases (or form sections, although the latter term suggests clearer sectional articulations than in fact exist). The reader should consult this graph together with the still more detailed graphs of the individual 'sections' that follow, much like a visitor to London or Paris, who in using the wonderful published guides to those cities first finds the street he seeks on a detailed map of its neighbourhood and then looks at the synoptic map of the whole city to find out where he is going in relation to where he is.

The march (bars 1–43)

Although the opening march is cast in the role of an introduction, it has little of the normal character of one. In no way an open-ended section obviously directed toward coming events (compare, by way of contrast, the introduction to the *Polonaise-fantasy*), the march is outwardly the most stable part of the piece. Though some of the phrases are linked together with Chopin's usual finesse, each one contains a strong closing cadence; each of the two strains leads the melodic line to a closure on Î; and there is even a codetta to round off the section.

And yet the march sounds not at all like a self-contained whole. Chopin's refined art can create an impression of completeness and, at the same time, subtly undermine this very impression. In the march, Chopin accomplishes this feat, first of all, through his treatment of register and dynamics. The repeated unison motto explores the lowest reaches of the keyboard in a way that prepares the listener for a work of vast scope. And the *fortissimo* outburst that momentarily shatters a dynamic level of almost unrelieved *piano* similarly tells us that the march must be merely a prologue to the main action.

Even more important than dynamics and register is the treatment of tonal structure, shown in Example 3, a foreground graph of the first strain. The *fortissimo* of bar 19, for example, underlines a harmonic tension that chafes at the confines of the march's closed form. And that tension, prophetically, is directed toward Ab major. The second phrase's cadence in Ab (bars 7–10) – in itself a perfectly normal prolongation of III in minor – is extended by two bars, creating far more emphasis than is needed for purely local harmonic purposes. The drive toward Ab resumes in the fourth phrase with greater urgency (hence the crescendo to *fortissimo*), but the promise of Ab is not yet to be fulfilled; the unexpected and irregular resolution of a seeming cadential six-four (bar 19) turns the motion back to F minor. Yet this urge toward Ab, frustrated for the moment, is the opening phase of a process that will ultimately topple the ostensibly unassailable F minor of the march.

The struggle between F minor and Ab major – a struggle carried out in the domain of tonal structure – is perforce reflected in the Fantasy's motivic design, for in tonal music the motive is never separable from the linear and harmonic forces that operate in the background. Chopin's instinct for the motive – his ability to connect contrasting ideas through what Schenker calls 'hidden repetitions', his related ability to connect large structure with detail through the enlargement of basic melodic figures – is one of the most striking aspects of his compositional genius.[6] It is given full play in the Fantasy.

Example 4 shows, in schematic form, the tonal matrix within which much of the motivic life of the Fantasy develops. It consists of nothing more than the tonic triads of F minor and Ab major, the beginning and closing 'keys'. As with any pair of diatonically-related triads with roots a third apart, two notes

---

[6] Heinrich Schenker, *Free Composition*, 93–107. See also Charles Burkhart, 'Schenker's Motivic Parallelisms', *Journal of Music Theory* xxii/2 (1978), 145–75.

Example 3. March, first strain

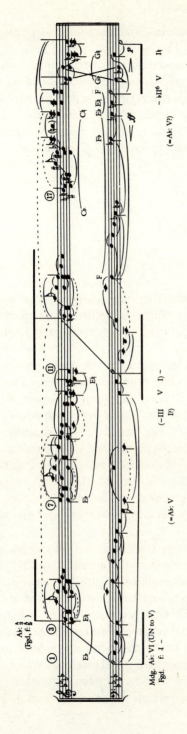

Example 4. 'Matrix'

above the bass – here, A♭ and C – are held in common, while the remaining one is constrained to move – F moves to E♭.

How does the Fantasy's motivic design concretise the abstract pitch relationships shown in Example 4? By placing emphasis on the motion of F to E♭, by doing so in both F minor and A♭ major contexts, and by incorporating the note-pair F–E♭ into melodic figures of significantly similar contour. This process begins with the Fantasy's first idea – the unison motto of bars 1–2 (Example 5). The passage spans a descending fourth, F–C, expressed as the

Example 5. Motives x and y

stepwise linear progression, F–E♭–D♭–C. The even pacing of this linear progression (two notes per bar) and the repetitive, sequential character of the melodic diminutions would normally tend to divide the passage's flow symmetrically into whole-bar segments. But the staccato sign given to the first note (and to neither of its sequential analogues) disturbs this symmetry, dividing the four-note linear progression into one note plus three (F/E♭ D♭ C). This is because the ear separates slightly the detached F from the sustained E♭, D♭, and C, and it groups the latter notes together. Thus if performed as Chopin wrote it, the opening motto projects an emphasised E♭ – potentially an element of the A♭ triad – between the principal notes, F and C. Unfortunately, many pianists and some editors slur the first two notes and, by changing this tiny detail, weaken the coherence of the whole piece. (Emerson's remark that foolish consistency is the hobgoblin of little minds certainly applies to those musicians who prefer a machine-like uniformity to the inspired diversity found here.)

Chopin's staccato has another far-reaching consequence: it reveals an important motive. Without it, the motto would be dominated completely by the descending fourth, F–C, an interval outlined by the first two notes, repeated sequentially, and filled in by step to form the structural outline of the whole motto. The descending fourth, in both its disjunct and its conjunct forms, is one of the leading elements in the design of the Fantasy; the symbol 'x' in the analytic illustrations will point out its significant occurrences. Important as it is, the fourth is slightly obscured in its initial presentation, for the staccato articulation makes it possible to hear another figure (marked 'y') starting with the second note. In later statements of the motto (bars 5, 11, and 15), figure 'y' is further emphasised by changes in register. As the Fantasy goes on, this figure – subordinate at first – takes on more and more importance until it finally assumes as important a role as the descending fourth.

The connection of the motto (bars 1–2) with the full chordal setting (bars 3–4) involves an indirect chromatic adjustment: the E♭ of bar 1 must give way to E♮ over dominant harmony (the E♮ is implicitly present over the C of bar 2 even before it becomes an actual sound). This chromatic relationship – here more hinted at than expressed overtly – becomes a decisive factor in the later unfolding of the Fantasy; the process begins in bar 10, and continues in bars 18–19, where E♮ and F♭, its enharmonic equivalent, are the principal tonal agents of the march's climactic event – the frustrated move toward A♭ major and subsequent resolution in F minor.

Of course the Fantasy, like just about any of Chopin's major works, will explore many different chromatic paths. It is a characteristic of tonal chromaticism, however, that a single altered note (often in association with its enharmonic transformation) will tend to function as the primary chromatic element of a given piece. In the Fantasy, that role is inevitably assigned to E♮ and F♭, because of their connection to E♭ and F, the diatonic pitches whose relationship helps to express the two-key scheme. Two additional chromatic sounds – B♮/C♭ and F♯/G♭ – are to assume special importance as the Fantasy unfolds; significantly, both receive some prominence in the march (bars 16–18, 19–20, 27, 25). The occurrence of important chromatic pitches is indicated in Example 3 and many later graphs.

Example 6 continues Example 3 with a graph of the F major strain, which emerges as if on the spur of the moment out of the unexpected major tonic of bar 20. Not counting the cadential flourish of the six-bar codetta, it consists of only a single repeated eight-bar phrase, and functions primarily as a pendant to the strain in minor. Although it lacks the sense of tonal conflict that characterises the first strain, it manifests a compensating density of contrapuntal and harmonic texture, so much so that graphs on two levels are required to give an adequate picture of its structure. The more reduced graph (Example 6a) gives the better preliminary orientation; note in particular that the D♭ chord of bars 25–7 becomes an augmented sixth chord that connects (through a chromaticised voice exchange) with the B♭ chord of bar 24. Thus the triads on B♭ and D♭ and the augmented sixth chord combine to express a prolonged subdominant harmony – a procedure very characteristic of Chopin.[7]

Note that the descending fourth F–C is expressed chromatically in the 'alto'. In terms of strict voice-leading, the chromatic line transfers into the bass and culminates in the D♭–C of bar 27; doublings of these notes also complete the

[7] See, for example, the Fourth Ballade, bars 169–94 and the Mazurka op. 56 no. 1, bars 1–12 for related, though by no means identical, procedures.

Example 6. March, second strain

motive in its original register. This reminder of the doleful opening motto falls like a shadow across the brightness of the F major (in addition the very low octave C of bar 22 connects in register with the octave F of bar 20 and also serves to recall the motto).

Unlike the march's two principal strains, both of which break off cleanly with well-articulated cadences, the codetta merges into the next section. The neighbour notes bb and db' of the last six-four chord (bar 42) are taken up into the figuration of the following arpeggio passage; their resolution is completed only with the F minor chord of bar 44. And the low octave Fs of bars 41–2 dissolve into the broken octaves that initiate the first arpeggio. In Example 6b, bars 36–8, note the indication of motive 'x' in registral expansion; the allusion is made possible by the descending register transfers of the right-hand part, which prepare the low register in which the arpeggios begin.

The transition (bars 43–68)

It was the late Oswald Jonas who first explained, more than fifty years ago, that the guiding idea of this wonderful passage is the descending fourth, F–Eb–Db–C, of the opening motto.[8] I have incorporated Jonas's idea into Example 7, a voice-leading graph of the section and a continuation of Example 6. In addition to forming the bass line of the passage (Jonas's point), the motto appears, in a huge registral expansion, in the colossal descending run of the right hand (bars 64–8) that leads from the keyboard's highest F to its lowest C. Within the run, the first four notes and its octave transpositions form a diminution of the motto; the last of the four notes, C, represents a suspended seventh that resolves to Cb. (Locally the suspension's preparation forms part of the subsidiary F minor chord that immediately precedes the run; in a deeper sense, the suspended C carries over from the structural F minor chord that begins the whole passage. The more reduced graph makes the large-scale connections clear.)

The orthography here is confusing but characteristic: the Cb really functions as a B♮, producing an augmented sixth above the bass's Db, and resolving into the C major chord that begins the next section. There is, I think, a significant association between this Cb (=B♮) and the uses of Cb/B♮, also members of augmented sixth chords, in the march (bars 18, 27, 35); the sonority of the augmented sixth and the rising semitone of its resolution mark many of the critical junctures in the Fantasy's development, and take on a motivic meaning. (Here and elsewhere in the article, I have changed Chopin's spelling to clarify the sense of the passage.)

[8] Oswald Jonas, *Introduction to the Theory of Heinrich Schenker*, trans. and ed. J. Rothgeb (New York, 1983). The first German edition (which included Jonas's discussion of the Fantasy) was published in Vienna in 1934.

Example 7. Transition

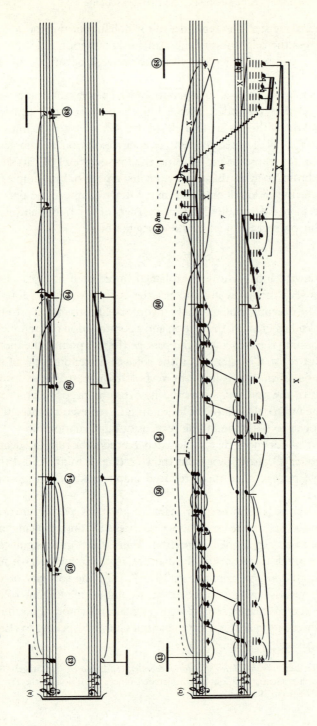

The large-scale descent of the bass is elaborated in a most unusual manner: through motion in consecutive rising thirds. Thus the move from F down to Eb (the first step in the descending fourth) is accomplished through the bass (and root) succession F–Ab–C–Eb–G–Bb – an eleventh (F–Bb) subdivided into five consecutive thirds; the Bb then becomes a preparatory dominant to the Eb that follows. It is surely no coincidence that the first of these rising thirds – F–Ab – expresses the urge toward Ab major that has already manifested itself in the first strain of the march, and that will determine the tonal direction of the whole work. And, as we shall see, transpositions of this primary rising third will play an important role in the Fantasy's middleground structure, so the interval itself becomes a design element.

As Example 8 shows, the motion in rising thirds is associated with the presence of figure 'y'. The first statement of the figure here is at the same pitch level – C–F–Eb – as its very first occurrence at the opening of the march. Note that the F is suspended over the Ab chord, resolving on the third triplet quaver of bar 45; as the bass moves up by thirds, equivalent suspensions appear over each new step. Chopin's autograph reveals an elaborately careful and lucid notation of the suspensions; his notation was ignored, or at any rate not reproduced, by most editors starting with the French first edition (the Henle edition has it right). How characteristic it is of Chopin to dissolve a kind of imitative counterpoint, fraught with motivic significance, into what might seem to be a merely pianistic transitional passage. As the tempo accelerates, the triplet quavers project more and more clearly not only the melodic shape of figure 'y', but also an approximation of its original rhythmic contour and duration. Eventually a partially new idea – a complete neighbour-note figure in dotted rhythm – grows out of figure 'y'; appearing first in bars 50–2, it will recur each of the many times an arpeggiated passage based on this one appears.

The three double octaves that punctuate the arpeggios in bars 52–3 will become another important articulative element in the Fantasy's design, recurring in bars 153–4, 197–8, and 233–4. They can be traced back – indirectly, but, I believe, unquestionably – to the octave sonority of the opening motto. The connecting links are better expressed in musical notes than in words (Example 9).

The first cycle (bars 68–155)

The contra C at the head of bar 68 is at once the last note of the transition and the first note of the first cycle.[9] This sort of overlap, which we observed first

---

[9] The larger metrical structure also shows a curious sort of overlap. The bar (or at least its downbeat) belongs metrically to the preceding four-bar group, to which it forms an appended downbeat bar. (Schenker illustrates such extra downbeats in *Free Composition*, Figure 149/3, 4, and 5.) Simultaneously, the right-hand part forms an upbeat to the eight-bar group that begins the cycle.

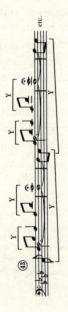

Example 8. Motive y

Example 9. Octave sonority

at the beginning of the transition, characterises all the phrase connections within the cycle. Although several phrases end with V–I progressions, all of these are so arranged that the V comes at the end of one eight-bar group and the I at the beginning of the next one (e.g., bars 100/101, 108/109, and 126/127). Thus even apart from the striking deceptive cadences and other unexpected chord successions at phrase junctures, the cycle is singularly free of 'normal' phrases – that is tonal/durational units in which the tonal goal falls within the time span of the durational unit.

And since most of the rest of the Fantasy is given over to restatements (partial or complete) of the cycle, the overlapping of phrases and of large sections pervades almost the entire piece. Indeed in the almost three hundred bars from the beginning of the march's codetta to the end of the Fantasy, there is only one phrase (bars 199–206) that cadences without an overlap – and its cadence lacks a conclusive melodic line. Avoiding strong cadences and closed form sections is a traditional trait of the fantasy as a genre; overlapping phrases to create continuity is a hallmark of Chopin's style; but surely this piece represents an extreme instance of these tendencies (perhaps *the* extreme instance) both in the tradition of the genre and in its composer's output.

In its thematic contents as well as its overlapped phrase structure, the cycle seems to have neither a definite beginning nor a definite ending. The first unit, an *agitato* passage in syncopated rhythm (bar 68), composes out a chord of dominant, not tonic, function; in addition, it has the character of a bridge passage, not a stable theme. And the unit that one would expect to close the cycle – a quick march (bar 127) – debouches through a deceptive cadence (bar 143) into an arpeggiated passage clearly derived from the one in bars 43–68; like that earlier passage, it leads into the *agitato* syncopations, and the cycle – again without a stable beginning – resumes.

The many sudden and surprising changes of tonal focus make the larger harmonic structure of the cycle very hard to grasp. In my view, a first step toward understanding this structure is realising that the splendid Ab major *cantilena* of bars 77–84 does not constitute an arrival at the structural tonic of the Fantasy's tonal background. The episode enters without harmonic preparation and closes without achieving a harmonic resolution; in no way are its eight inconclusive bars – striking and beautiful though they are – sufficient to replace the powerful F minor that has dominated the piece so far. Like the moves toward Ab in the march and transition, this one is rather a vision of the Promised Land than an arrival in it; this time, however, the vision is on the way to becoming a reality.

Example 10 forms a continuation of Example 7, and shows on two levels the linear–harmonic contents of the cycle. In the less detailed graph (10a), we can see that the origin of the Ab chord is contrapuntal rather than har-

Example 10. First cycle

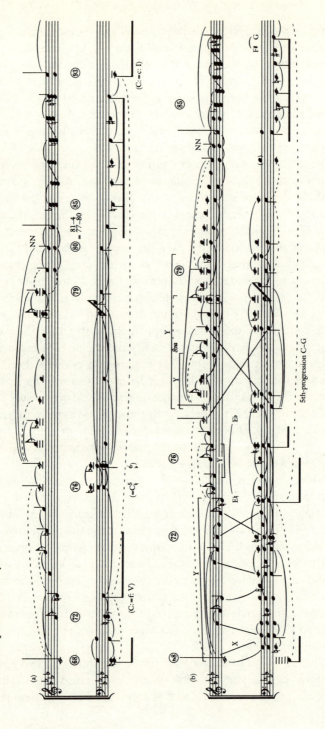

Example 10. (*cont.*)

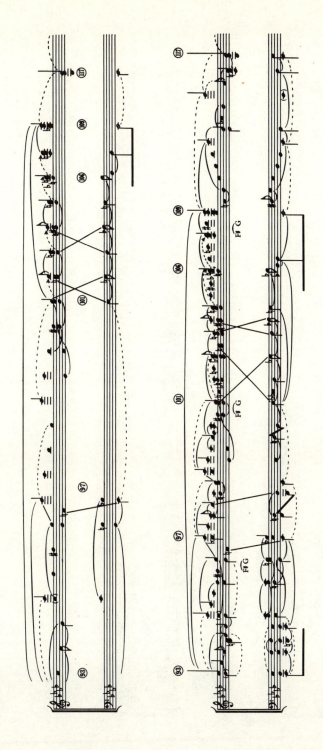

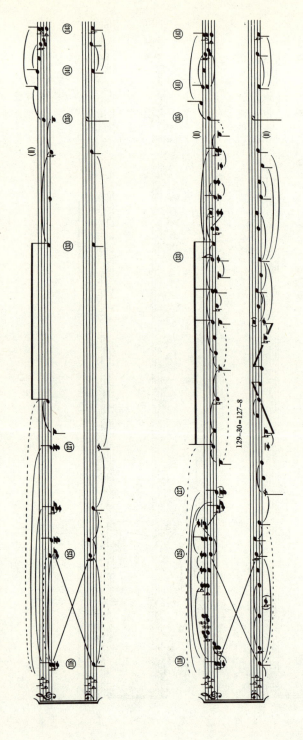

Example 10. (*cont.*)

monic. It results from an interval-progression 5–6 above C accompanied by the chromatic inflection E♮–E♭ (again note the use of E♮ as primary chromatic); the addition of the root A♭ in the bass produces the stable five-three position of the A♭ triad.

Example 10 indicates that the A♭ passage occurs within a broad and eventful prolongation of a C-triad that changes its quality from major to minor and its local harmonic function from dominant to temporary tonic. It is in the bass line that the coherence of this C-prolongation is most readily apparent; the ascent from D to G of bars 85–92 continues from the earlier C (bars 68–76) almost as if the passage in A♭ had never taken place. A fall to C balances the earlier stepwise ascent and stabilises the C minor with a dominant to tonic resolution (bars 92–3). Note, by the way, how the accompaniment figure of bars 93–4 resumes the pattern of bar 68–73; this textural association under-scores the connection between the C minor and the earlier C major.

With respect to the logical motion of the bass, the A♭ episode is a kind of digression or parenthetical interpolation. But its appearance marks a critical point in the struggle of A♭ to assert itself as the governing tonic of the Fantasy. The passage follows a pedal on C (bars 73–6) that proclaims itself a preparatory dominant to some kind of big statement in F minor. That statement, of course, is never made. Thus the A♭ theme, though not yet the expression of a stable underlying tonic, does represent the negation of what has seemed, up until now, to be such a tonic. At no further point in the cycle will F function as a strong centre of tonal gravity; the weakening of F minor leaves the field open for other forces to emerge. How fitting, in a fantasy, that it is this visionary episode that transforms our sense of tonal realities![10]

The prolonged C-triad of bars 68–93 has undergone two transformations: from major to minor quality and from dominant to tonic function. It will soon experience a third change, for its term as tonic is very brief; it must yield to the E♭ major that is about to emerge as an important new centre. Indeed from the perspective of tonal structure, the main purpose of bars 93–142 is to introduce the E♭ and to stabilise it so that it takes on a weight commensurate with that of the opening F minor. Chopin's manner of accomplishing these tasks is highly unusual, yet highly suitable for a fantasy – that genre where the unusual almost becomes the norm.

A superficial reading of the Fantasy might lead one to infer a structural arrival on I of E♭ in bar 97; a prolongation of E♭ would underlie the rest of the cycle. Yet the E♭ of bar 97 hardly sounds like a point of arrival at all, let alone one that initiates the prolongation of a structural harmony. In the first place, it enters without any harmonic preparation. In the second place, it brings with it no

---

[10] Harald Krebs also recognises the A♭ episode as a turning point. See 'Third Relation', 139.

change in design: the upper voice merely repeats a third higher the melodic line of bars 93–6. Now the E♭ that recurs at bar 100 does follow a dominant, and does introduce a new left-hand figure. But the V is brief, the new left-hand figure accompanies a melodic line that continues the motive heard just before, and most important, the entire phrase is still clearly on the way to something more stable.

That 'something' is, of course, the big E♭ chord of bar 109, which undoubtedly does sound like a point of arrival, and the most important one so far in the piece. That this is so is mainly due to the preparatory V pedal of bars 106–8, whose insistence is emphasised both by the crescendo and by the contrast between the repeated B♭ octaves and the very active bass line of the immediately preceding bars. As I hear it, the bass line of the cycle has as its deep structural core a motion from C through B♭ to E♭: that is, from the prolonged C of bars 68–95 to the B♭ pedal of 106–8 to the E♭ that continues from 109 to the end of the cycle and, as we shall see, beyond. This bass structure forms the first of the subordinate auxiliary cadences shown in Examples 2b and 2c.

The E♭ triad of bar 97, then, would function rather as the upper third of the previous C minor than as a harmony of deeper structural significance. (In this connection, compare Schenker's reading of Mozart's Symphony no. 40, first movement, bar 28, where he does not interpret the B♭ chord as structurally connected with the coming prolongation of B♭.)[11] Here the vehement E♭ of bar 97 enters as if to overthrow the C minor – an ingemination, in the region of the dominant, of the Fantasy's F minor/A♭ major conflict. (And in the last cycle, the conflict will be replicated at its primary pitch level: F/A♭ instead of C/E♭.) An E♭ major stabilised by a preparatory V, like the one of bar 109, would not convey a sense of conflict, hence the 'premature' and, I think, non-structural E♭ of bar 97.

From the perspective of larger tonal structure, the next phase of the cycle contains a cadence in E♭ ($\hat{3}$–$\hat{2}$–$\hat{1}$ over I–V–I, bars 109–27) made more emphatic by the rhythmic expansion that delays the arrival on the final I. The expansion takes the form of a passage interpolated within the prolonged V of bars 116–26. Note that the first move of the passage is to a six-five chord on B♮ (bar 119) – a chord whose contrapuntal meaning emerges clearly enough from Example 10b. The graph, however, does not tell the whole story, for the association of the chord with C minor is unmistakable; thus the struggle between C minor and E♭ (F minor and A♭ in the third cycle) flares up briefly just before the latter key celebrates its triumph.

[11] Heinrich Schenker, 'Mozart: Sinfonie G-Moll' in *Das Meisterwerk in der Musik* (Munich, 1925, 1926, 1930), ii, 110. The three volumes of *Meisterwerk* were reprinted in facsimile in one volume (Hildesheim, 1974).

As always in the Fantasy, the goal tonic of the cadence overlaps the beginning of the next unit – a march-like parallel period composed almost in strict antecedent-consequent relation. I say 'almost' because of the overlap that binds the goal V of the antecedent to the opening I of the consequent (bar 135) and because of the startling deceptive cadence that, in denying the expected resolution on E♭, prevents the cycle from closing and propels the piece into a transitional passage based on the one of bars 43–68.

The function of the dissonant chord (bar 143) that creates the 'deception' is not immediately clear. Indeed only when we approach the second cycle shall we see that it results from the chromatic inflection of the II⁶ that arrived in bar 141. (In graphing the deceptive cadence, I have once again attempted to clarify the meaning of the passage by using enharmonic equivalents of some of Chopin's notes. I shall have recourse to this procedure in some later illustrations as well.)

The larger melodic contours are clearer and less problematic than the bass line and large-scale harmonic organisation. In studying Example 10, note the frequent use of voice-leading devices – upward register transfer and reaching over – that carry the upper line into higher regions. This upward tendency characterises the leading of the upper voice throughout the Fantasy. In this connection, the first two phrases of the march and the arpeggios of the transition are emblematic; the rising thirds that we encountered there are mirrored in the cycle, but spread out over huge spans of time.

The ascending impulse of the Fantasy's upper line relates both to the two-key scheme by rising third and to figure 'y', whose rising fourth and falling second also produce a third between the first and last notes. Example 11 traces this

Example 11. Motive y

figure in its various incarnations from the opening of the piece through the A♭ episode. Particularly impressive is the contrast between the *agitato* C–F–E♮ of bars 73–5 and the songful C–F–E♭ that begins the A♭ theme. Unlike the 'y' figure, which takes on a prominent role especially in the first half of the Cycle, the 'x' figure of the falling fourth is much less in evidence than earlier on in the Fantasy. Two important episodes, however – the *agitato* passage (bars 68ff.) and the closing quick march (bars 127ff.) – begin with leaps of a descending fourth, and its influence can perhaps also be traced in the octave bass of the march and the upper line of the A♭ episode (especially bars 78–81).

After the A♭ episode, the cycle is strongly coloured by the chromatic pitch F♯, which leads to G, usually as the culminating event of a rising line. Example 10b shows the significant instances; note especially the bass of bars 85–92, and the upper line of bars 106–9. The very Chopinesque chromatic sequence that begins in bar 101 is clear in its general orientation but far from easy to understand in its details. The problems are both notational (Chopin's typical enharmonic spellings) and compositional (the use of *rhythmic shifts* to create pseudo-chords out of passing notes). In Example 10b I have tried to disentangle the voice-leading of bars 101–2; the sequential repetitions would follow the same principles.

The second cycle and the Lento sostenuto (bars 155–235)

The dying away of the incomplete second cycle, the surprising advent of a fragmentary 'slow movement' in triple time, the almost brutally abrupt resumption of *alla breve* metre and quick tempo in the transition to the third cycle – all of these produce the highest concentration of surface contrast in the Fantasy. Yet underlying this kaleidoscopic surface is the elaboration of a single prolonged harmony whose unifying power fuses the contrasting passages into one large formal component. The prolonged harmony is the dominant, E♭ major, that governs the end of the first cycle; somewhat like the development of a sonata movement, this composite section moves within a previously established structural harmony, transforming it from a local tonic into a dissonant chord requiring resolution.

But the tonal path taken here differs from any found in a normal sonata development, for the two-key scheme of the Fantasy does not permit a resolution to the primary tonic, A♭, at the beginning of the third cycle. It is therefore to the F major chord that begins the next cycle that this prolonged dominant must find its way. Chopin's solution to the compositional problem posed here is shown in Example 12; he alters chromatically the E♭ harmony so that it becomes the augmented sixth chord G♭–B♭–D♭–E♮; the augmented sixth, in turn, resolves into the F chord (Example 12a). (Note that each of the three cycles is introduced by an augmented sixth.) As I mentioned in connection with Example 2, a chromaticised voice exchange effects the connection of the diatonic E♭ harmony and its altered derivative; voice exchanges are frequent occurences in the Fantasy, both on a huge scale like this one, and as surface events, as in bars 101–2, which express almost the same tonal contents within a two-bar span.

The Lento sostenuto passage in B major (a notation of convenience for C♭) leads directly into the augmented sixth; Chopin utilises the enharmonic equivalence of dominant seventh and 'German' augmented sixth by transforming the unresolved V^7 that ends (or rather fails to end) the Lento (bar 222)

Example 12. From first cycle to third

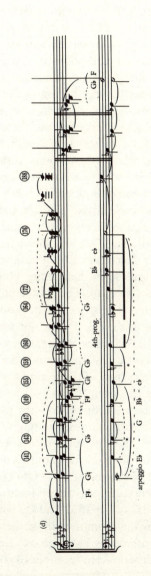

into the German sixth (bars 227–34) that prepares the third cycle. (As so often with Chopin, the notation does not reflect this change in function.) Example 12b reveals the voice-leading origin of the B♮ (C♭) major in a 5–6 motion combined with the downward inflection of a major third, G♮, into the minor third, G♭. The addition of a root in the bass and the introduction of a preparatory dominant stabilise the C♭ triad so that it can serve as the basis of a relatively self-contained passage.

Much of the dramatic intensity of this part of the Fantasy grows out of its chromaticism, and the chromaticism here hinges on the various functions of the single sound F♯/G♭, as can be seen in Example 12d. We have seen how the first cycle gives prominence to rising chromatic lines that culminate in F♯–G. As Example 12d points out, the arrival of the second cycle is marked by the same chromatic succession (the F♯ notated as G♭, bars 149–55 – again note the augmented sixth). How beautifully does Chopin stabilise this sound in its G♭ incarnation when he turns to E♭ minor and G♭ major in the passage that serves as a kind of codetta to the cycle (bars 184–98). The stabilised G♭ (written as F♯) continues throughout the Lento episode, but its stability turns out to be deceptive – the still point at the centre of a storm – when the sound is incorporated into the dissonant augmented sixth that hurls it down to F. (Compare the three G♭ octaves in bars 197/198 and 233/234.)

The second cycle is not an exact transposition of the equivalent portion of the first; harmonic necessities impel substantive changes in two passages (see bars 158 and 172/180). These necessities involve the prolongation of the E♭ chord that was mentioned above. As Example 12d indicates, the harmonic path leads from the opening G major (bar 155) to B♭ major (bar 160) and E♭ major (bar 176). The episode in G♭ (bar 164) is interpolated between the B♭ and the rising sequence that continues it. Like the equivalent passage in A♭ of the first cycle, it does not form part of the harmonic framework; but, again like the earlier passage, it foretells important future developments – the turn toward G♭ as a preparation for the B (C♭) episode and the directing of the larger structure of the section toward the augmented sixth on G♭.

The movement from the end of the first cycle through the transition into the second cycle is composed with extraordinary subtlety into a sequence of events rich with multiple meanings (Example 13). To begin with, the dissonant chord that interrupts the expected cadence (bar 143) could resolve either as a four-two to F♭ major or (as a diminished third chord) to B♭; the latter is by far the likelier possibility. Of course the chord does neither; through chromatic inflection, it is transformed into the augmented sixth on A♭ that moves to the G of bar 155. And yet when B♭ arrives in bar 160, it fulfills the seemingly broken promise of the earlier passage; even the diminished seventh on A that introduces B♭ serves as a reminder of the earlier sonority. (The asterisks under the As in Example 13 convey this association.)

Example 13. Second cycle

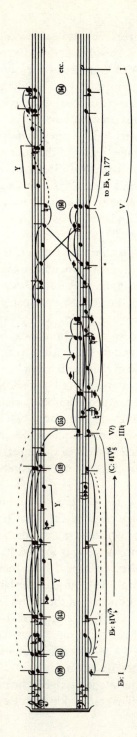

And the G chord that begins the new cycle (bar 155) also carries a double meaning; eventually it turns out to function as an altered III of E♭, but at first it sounds like the V of C minor. The hint of C minor at the outset of this cycle looks back to the C minor/E♭ major conflict of the preceding one. And finally, the strong tendency toward G♭ transposes to a new pitch level the movement by rising third that permeates the entire Fantasy.

After it achieves a harmonic closure on E♭ (bar 176ff.), the cycle moves on to a variant of the arpeggio passage that, this time, seems to die away in the manner of a codetta rather than moving forward (bars 180–98). However the G♭ harmony on which it dies away does not form a natural goal, and it enters quite without the kind of preparation that might stabilise it, at least temporarily. In retrospect, therefore, the G♭ is understood as a preparatory dominant for the B (C♭) of the Lento sostenuto.

Except for the sixteen-foot doublings of the bass line, the Lento episode is written almost entirely within the range of the human voice and in a texture close to that of four-part choral music. With its simple ABA form (3 × 8 bars) and meditative, hymn-like character, it presents the greatest imaginable contrast with the tempestuous passages of the preceding cycles. And yet it is as intense as any part of the Fantasy. That this is so results from two factors: the relation of the episode to its larger context and its highly chromatic tonal fabric. A glance back at Example 12b will remind us that the B major harmony that governs the Lento originates out of the combination of G♭, a chromatic passing note and C♭, a chromatically inflected upper neighbour; elements of tension and flux freeze for a few moments into the semblance of a stable structure. The two generating notes (written enharmonically as F♯ and B) are, of course, two of the three main chromatic elements of the Fantasy (see above, p. 231); E♮, the third element is a prominent feature of the melodic line (bars 202, 205, etc.).

The eight-bar phrase that begins the Lento is not very chromatic, but the B section (bars 207–14) manifests the complex chromaticism of Chopin's late style in all its power and beauty. Example 14, which gives a comprehensive picture of the Lento and the brief transitional passage that follows it, does not have enough levels to explain this chromatic passage; I have therefore added a graph of part of the B section (Example 15). As I understand it, much of the chromaticism results from the introduction of the sound G♭/F♯; in particular, the succession G♮–F♯ mirrors the G–G♭ that helps to connect the end of the first cycle to the beginning of the third one (again consult Example 12). How moving is the effect of the F𝄪 and G♭ that Chopin adds to the reprise in bars 216 and 220 as an echo of the B section.

Another essential key to understanding the chromatic passage is the notion of rhythmic displacement (or shift) already cited in connection with Example

Example 14. Lento sostenuto

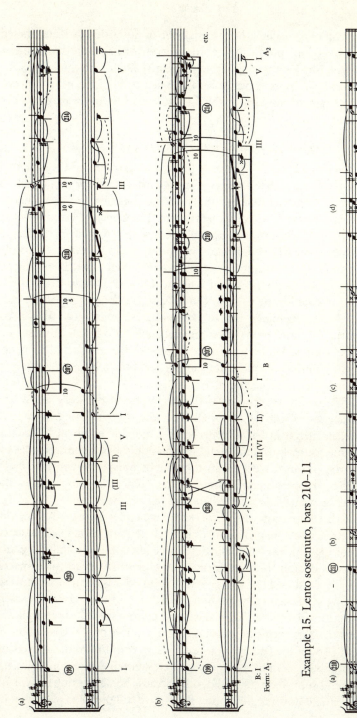

Example 15. Lento sostenuto, bars 210–11

10b. This technique creates simultaneities out of notes that lack an inherent harmonic connection, producing chordal successions that are harmonically non-functional, obedient to a purely contrapuntal logic. I am thinking particularly of the last two beats of bar 210 and the first two of 211; note, however, that the larger framework within which these sonorities move makes perfect harmonic sense.

The third cycle, extended cadence, and coda (bars 235–332)

Although the third cycle is an almost literal transposition of the first, it is in no way a mere copy. Its different position within tonal space and musical time gives it an altogether different function and meaning and even changes the local effect of some of its component parts. The C major harmony within which the first cycle begins, for example, is strongly rooted in the key of F minor, which it seems to continue. The corresponding F major chord that opens the third cycle does not follow a previously established Bb minor; instead it follows the foreground key of B major (Cb) – as drastically unrelated a sonority as one could hope to find. (To be sure, the beginning of the cycle suggests the key of Bb minor, but the key never becomes more than a suggestion, for the Bb minor triad occurs only in passing.) Whereas the first cycle forms a direct connection between the F minor of the march and Eb major, the third cycle connects directly only with its goal – Ab major – and not with the events immediately preceding it.

The lack of a strong focal point at the beginning of the cycle makes the magnetic attraction of the Ab major all the more overwhelming; in a good performance, its arrival in bar 276 becomes a veritable epiphany. That this is so is also due to the long and careful preparation that Chopin provides for this arrival: the moves toward Ab in the march, transition, and first cycle, and the return to a prolonged F chord in the third cycle, which makes the cycle replicate on a smaller scale the structure of the whole piece.

Even a casual comparison of the two complete cycles will reveal many differences of detail; these involve changes in pitch content, dynamics, articulation, and voicing. Although no single change alters the musical substance very much, their combination produces an intensity that reflects the climactic position of the third cycle in the Fantasy's form, the last curve, as it were, in an ascending spiral that culminates in the arrival on the Ab tonic. Precisely for reasons of form I believe that pianists and editors should observe all textual differences. This includes avoiding the alteration of the bass notes in bars 112 and 116 (of the first cycle) to make them conform to the Ab version (bars 279 and 283). Chopin may perhaps have written octaves on Eb in the earlier passage, as some have suggested, only because he was writing for a piano that did not extend down to Subcontra Bb, but we still ought to play what he

wrote and not some conjectural 'improvement'. And there is something to be
said for saving the admittedly more effective later version for the triumphant
tonic statement at the close. Similarly the *piano* dynamic that Chopin requires
for the quick march that begins in bar 127 must be strictly observed despite –
or indeed because of – the *sempre forte* in the corresponding passage at the end.

Example 16 depicts the final part of the Fantasy – the interrupted cadence
of bars 308–10, the resumption of motion toward harmonic closure in a
passage that incorporates the transition and a quotation of the Lento sostenuto's opening bars into the work's structural cadence, and the brief coda,
based on bars 188–98. (For reasons of space I have omitted detailed voice-
leading graphs of the third cycle; anyone who wanted to could construct his
own, using Examples 2c and 10 as models.) Unlike the corresponding deceptive chord at the end of the first cycle, the one in bar 310 leads fairly directly
into the dominant harmony that forms its goal; in so doing it expresses the
Fantasy's primary chromatic element, F♭, and makes good the promise of the
opening march's frustrated moves toward A♭. A comparison of bars 319/320
with 18/19 and of the descending chromatic run of 316–18 with the one in
64–8 will begin to show how many threads are tied together in this climactic
passage.

In a piece whose main tonic arrives only after a long struggle and whose
large formal components, almost without exception, fail to achieve closure,
a quick and facile final cadence would be disastrously out of place. The deceptive progression that extends the final cadence, therefore, is a compositional
necessity. Its effect is far more powerful than that of its analogue at the end of
the first cycle, or any of the other interrupted cadences in the Fantasy. This is so
precisely because the progression it interrupts is perceived by any experienced
listener to be a motion toward final closure.

That closure represents the resolution both of immediate tonal tensions and,
indirectly, of all the processes whose lack of resolution has kept the Fantasy
in a constant state of flux almost without parallel in the literature. The closing
V and I, therefore, must enter like characters in a drama; no simple cadential
formula would suffice here. But a dramatic gesture without musical content
would prove even more inadequate – I need not cite as evidence any of the
countless programmatic pieces whose musical emptiness turns their dramatic
discourse to bombast. Chopin's solution to this compositional problem is as
fulfilling musically as it is dramatically; it includes the final transformations of
the Fantasy's two main motives. As Example 16 shows, the upper line moves
into the Allegro assai of the coda with the notes f″–e♭″–d♭′–c′ – the descending
fourth of the opening motto with pitches untransposed but now expressing
A♭ major as clearly as it once did F minor. (The g″ just before the f″ is an
accented neighbour or appoggiatura; this is one of the few configurations in

Example 16. Final (structural) cadence and coda

tonal music where a neighbour note is embellished by its own neighbour.) And the rising arpeggios that follow carry figure 'y' into the highest possible register, dwelling for a moment on the crucial notes F and E♭ before disappearing into the blue. The F♭ of the penultimate chord seals the victory of E♭ and of the A♭ harmony to which it belongs – no trace of F♮ remains!

In reviewing a Chopin biography, Bernard Shaw disputed the ridiculous notion that any piece not in sonata form must be programme music. He wrote, 'Now a Chopin ballade is clearly no more programme music than the slow movement of Mozart's symphony in E flat is.'[12] The statement holds true, needless to say, for the Fantasy as well. This does not rule out the possibility that extra-musical ideas might have played a part in the creative process that led to the Fantasy, the Ballades (Mickiewicz's poems), or, for that matter, the Mozart slow movement; once achieved, however, the works stand on their own, sustained by their extraordinary musical values.

Among the musical values of all of these works is their narrative quality; but the narration is a musical one, carried out by tonal structure, texture, form, and motivic design. To my way of thinking there would be nothing wrong in imagining a programme to make more vivid one's image of the musical narration so long as one did not take it too seriously or begin to believe that the piece was 'about' one's concoction. For the Fantasy, in particular, it would at first seem easy enough to construct a fairly convincing, though inevitably trite, programme – probably something along the lines of *Les Préludes* or *Tod und Verklärung*. After all, Chopin himself calls the opening section a 'march', and it is clearly a march of solemn – even funereal – character. The subsequent course of the piece – the struggle between the two keys, the victory of A♭, the celebration of that victory in a march-like episode of triumphal character – is almost impossible to describe except in metaphors that come close to suggesting a programme.

But the Fantasy mocks at any attempt to force its musical narrative – fraught though it is with human feeling – into a story of victory over death or tragedy and triumph. For in the end there is neither tragedy nor triumph, but only the unfathomable magic of a dream. The deceptive cadence interrupts the victory celebration like the Red Death at the Masque, but the interruption does not lead to the sort of violent conclusion to which Chopin was so often drawn.[13] (And a violent conclusion would hardly fit the Fantasy's 'optimistic' move from F minor to A♭ major.) What follows instead is the urgent appeal of the Adagio sostenuto, an appeal to which the final tonic yields no definite answer, for the piece ends like a dream, its elements dissolving into nothingness just when we think we have finally grasped their meaning.

---

[12] Bernard Shaw, *Music in London* (London, 1932), ii, 209.

[13] As in the First Scherzo, all of the Ballades except the third, and the Finale of the Third Sonata.

Index

CA.